The Motorist's Bedside Book

The Motorist's Bedside Book

Edited by Anthony Harding

B. T. Batsford Ltd
London

First published 1972

© B. T. Batsford Ltd 1972

ISBN 0 7134 0470 1

Made and printed in Great Britain by
C. Tinling & Co. Ltd, Prescot, Lancs
for the publishers B. T. Batsford Ltd
4 Fitzhardinge Street, London W1H 0AH

CONTENTS

Contents

EDITOR'S NOTE

For newcomers to this series of motoring symposia the point must be made that this book is not an anthology in the usual sense of the word as all the essays are new and have been specially written for it.

Readers of *The Motorist's Weekend Book* (1960), *The Motorist's Bedside Book* (1962) and *The Motorist's Miscellany* (1964)—all long since gloriously out-of-print*—will now no doubt be showing signs of the long tooth, the fallen arch, the balding pate and other less obvious chassis defects. Their motoring habits and prejudices will have been bitten deep into their souls (and faces) by the dyspeptic upsets born of many years of acidulating experience of the merry motoring pranks of their fellow dupes, and the frustrations of hour-years sitting in stationary lines of traffic.

Take heart once more, ladies and gentlemen, the Old Guard (*Vieux Equipe?*) are here again in force, full of that great old reactionary thinking which cannot fail to appeal.

Yet... the New Blood—those chaps who can see a Grand Prix car in, for instance, a Tyrrell-Ford—are fully catered for as well, by a number of fresh, switched-on, with-it, groovy young contributors oozing with high-octane enthusiasm, plus a dash of vitriol, for modern motoring and today's racing drivers and competition cars. And why not, pray? A damned sight better than walking, footballers and bingo, don't you think?

It's up to you, of course, to decide who are the New Blood and which the Old Guard....

Midhurst, *Autumn,* 1972   A.H.

* Gloomily remaindered, more like.—*The Publishers.*

ACKNOWLEDGMENTS

The Editor and the Publishers are indebted to the following for the photographs which appear on the pages given after their names, and for their permission to reproduce them in this book:

Associated Press Ltd, page 63 top; the Editor of *Autocar*, pages 51 bottom, 52 top, 54 bottom, 55, 57 bottom, 145, 148 bottom; the Editor of *Autosport*, page 62; British Petroleum Co Ltd, and Maxwell Boyd, page 54 top; the H. G. Conway Collection, page 146; Michael Cooper, pages 49 bottom, 56 bottom, 151; Geoffrey Goddard, pages 53 top, 150, 152 left; Louis Klemantaski, pages 49 top, 52 bottom, 53 bottom, 57 top, 149 bottom; London Art Tech, page 56 top; Michelin Tyre Co Ltd and Brian Worth, page 64; the Editor of *Motor*, pages 58 and 59; David Ogle Ltd, page 147 bottom; Phipps Photographic, page 50 top; Planet News Ltd, page 63 bottom; Spencer Smith, page 148 top; Nigel Snowdon, pages 50 bottom, 51 top, 152 right; Michael Ware, pages 147 middle, 149 top.

They also acknowledge with thanks the permission of the following to include quotations:

The Editor of *Autocar*; the Editor of *Car*; the Editor of *The Daily Telegraph*; Messrs. G. T. Foulis & Co Ltd; the Editor of *Highway Times*; the Editor of *Motor*; the Editor of *Porsche Post & Lancia Journal*; the Editor of *The Vintage Sports-car Club Bulletin*.

The cartoons by Russell Brockbank are reproduced by permission of the artist, who also designed the dust jacket, and the text decorations were specially drawn for the book by Alan Roe.

THE PLATES

THE CONTRIBUTORS

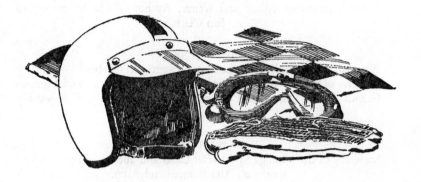

RONALD BARKER

Special Contributor to *Autocar*; also to Japanese and Scandinavian magazines; a Past President of the Vintage Sports-Car Club.

ANTHONY BIRD

An antiquarian horologist, antique dealer. Author of *The Motor Car, 1765–1914*, *The Rolls-Royce Motor Car* and other works.

WILLIAM BODDY

Editor of *Motor Sport* and author of the standard work on *The History of Brooklands Motor Course*.

JOHN V. BOLSTER

The Technical Editor of *Autosport* and well-known as a B.B.C. commentator on sound and television.

RUSSELL BROCKBANK

Internationally renowned motoring cartoonist with seven books to his credit. Art Editor of *Punch*, 1949-60.

MICHAEL BROWN

Sometime 'D.A.W.' of Ireland's *Motoring Life*; a motor insurance expert and editor of the *Policy Holder Insurance Journal*.

PAUL FRÈRE
Engineer, journalist and works driver for Ferrari, Aston Martin and Jaguar. Winner of Le Mans and South African Grand Prix, both in 1960.

GRAHAM GAULD
Scottish motoring editor and writer. Author of the biography of Jim Clark.

DAVID HODGES
An author in publishing, he has written several books including histories of the Le Mans 24-hours Race, and the French and Monaco Grands Prix. The British Correspondent of the Italian weekly *Autosprint.*

PETER HULL
Secretary of the Vintage Sports-Car Club and author of the standard works on Alfa Romeo and Alvis.

DENIS JENKINSON
Continental Correspondent of *Motor Sport.* Author of many motoring books including *The Racing Driver.*

PATRICK MACNAGHTEN
Novelist, motoring writer and broadcaster, who has just written a book about antique furniture, and is about to do one on architecture.

F. WILSON MCCOMB
Freelance writer, broadcaster and photographer. Author of the standard work on M.G. cars, and a specialist in their history.

HENRY N. MANNEY
American author resident in California. Editor-at-Large for the pre-eminent motor sporting magazine of the u.s.a., *Road & Track.*

RICHARD O'HAGAN
A mystery man of Hibernian letters; recently a regular contributor to *Motoring Life* of Dublin.

CYRIL POSTHUMUS
A motoring historian whose many outstanding books include *The British Competition Car*, a biography of Sir Henry Segrave and *Land Speed Record.*

'S.B.'

The chosen nom-de-plume for this volume of a very well-known motoring writer who wishes to remain anonymous for personal reasons.

MICHAEL SCARLETT

A member of the Road Test and Technical Staff of *Autocar*.

MICHAEL SEDGWICK

Motoring historian and writer. Curator of the Montagu Motor Museum, 1958-66 and now its Director of Research. Assistant Editor of *Veteran & Vintage Magazine* and author of a number of outstanding books including *Cars of the 1930s* and a history of the Fiat Company and its products.

L. J. K. SETRIGHT

Freelance contributor or technical editor to *Car, Cars & Car Conversions, Journal of Automotive Engineering*. Author of $9\frac{1}{2}$ books on aero engines, cars, motorcycles, tyres, etc.

SANDY SKINNER

Editor of *The Vintage Sports Car Club Bulletin*; G.N. Fancier, Owner and Expert.

RODNEY L. WALKERLEY

The illustrious 'Grande Vitesse' of *Motor*. Author of many books to do with motoring, and one to do with pubs—of Sussex.

MARTYN WATKINS

Motoring journalist and author, wildfowler and yachtsman. Sometime Editor *Cars Illustrated, Cars & Car Conversions*, etc. Monumental work on post-war sports-cars shortly forthcoming.

W. G. S. WIKE

A textiles manufacturer with an eye for a motor-car! A very early member of the Vintage Sports Car Club.

EOIN S. YOUNG

Freelance motor racing journalist and consultant from New Zealand. McLaren expert, and topical motoring columnist for *Autocar, Car, Road & Track*, etc.

The Motorist Ill-Defined

MICHAEL BROWN

It was only when I found myself in a traffic jam stretching fore and aft into what is euphemistically called 'the distance' of an English winter day that the loss came home to me. Ahead of me was a car radio housed in a Mini, which, at Strength 5, was not only loud and clear but also as hideous as only Radio One can be. To port a female, thin of face and flared of nostril, beside whom sat a pouty small boy on his way to a term at prep school costing more, no doubt, than the Jaguar in which he squirmed. I'll bet his name was Jeremy and that Nanny was looking after sister Joanna in the morning-room back home. To starboard was a Thing in another Thing labelled GT and what might have been a telephone number before STD: it (the first Thing) had shoulder-length wavy hair from the tresses of which peeped a pink blouse (shirt?). It drove something nondescript from the Midlands—and where better to go for the nondescript?—and it occupied the enforced interval in life by scrutinising long, white, be-ringed fingers. Forty years ago it might have been a débutante, now it was probably a pop singer on the way to a recording and that. Behind me was something portly which had opted out of the strains of modern life and was reading the City's *Pink 'Un*—probably the last paragraph of 'Men and Matters'. As I say, this was my moment of truth: 'Not a blessed motorist amongst them'.

Now I am an argumentative fellow. Make an assertion to me, and my first instinct is to deny it, and the surprising conviction of this piece of didacticism was a splendid opportunity for doubt and questioning. Motorists? Of course they're motorists. They're driving cars, and what more do you want? What indeed? The question, as they say, arises. What, in these modern days, constitutes a motorist?

For a start, he must, I feel, be a descendant of tradition, and the traditional motorist is still a fairly vivid picture. Vivid, yes. Listen to the Baron de Zuylen de Nyevelt writing on 'Dress for Motoring' in 1902: 'One of the principal waterproofers in the City of London has devised a kilt made of strong indiarubber material which is absolutely waterproof. This kilt is worn high round the waist, buttons down the side, and reaches below the knees. It is intended to be worn with gaiters.' Well, well. Vivid enough. But wait. Its fitness for purpose causes it to challenge the cataracts of the world as a spectacle: 'If the driver's seat becomes a pool of water the wearer of this kilt remains in blissful ignorance of the fact. Furthermore (The Baron must have been a leader-writer for *l'Équipe: "D'ailleurs . . ."*) the draining of water from the front openings of the coat—which is apt to take place where the legs bend from the body—is shot off by means of the kilt.' I leave the lewder imaginings to draw parallels to this picture of the motorist of 1902. Vivid it certainly is.

The astonishing thing about these earliest examples of the species was that they rarely drove themselves. Mr Alfred Harmsworth who, we are told, was one of the leading pioneers of automobilism in England, wrote a dashing piece on side-slip for the *Badminton Magazine* at the turn of the century. 'Personally,' he declaimed (and being Alfred Harmsworth one was obviously intended to give the word its proper weight), 'I regard a twelve-horsepower automobile as almost as dangerous as a four-in-hand. I object to driving behind a spirited team unless in proper hands. I refuse to drive in a motor-car unless I know the abilities of the driver.'

So it was in later years than these that the terms 'motorist' and 'driver' became synonymous; in the days of the dreaded side-slip he was not necessarily to be found in the driver's seat. Indeed no: a contemporary wash drawing by Holland Tringham shows a side-slip at Hyde Park Corner where a combination of oversteer and high pressure tyres has brought the automobile into sharp contact with the base of a Victorian lamp post the top of which is about to fall as it sheds its glass on all and sundry. The chauffeur has left his seat to take up the stance of a Welsh lock forward over the bonnet. The motorist, however, remains seated at the rear, dignified and with only the slightest look of alarm. But perhaps he was wearing his seat belt. The O *tempora, O mores* aspect of this drawing is that one policeman is already standing by the bonnet of the car doing a Now-look-here-my-man with the Welsh lock forward while another is hoofing it west along Piccadilly towards the scene. And don't forget that the broken glass of the lamp hasn't yet reached the ground. Our policemen in those days were indeed wonderful.

I would not, for one moment, be thought to be taking the Mickey out of the pioneers. At the same time as the Honourable Evelyn Ellis was driving 'from Datchet to Windsor, and from Windsor to Malvern', twice satisfying the police by producing his carriage licence and once amazing a roadman who 'threw up his arms . . . and said, "Well, I'm blest if Mother Shipton's prophecy ain't come true! Here comes a carriage without a horse",' men like Jenatzy, De Knyff, Farman, Gabriel and S. F. Edge were averaging nearly 50 m.p.h. in the Gordon Bennett Cup race in 1903. When I was a small boy in the 'twenties, 'Gordon Bennett!' was an expletive conveying amazement and awe. No wonder.

It was the racing drivers, in fact, who ultimately lifted the actual driving of the vehicle from the servants' quarters into the drawing room and gave it a standing alongside the saddle of a horse. By the time the Bentley Boys were winning at Le Mans—wealthy amateurs all—the motorist as a species needed to suggest an affinity with the great ones of the Sarthe circuit—gauntlet gloves, a leather helmet, and a 'mount' with some suggestion of W. O. Bentley's functionalism about it. Even Herbert Austin's Twenty was given a dashing look, and if you knew Herbert's Midlands conservatism—and where better to go for conservatism?—you will not underestimate the significance of the sporting influence. Those of us who were trying to reconcile the earning of a pittance in the City of London with ownership of a motor car were in no doubt about where our loyalties lay. I worked for Iliffe at that time, who had deteriorated (in my opinion) from the competitor in the 1900 Thousand Miles Trial to the occupant of a chauffeur-driven Rolls-Royce, but my motor car yearned towards Parry Thomas and Major Henry Segrave. It was a Grand Prix Salmson costing all of £27 10s, with a St Andrew's cross on the radiator grille, a straight gear box, a solid rear axle with hand brake on the off-side rear wheel and the foot brake on the near-side rear wheel. It had an exhaust note like the boom of Concorde and was not at all the menace that it sounds. There is nothing to instil caution in a driver like the absence of brakes.

I digress. Were we motorists? We owned and adored our cars; we tinkered with them; we wore the accepted garb, and when we had a journey to make we no longer thought in terms of the Great Western, the London & North Eastern Railway, or even the London, Brighton & South Coast Railway. We were uncomfortably short of the spondulicks that had characterised the earliest motorists but petrol was only about a shilling a gallon and a daily load of clerks *en route* to and from The Office ('commuters' crossed the Atlantic years later) maintained a reasonable motoring fund. *Coward v Motor Insurers Bureau* belonged to the far future. I suppose, in fact, we were motorists—until someone decided that the future of motoring lay with the saloon. This was a sagacious decision which I have never ceased to applaud, but it made nonsense of gauntlet gloves, leather helmets and the $3\frac{1}{2}$-litre look. With the wisdom of hindsight one can see that this was the point at which we altered course for Jeremy's mother and Joanna's nanny. Perhaps it was the point at which the motorist disappeared behind a shadowy veil like Siegfried and Odette in the last scene of 'Swan Lake', drawn by a six-swan-power landaulette. Perhaps. But I don't think so.

One of the most curious features about the motor car had been the absence of a literature around it. There was plenty of motoring journalism but no literary writing about the device apart from one or two exceptions to prove the general rule. I discount Iris's Hispano-Suiza in *The Green Hat* because it was only incidental to that improbable girl's character, a foil introduced by Michael Arlen which would be dismissed as a gimmick today. In fact, I can recall only John Prioleau writing about Imshi in a manner that gave the car a personality without making one's toes curl up in embarrassment at the coyness which seems inseparable from this particular exercise. Why this should be I do not know. It does not exist with boats. I shared William A. Robinson's affection for *Svaap* and identified easily with Gerbault's *Firecrest*. I was even moved to pay sixpence to go aboard *Idle Hour* when she lay at Westminster Pier earning Dwight Long his keep. When I eventually found myself at sea I fell for the United Africa Co.'s *Guinean*, loading massive mahogany trunks into the hold 80 miles up the Niger delta with the aid of her jumbo boom, and for the sleek dachshund hulls of loaded tankers, thirty or forty of them, decks awash in a winter North Atlantic convoy. No sentiment, you understand; more respect and admiration, not qualities that I, or even John Prioleau, seemed to have felt for motor cars. Was I, then, a sailor rather than a motorist? Could a motorist be equated with a sailor?

Probably the absence from the road during the war gave time for one's ideas to crystallise on the subject. I was a sucker for distant places and can recall the almost physical pang of jealousy when I used to read the Booth Line's advertisement for their cruise 'One Thousand Miles up the Amazon'. Who goes to sea opens the oyster of his world. I swam in the Suez Canal and dived from the rail into Colombo Harbour. I cycled in the Nigerian bush and ate hot dogs from the stand at the Harlem end of the George Washington Bridge. I recalled that John Pratt in *Vagus* had preceded me across the Gatun Lake and out at the Pacific end of the Panama Canal, and I was on watch one dawn and sunrise off Curaçao when the sea and sky were of such rainbow radiance that one's emotional reaction made the voice too tremulous to risk.

The war, additionally, rocketed the aircraft from something that lumbered from Heston to Paris with film stars and socialites on board to something that put a girdle round the earth in forty minutes, and before long I was flying over a brown-baked Greece as the sun prepared to dip behind the Pillars of Hercules, taking off from Darwin with a pilot who possessed a dramatic eye for Indonesian volcanoes, banking over the Victoria Falls, and dropping into the night jewels of San Francisco Bay. I even trod on a South Sea Island, surely the ambition of every would-be traveller.

Now what on earth has this boastful catalogue to do with motorists, you will ask? I think I have at least a personal answer. For motorist read obsessional traveller plus means, because the new joy of car ownership after the war was that outside in the garage were the private seven-league boots to replace the professional ones that had enlarged the wartime horizons. In those still-youthful years the sporting influence had not dwindled. How could it when one of the greatest of the Bentley Boys, S. C. H. Davis, was always arriving simultaneously in the car park with a 'Hello, old thing' from alongside the tonneau cover of his red Aston Martin? I lived with and loved a Cecil Kimber MG, a Riley Brothers' 1½-litre and a W. Lyons' XK140—all cars that told you precisely what they were doing as you drove them as quickly as was safe along the roads of post-war Europe.

Other drivers, I freely acknowledge, drove such cars faster, and one or two of them emulated Holland Tringham's side-slip in the process, though not at Hyde Park Corner. Tugging at my sleeve on the long descent through the Alpes Maritimes at the end of a Monte Carlo Rally were the Alpes themselves demanding that one's eyes should leave the hairpins to take in the glory of the summits against the late afternoon sky, and that is best done at less than maximum speed; and if I drove fourteen times round the Le Mans circuit it was not because I fancied myself as a racing driver but because I wanted to know exactly where Gonzalez was at any given moment in the race that he was going to win on Saturday and Sunday. Such tastes, such activities, defined, I suppose, the motorist of that era, before Professor Rostow began to talk about 'take-off point' for the national economy after which growth comes easy, the theme music is Strauss' 'Acceleration', and Everyone, as the Pressmen say, owns a car.

From this point the image becomes more shadowy than ever, like those denizens that used to ride the sky above Jules Verne's *Castle in the Carpathians*. By contrast, R. J. Smeed of the Road Safety Section of the Road Research Laboratory was reducing to science all those imponderables of vehicle behaviour which we had delighted to explore as drivers, like lovers with a mistress. The side-slip came out as a bigger slip angle at the back than at the front tyres, generating cumulative centrifugal force. The distance which we so carefully judged when we drove behind another car crystallised into a formula derived from fitting a quadratic to observed results. Behaviour under braking became a matter of which wheel locked and the camber of the road. You could look up the certainties like a TV repairer armed with a fault chart. But the reasonable man could not withstand Smeed and was forced by his own conscience to drive at the safe speed which the circumstances demanded, and as he was doing this on roads which were never free from other vehicles he severed thereby the umbilical cord that had previously tied him to the racing circuits.

Much of tradition had to go too. A driver with half the politeness of the 'thirties found himself bullied. Observe Smeed's 'distance off' formula and two other drivers would overtake and occupy the gap. Drive at the speed which the fog demanded and you would get a flare of quartz-iodine lights from behind which, reflected from the fog, would induce snow-blindness as well as telling you that someone felt that he could get home to the telly more quickly than you. Try to change lane in a strange town because you had made a mistake and it became possible to observe the unforgiving attitude of your fellow-drivers. 'When in Rome do as Rome does'? Yes, but who wants to become a selfish lout, foul of mouth and brutish of action, prepared to inflict a hundred pounds-worth of damage for the sake of demonstrating that courtesy is a word unknown to the modern vocabulary? Besides, such behaviour reverses the tenets of the true motorist. This

modern spawn of the age of violence earns no such title; he is a
mere thug on wheels.

Perhaps motorists are like so many of the world's splendours—
becoming rarer and threatened with extinction? The environment
is hostile and thick with the enemies of our kind—the first away
from the traffic lights and the carriers of dolly-birds from pub
to pub, not to mention the $4\frac{1}{4}$-litres and the dammit-I'm-the-
company-chairman type making full use of 'Continental' horns
and 260 b.h.p. Occasionally, however, one can return to the
kindly, gentle world of the 'knight on wheels' and his con-
sideration for the rest of us. One of my more frequent after-
midnight journeys is the climb from Huddersfield up through
Holmfirth, Holmbridge and Holme up to Holme Moss at
1,723 feet where the BBC has its TV aerial. It is a world of vast
panoramas, followed by black peat, swirling mist indicating
that you have gone above cloud ceiling, and ghosties and
ghoulies, if not long-leggity beasties, although the chequered fog
and snow-depth markers on both sides of the road could easily
be the stilt-like limbs of animals inhabiting a Wagnerian twilight.
No-one follows you up this hill after midnight and you can
savour your own judgement in the fog, conscious of the potential
death-roll down into the valley if you leave the road and your
chances of a headline in the local paper a week later, and mindful
of the maxim that the master must never hazard the ship.
Eventually you leave the mist and lower the car gently down
Heyden Moor towards Woodhead, past the escape road for
brake failure and into the hairpin above the stone bridge that
makes a wasp-waist of the road over the stream.

Once in a hundred journeys you will meet another car at this
spot, that late. With instinctive courtesy you hover with dipped
headlights while he takes the bridge and the one-in-four corner
and climbs past you with a flick of appreciation. The encounter
is brief but significant. The post-midnight loneliness of the road
is gone, the wet cold air of the Western Pennines is suddenly
warm with the reward of courtesy. Just for a moment, two
motorists have reaffirmed their principles and justified their
soubriquet in a congenial environment.

Chez Brockbank

'Since we left Oulton Park for the horses we have seen them walk round and round, the blankets taken off, the saddling up, the owners' last instructions, the jockeys mounting, the cantering up the course, the circling round and the tightening of girths, the eventual start, two minutes of racing, the plodding back to the paddock, the jockeys getting off and the blankets going on, the hanging around for the results, the winning prices announced—since then, as I said, the leading cars have swopped eighteen times, one driver has swum out of the lake, there has been a phenomenal avoidance at Old Hall involving four cars, a fire at the pits, and here come the three leaders neck and neck for the finish of the century while we go over to Wigan for the Rugby League match, where a muddy man is digging a hole with his boot with infinite care . . .'

'With only two hours to go No. 61 has a comfortable lead.'

'Brace yourself, dear: in addition to the big race they have for our delight no less than five separate feasts of speed and daring.'

'Says his last job was the Paris–Madrid.'

'From now on I don't care a damn whether it rains, shines or snows.'

'It's just your word against OURS.'

'Ask him which symbol he's pointing at'.

'Fancy ruining a great old car like that with grotty mod wheels.'

Motoring Nights

RONALD BARKER

Today it's Watford 24498K, and you have to feed it with Two or Ten New Pence to set it chattering. Coppers and tanners are out, Button A and Button B have disappeared without trace, and probably the number's changed in the 31 years since I last called here, but the red kiosk looks just as it did—and no cleaner, although the cigarette stubs and other dropsam have been changed regularly through the years. Every time I pass this way a shiver of cold memories still runs up and down the spine, of a bitter February night in '41 when no Samaritan's masked head-lamps shone discreetly through the wartime blackout to lift a stranded hitchhiker.

Sleet was beginning to soak through the RAF 'other ranks' coarse cloth, and already the trouser legs had become creaseless blue-grey tubes, so heavy with moisture that the plaster cast encasing my right leg from thigh to toes must soon turn flabby and disintegrate around its fragile contents like a hollow tree in a storm. So I decided to take refuge in this telephone box and spend as little of the night as possible as the GPO's uninvited guest. Weakened by long months in hospital, only an idiot would chance bumming a ride home for sick leave but I dreaded the sympathy of civilians on railway platforms rushing to assist the poor wounded airman, although they weren't to know there was nothing heroic about being unsaddled from a Norton by an armoured truck in Cheltenham, even if it was in the middle of an air raid alert. I could have knocked up a nearby household, but my folly scarcely justified disturbing some family already bedded down; and if I dialled 999 for help the police might contact my station commander and make matters worse.

They were very long hours I spent propped on crutches or leaning on the sharp-edged coin box in that impromptu, vertical bedroom, unable to double up and squat on the concrete floor. I was chilled right through, shaking like an aspen, while the fractured leg had swelled tight in the plaster and throbbed violently with the effort to slough it and break free. Probably I hadn't slept a wink when, soon after daybreak, an old truck suddenly materialized through the gloom outside, and going my way. I pushed open the door and waved a crutch as a feeble signal, suddenly knowing then how Wellington must have felt when Blucher arrived, except that the smell was different; not sweating men and horses, but dog manure seeping out from wooden casks on the open platform whose stench somehow permeated forward to the cab. The driver told me he was heading for a leather tannery, and that his route took him straight past my front door. He apologised for the smell, and vainly tried to counter it with occasional splashings from a huge bottle of Eau de Cologne. But it was hot as a Hilton suite in there beside the busy engine, and by the time we reached home I was warmed through and revitalized with its vibro-massage.

In the early '50s I was back to live in Cheltenham for a while, and once a month rode to the RAC in London for Vintage Sports-Car Club committee meetings on my Vintage 2-stroke Scott. After the meetings we would wash down sandwiches and Cornish pasties with a few pints in a nearby pub, and then the committee would push-start me down Piccadilly. In those days A40 was almost free from traffic around midnight and I would ride home flat-out, but the Scott fuel tank was microscopic, and the twin-cylinder 2-stroke responded to full rein with galloping consumption of its smoky brew. I recall two all-night filling-stations but it could not always make the distance between them, and I came to know other tiny GPO hotels on that route.

Later I bought a 1928 overhead-cam KE Velocette which went like a bat out of Lords, discharging oil not as smoke from the exhaust but as a fine spray from the engine joints, to such an extent that competitive opposition in its wake was soon part-blinded and thrown off in disarray. So, sometimes, was its rider. The first time was following yet another night in a telephone box near Swindon, when bound for heaven knows where from somewhere else. I propped it up outside this friendly refuge and cuddled up knees to chin on the floor to await the rosy-fingered dawn. Come morning, a small Ford van materialized, and the driver suggested tying one end of my long woollen scarf to the rear door handle while I hung on to the other. This was so tiring, what with the combined weights of Barker and bike, that after very few miles I suddenly lost hold and the Velocette swung violently to port.

I crashed against a grassy bank and rolled back on to the road, but luckily the driver felt his van shoot forward as the dead-weight was released. He reversed, helped sort me out again and towed me the last mile or two to a country garage. 'Why didn't you walk here last night and knock me up?' the proprietor asked. 'For one thing I didn't know you were here,' I said, 'and for another, you wouldn't have been pleased to be dragged out of bed at 1 a.m., would you?' 'I'm glad to help people at any hour. It often happens, and that's what I'm here for—a service to travellers!' He must have been unique.

The last of my GPO nights was spent on the short stretch between Salisbury and Downton, when I was (of course) very nearly out of petrol but was actually stopped by two flat tyres. The car they were failing to prop up was a Type 30 straight-8 Bugatti with which I was undergoing a love-hate relationship at the expense of my toenails; the successive engine vibration periods were making them ingrow, starting with the great big piggy at about 2,000 r.p.m. and running down to the littlest piggy at three-eight. There was one critical frequency range that got them all going together, but the engine would never let you stay in one frequency for long; a plug would die and change it, or all the plugs would die and stop it. The tyre problem was beaded-edge covers, hard and perished, with miniature Cheddar Gorges in the walls through which the tubes tried to escape but were pinched, as you might say, in the nick of time, and I didn't fancy a major strip and repair job by the road-side at dead of night. Why not sleep in the Bugatti? I tried to, but it let too much weather in.

Reverting to the Velocette, which I ran concurrently with the Bugatti, some of my worst nights were spent with that, right from the start of our association. I had done a complete rebuild before running it, apart from farming out the engine job to a professional Velocette expert in Cheltenham, and its very first outing was to be a European tour taking in France, Germany, Austria and Italy in company with a chum riding a new BSA. An air passage was booked from Lydd to Le Touquet before the work was finished, and it began to look like I would never make it. For two nights running I slaved right through without sleep or rest, spending the days between at my professional work, and on the third night we set off from Cheltenham about 10 p.m. in heavy mist. Almost immediately the dynamo ceased to charge so the headlamps could only be used for any emergencies one was sharp enough to foresee. At a brightly-lit filling-station in High Wycombe we tried to sort out an accumulation of breaking-in problems, including the dynamo, but after an hour or two had to restart without amps. Mist and fog persisted right through the night to Lydd, which combined with intense fatigue made that a journey best forgotten. We caught our flight without a minute to spare, but when they handed the Velocette back to me at Le Touquet, it fell on me—quite hard. We rode the few kilometres to Berck Plage, bought some chocolate patisseries and made for the beach, where we slept for hours and woke with one side of our faces à *point*.

Our next nocturnal adventure was to arrive in darkness at the crest of the Brenner to find the descent into Italy blocked by landslides, so we parked our mounts in a straw-strewn barn with some cattle and found beds in a tiny pub there. Next morning there was nothing for it but to ride westwards into Switzerland and try to cross by the Maloja. On this route lay St. Moritz, its streets swarming with the rich and fashionable. Some of them watched as we rode into a parking area in the centre, with saliva welling up in our mouths at the prospect of cream cakes and hot chocolate, and open tarts filled with succulent black cherries. As I heaved a leg over the Velocette saddle to dismount, the belt supporting my slacks snapped and they fell around my feet. . . .

There was one terrific night in Italy, in a tiny albergo high above a mountain village. We had come to a halt because the Velocette had no lights and it was pitch dark, so any haven was welcome. It so happened the landlord and his customers were mostly ex-partisan fighters who had shared the latter part of their war with British fugitives and Commandos, so the night was festive and alcoholic to excess, and the take-off next morning correspondingly erratic. We made for Genoa and a lobster lunch, but arrived there in the middle of an international motor-cycle rally. Like widdershins, it drew us three times anti-clockwise into the central assembly point before we managed to break clear and ferret out our fish restaurant, if you'll forgive the terminological contradiction.

From Genoa it was a short run to the French border and Monaco, but here all the many small hotels and pensions we tried were *touts complets*, perhaps because long-distance motor-cyclists tend to look battered and impoverished, scarcely respectable enough to mix with well-washed company. So we rode through gathering dusk towards Nice, finding nothing on the way; before reaching the Promenade des Anglais I stopped to warn Hugh that the police were sure to whistle me for riding without lights, and not to worry—it was my problem. I would ride flat-out and wait for him if necessary beyond the town. Sure enough, the flatfoots whistled like mad but luckily no *mobiles* were saddled for the chase. It was a super warm night, so I suggested sleeping under the stars for a change. On the right was some inviting scrub, but on closer inspection it showed up filthy with litter and human excrement. On the left, though, there was a slight

c

drop from the road, some heavy shingle and then a broad expanse of clean ground as far as one could see in the BSA's lamp beam. Extraordinary! We wheeled our mounts down off the road and rode them well into the middle of this welcoming expanse, towards the sea. Propping the bikes, we were soon fast asleep beside them.

About 3 a.m. I was jerked from my dreams by a dig in the ribs and Hugh screaming 'Run for it!' above the roar of aeroplane motors. Dazzling lights were rushing straight towards us, and as we ran a DC3 lifted steeply to clear the two machines now brilliantly lit in its path. Of course it's different now, and Nice Airport is properly fenced off from intruders. Quick as gazelles fleeing from a ravenous lion we were up, up and away before any frantic reaction to the pilot's alerting the control-tower.

May 16 1954 was, I believe, the day the Queen returned from a long tour of her overseas dominions (which wouldn't take her so far these days) and the pubs were open late that evening to celebrate her homecoming. They were discharging droves of inebriated customers sometime after 11 p.m. when a 1907 Gobron-Brillié fire-engine rumbled through the streets of Bridgwater on solid tyres en route from Exeter to Cheltenham, just 120 miles. Their reactions were extraordinary; seeing that apparition through the alcoholic haze was not believing, and understandably. (It's the same vehicle, incidentally, that now belongs to Lord Montagu and can be seen in his Museum at Beaulieu.) I had gone down to Exeter early that morning with three friends to try to get the old thing going and drive it back, but the daylight was frittered away dealing with a succession of snags—water cascading from a cracked cylinder block; the gear lever coming readily to hand (which meant dismantling all the selector mechanism to repair it), then some carburettor problems.

Finally we thundered away about 6 p.m., travelling hopefully but scarcely expecting to arrive. After long years of idleness sitting on its airless tyres, they had each developed a deep 'flat' which came down to earth in a varying sequence that changed at every bend in the road, thump—thud—bump—bang, or bump—bang—thump—thud, *ad infinitum*. With 7.6 litres and a pair of opposed pistons coming together but never quite meeting in each cylinder, we had plenty of crude urge but low overall gearing through side chains and sprockets, and about 18 m.p.h. was all the human frame could stand. The worst problem was to keep the escort car's crew awake, and every time my riding mechanic saw it veer off course, he dropped a length of fire-fighting hose in its path to jolt them out of their dreams. On board the Gobron-Brillié we suffered agonies from freezing faces, the reason becoming clear when a cracked fuel line from the gravity tank above the bulkhead just in front of us finally sheared a few miles from Cheltenham, where our masochistic journey ended at 5 a.m. next morning.

It was probably earlier than 1954 that Nigel Arnold-Forster and I had the lunatic notion to drive to Spain for a holiday in my tiny 1922 Peugeot Quadrilette, and we did in fact get there and back. Once again there were problems getting it ready in time after a rebuild, and once again we were booked to fly Silver City, but this time from Southampton to Cherbourg. The arrangement was for me to drive it over to his home near Swindon for the night and we would set off early next morning, but the last-minute finishing touches seemed never-ending. At last all appeared to be ready, but I crept into Cirencester at a late hour with desperate misfiring under the bonnet and the 10-odd b.h.p. practically decimated. There I roused a cycle shop proprietor to sell me a torch (God! Not even a torch in the going-away kit?), and brought back enough life to reach the Arnold-Forster mansion sometime after midnight. In their garage I set about fitting the spare magneto, only to find it had 'opposite rotation'. So then I dismantled it to modify the internal timing, and dammit if one of its minor entrails didn't fall to the floor, roll gracefully through a drain grid and drop into the mush below. Perhaps it is still there. By about 5 a.m. one working mag had somehow emerged from two duffers and all systems were more or less 'go'—including the brakes, which were powerless to prevent it. (It was not until days later, when we had descended the Pyrenees into Andorra at unbelievable personal risk, that we solved this problem by dismantling the rear transmission casing to reverse the axle shaft and hence the rotation of the oil-retaining scrolls.) Anyhow, after another sleepless night we caught our air ferry to Cherbourg.

You may hardly credit this, but in 1970 I had similar magneto traumas with the same car in a small village just outside Marseilles. Before I left for that trip Nigel offered to lend me a Fordson magneto which he swore was the very one that had sparked us home from Spain on that earlier trip, when the one I had rebuilt in his garage ultimately failed. If it was the same, its rotation had mysteriously reverted in the interim, because I spent all of a night in a small hotel bedroom with a kit of tools retiming it internally before I could progress to Monte Carlo for the Grand Prix.

August 29, 1959 was a great day for Alec Issigonis, the day his Mini was unveiled to an astonished but extremely sceptical public. A little thing like that, they thought, was purely a short-term expedient to meet a fuel crisis (Suez, remember?). It was far too small and toy-like for serious motoring—just a shopping car. It was also the day World Champion Jack Brabham went to the Festival Hall in London and was given a flag. His job (the penalty of fame) was to wag it at a little red Mini. Somewhere inside this Mini, packed among all the baggage and water cans and spare parts and other paraphernalia, were Peter Rivière and Barker. Our job was to drive the thing right round the Mediterranean. All went tolerably well until we approached the Turkish-Syrian border late one night, at the summit of quite an exciting little Alpine pass.

Here I was accused of a currency fiddle. Even had it been my own money, I certainly should not have risked a fiddle, and the customs men knew well enough that it was no more than a simple mathematical error. But they said I must pay a £95 fine or stand trial. They even got the village magistrate out of bed to adjudicate. He arrived in the little courtroom around 11 p.m. dressed in a snappy pale grey suit and Panama hat, and expressed his displeasure at being disturbed by supporting their accusations. Unwilling to squander *The Autocar*'s money on a Turkish chicanery, I opted for trial and was promptly arrested. My report to London read: 'We are provided with an armed escort, very high (e.g. smelly), who carries a statement which Barker has refused to sign, since it was written on a Turkish typewriter. At 11.30 p.m. we somehow immerse the Good Soldier Schweik under luggage on the back seat and open all windows. Barker now gets his own back by a demonstration to Schweik of the Mini-Minor's chamois agility on the brinks of precipices by night. There is distinct evidence of full success; later, when the road has levelled out, Rivière notices him fast asleep but with eyes still wide open. . . .

'At 4.30 a.m. we arrive at Mersin (165 miles from the frontier), utterly exhausted and depressed, and find a filthy little hotel where a Turkish flea-circus performs on Barker for two hours. At 7.30 we are escorted to a ramshackle courthouse, where we sit on a hard bench among the pick of local thieves and seducers for 5½ hours. At 1.15 Barker is taken before a tribunal—one woman and two men—all wearing comic-opera red and black cloaks and smoking cigarettes. It is pure Alice in Wonderland, except that no attempt is made to put a dormouse into a teapot. Rivière is told off for crossing his legs in the public gallery, Barker for not standing to attention. . . . At 5 p.m. Barker is told: "You are not condemned".'

That, in fact, was after a second hearing. All this happened at a time of student uprisings in Turkey, and just before we left England I had read a report that students were being murdered, minced and fed to animals. Believe me, that night I would have given the whole of lousy Turkey for a cosy little telephone box near Watford.

Of all the motoring masochisms in which I have ever indulged, the most long drawn-out was a journey in 1969 from London to

Sicily via Amsterdam, Paris, Turin and Rome, and back again to Rome, in a monstrous straight-8 Daimler limousine of the late 1940s, one-time property of Prince Rainier of Monaco, a Midlands municipality and finally a string of undertakers. By the time it reached my hands it was knock-kneed and down at heel, with countless extra maladies that came to light in unison or succession during this marathon. In fact, it was overdue for consignment to a motor mortician.

For brevity's sake we'll overlook the whys and wherefores of buying such a car and using it for such an excursion, except to recall that it was done for an Italian friend who despatched his son to buy the car and share the action. In nine days we covered 2,300 miles, using over 200 gallons of fuel, 10 gallons of oil, measureless quantities of water and three screenwiper blades. Some of the water was used to dowse a fire in the driver's door just before setting off, and more in the middle of Paris when the limousine division was set alight by the electric motor intended to drive it up and down.

The first evening, hurrying in the rain to catch a ferry at Harwich, we experienced a 75-degree sideslip in a lane not wide enough to accommodate our full $18\frac{1}{2}$ feet at 90 degrees; getting out of that one without entering the scenery, we wondered whether the skipper of the QE2 has ever had a moment like that in Southampton Water. Most of the next night was occupied in 'moving house' between Amsterdam and Paris in miserable conditions, and another sleepless nocturnal stint was spent somehow lifting its unbelievably cumbersome three tons over the mountains into Italy.

In Naples, just when we were due to catch the Blue Kangaroo ferry to Palermo, my friend Massimo managed to wedge the Daimler with three-point contact across a T-intersection in one of those narrow gorges in the slum area, and half the population soon gathered to laugh and shriek conflicting directions. God knows how we got out of that one, overcome as we were by the infectious hysterics of the Neopolitan. After countless other adventures the last straw was a nightmare run, taking turns to kip in the royal apartment behind, from Reggio Calabria north to Naples (before the *autostrada* had been completed) and thence to Rome.

Then there were two traumatic nights somewhere in Morocco late in 1970, when testing a Range Rover with Doug Blain of *Car* magazine. Being unseasoned travellers, we carried no food, no water and no compass on board, and neither of us could read the stars. We had this notion to try crossing into Tunisia although one of us lacked the necessary papers; being a Tasman and brimming with self-confidence, he reckoned no border guard could stop him, but actually we never reached the border. We had picked on a point marked Figuig. Maybe it really exists, or is it merely a Figuig of the imagination?

Rather suddenly the light went out when we were on a 'road' indicated by the map but otherwise practically undefined. It kept arriving at dried river beds with no indication of where the trail restarted on the far side, and ultimately we reached a rather wet and very rocky one. After roving up and down this for some time at some peril without finding a rift in the far bank, and having approached the point of no return in our fuel tank, we had to surrender and retrace our steps. But how? In places the track forked into two or three prongs, and repeatedly Blain had to search on his knees in the dust with a torch to detect our tyre marks patterns. Eventually we reached a small Berber mud village in the small hours, completely dark, but luckily came across a youth still about with his dog. He banged and thumped on the door of a small café until, after much muttering within, an ancient biblical character carrying an oil lamp staggered out. The place was crammed with sleeping figures, but he cleared a space for us and laid rugs on the dirt floor, and in the morning fed us with rough bread and coffee.

The very next night we engaged a young guide to help us pick out another route, not towards Tunisia this time but looping south and west between the rocky foothills of the Atlas mountains and the Sahara. Again our Michelin map showed it clearly in white framed between black lines, and again it disappeared among the wadi. But our guide knew; hadn't he helped to guide many foreign tourists on behalf of this and that company? He knew all right and would point first this way, then that, with never a moment's hesitation, while we accompanied his Berber songs with super imitations of the mouth organ and other musical instruments. When he did ask the odd nomad shepherd, it was only to confirm his convictions.

By and by we arrived at a cluster of mud huts, miles from any other habitation (it was dark by now, as usual), where a friendly tribesman offered to ride half a mile with us to put us on the right track. Our guide thanked him in Berber, we said good-night in perfect English, and motored off. About 2 a.m. we found another lonely shepherd with rifle slung to guard his flock from wolves, and this man argued strongly with our guide, pointing to the stars to emphasize his directions. Our guide told us he was an ignorant fool; our guide knew better.

It must have been two hours later we came upon a cluster of mud huts, and a tribesman standing there who might be worth approaching, He was very surprised, because he didn't see vehicles pass that way more than once a blue moon and this was the second within a few hours. Moreover, it looked just like the other one—in fact it *was* the other one! We learnt that night what Berber hospitality to total strangers means. We were desperately hungry so they produced two tins of sardines which were opened with a sword and poured into a white enamel basin, to be scooped out with hunks of their delicious bread and swilled down with endless glasses of mint tea. After breakfasting next morning on a sort of gruel topped with melted butter, we were glad to carry one of the tribesmen about 60 miles over the rocky wastes to the nearest market town. That way we actually got somewhere, despite our guide.

There have been lots of other motoring nights to remember, of course—in a 1911 Fafnir, a 1920 40-50 Napier, various Lancias, and even a three-wheeled BSA; but now, if you'll excuse me, I'll just have a quick night-cap and crawl under the electric blanket. . . .

Design in Excelsis

or

What makes Racing Cars go fast

PAUL FRÈRE

'And still the Queen kept crying, "Faster! Faster!" '—
LEWIS CARROLL

This study deals mainly with the development of racing cars designed to participate in the two World Championships: the Drivers' (in Formula I) and the Manufacturers' (in what is commonly called 'sports car racing').

Racing car design is primarily governed by the rules devised by the relevant body, in this case the International Sporting Commission (CSI) of the 'Fédération Internationale de l'Automobile' (FIA). Unfortunately, these rules are usually far from simple, being a compromise of various, often diverging, lines of thought with a lot of added afterthoughts. They are not necessarily logical either, because often tradition interferes with logic. There is no other explanation to the requirement that 'Formula cars' must have their wheels uncovered by the car's body, for example. If it were not for that rule, it is obvious that today's single-seaters would look very much like Sports Proto-types in order to reduce the enormous air drag of the current racing tyres.

The rules being what we start from, let us have a quick look at their main outlines.

Formula I. The current FI has been in force basically since 1966. It calls for an engine of no more than 3 litres displacement (or a gas turbine or a NSU-Wankel rotary piston engine of a size governed by equivalence formulae) burning commercial pump fuel (or kerosene in the case of gas turbines) and a minimum weight which, from 500 kg, has gone up in steps to 530 kg in 1971 and 550 kg in 1972 in order to accommodate various safety features that have been introduced.

Sports Cars and Prototypes. The formula enforced from 1968 to 1971 allowed two categories of cars to compete simultaneously for the Manufacturer's World Championship. In principle, it limited the engine displacement to 3 litres with a sliding minimum weight scale that went up to 650 kg for 3-litre cars, and pump fuel was compulsory. A windscreen was compulsory, having a minimum height of 25 cm measured along the longitudinal axis of the seats (of which there were to be two) and a minimum width of 90 cm at half height. A spare wheel was compulsory.

As the engine displacement limit had been imposed at very short notice, there were only very few competitive cars available at the beginning of 1968 and, as a consequence, it was decided to accept cars with an engine displacement of up to 5 litres with a minimum weight of 800 kg, provided 25 had been built, thus qualifying as 'Sports Cars'. In practice, this made the Ford GT40s and the Chevrolet-engined Lola T70s eligible and these heavier cars powered by basically production American pushrod v8s proved to have, in fact, a performance about equal to that of the more exotic 3 litres.

This (technically regrettable) equivalence worked reasonably well until Porsche let the cat loose among the pigeons and decided they could afford to build 25 'Sports Cars' to full racing specification, and the well-known 917 was the result. In practice, these just made a joke of the 3-litre limit, and as Ferrari immediately joined in with the 512S, there was pretty little the CSI could do to give the 3-litre cars a faint chance of remaining competitive, but to abolish all restrictions, except on engine size. So overboard went the windscreen specifications, the minimum weight and the spare wheel in a desperate effort to reduce the the weight and the drag of the 3-litre cars, while the fuel tank capacity of the 5-litres was reduced to 120 litres, as for the smaller cars. Eventually however, it was decided to ban the 5-litres and restore the 3-litres in their own right, reimposing the 650 kg minimum weight limit, but not the other items required heretofore, so that the manufacturers now really don't know what to do with all that weight. The ban on the over-3-litre cars came into force on 1 January 1972.

Developments of structure and chassis design. The performance in terms of speed and acceleration of any car is mainly governed by two major performance factors:

(*a*) the power/weight ratio;
(*b*) the ratio of power to frontal area × drag factor.

The power-to-weight ratio has a direct bearing on acceleration. If the air drag were nil, the acceleration would be proportional to the power/weight ratio.

The ratio of power to frontal area × drag factor is what determines a car's maximum speed. It has little bearing on the acceleration at relatively low speeds, when air drag is comparatively small, but as the speed goes up, so does its effect on acceleration. This is easily understood if you take the case of a given car, having a maximum speed of, say, 150 m.p.h. If this is the maximum speed, it means in other words that, at that speed, the acceleration is nil. Now, if the car is modified to take a more powerful engine or by reducing its frontal area or giving it a more wind-cheating shape, it will be able to reach a higher maximum speed. So at 150 m.p.h. it will still be accelerating, which proves the point.

As far as absolute performance is concerned, any increase in engine power will bring returns at both ends of the speed scale; drag reduction (by reducing the frontal area, the drag factor or both) will bring returns mainly in the higher speed ranges and weight reduction in the lower speed ranges. Weight reduction is not applicable to Grand Prix racing however, as most of the cars have been pretty near the minimum weight limit since this has been introduced.

In Grand Prix racing, where the rules require that the wheels should not be covered by the body, there is little the designer can do about the drag factor C_W of the car which is very bad due to the turbulence caused by the wheels and their interference with the body. As a consequence, the total drag being governed by the product $S \times C_W$, they have been concentrating mainly on reducing the frontal area S, which is the only reason why a Grand Prix driver has to lie down in his car instead of sitting reasonably upright. The Lotus 25 was really the ultimate in that line of thought.

When the current 3-litre Formula I was introduced, the same line was followed, though doubling the engine capacity called for wider tyres and larger capacity tanks which inevitably increased the cross section of the body. Very soon however, tyre development played complete havoc with the frontal area, with rims widths going up from some 10 inches to 16, and even 17, inches on the rear wheels in the short span of five years, from 1966 to 1970, when the tyres alone were evaluated to account for about 70 per cent of the drag of a FI car.

It is during that period too that aerofoils were introduced to create down thrust and increase tyre adhesion and these aerofoils, though quickly limited in width and height by appropriate regulations, also contributed to increased air drag, so that in the end, the increase in maximum speed was not nearly as high as the difference in power between the 320 HP Repco engine of the Championship-winning Brabham of 1966 and the 450 HP Ford-Cosworth engine of the Championship-winning Lotus of 1970 should have produced.

By 1970, it was high time something was done about the enormous drag caused by the tyres. Already most manufacturers had been using 13-inch diameter wheels at the front, just to reduce their height, but for 1971 the tyre manufacturers came out with tyres which, even on very fast circuits like Monza, would not shed their tread on rear wheels of only 13-inch diameter and of which the profile ratio was as low as 30 per cent (which means the tyre's height was only 30 per cent of its width). Compared with the 40 profile, 15-inch tyres of 1970, this means a reduction in overall diameter of about $3\frac{1}{2}$ inches and a reduction of 12.5 per cent of the frontal area of the tyre.

The outcome of all this are extremely spectacular increases in the speeds reached by Grand Prix cars around given courses, as the following race winning speeds exemplify, the examples being chosen from races run in dry weather on circuits which were not materially modified in the meantime, though it must be said that race distances were reduced over the period:

Circuit	Year	Car	Speed	Increase	Comment
Monza	1966	Ferrari	135.5 m.p.h.		⎱ No aerofoils
	1971	BRM	151 m.p.h.	11%	⎰ used
Nürburgring	1966	Brabham-Repco	86.6 m.p.h.		⎱ No aerofoils
	1971	Tyrrell-Ford	114.4 m.p.h.	32%	⎰ Aerofoils very effective
Monaco	1966	BRM	77.3 m.p.h.		⎱ No aerofoils
	1971	Tyrrell-Ford	83.5 m.p.h.	9%	⎰ Aerofoils of little effect

This comparison shows what sort of benefit can be expected from the aerofoils. At Monza, where bends are few and fast, the advantage of aerofoils is at least debatable because the increased cornering speed and reduction of braking distances they allow is just about cancelled out by the reduced speed on the long straights. The fact that the 1971 winner had discarded them enables us to state that the 11 per cent increase in race average is due entirely to the increase in engine power and the better tyre performance. Comparing the speed increase at Monza with that on the Nürburgring (where the improvements made to the circuit are just about cancelled out by the chicane built on the straight, in 1969) indicates that on a medium fast circuit with many fast bends, the aerofoils have an enormous effect. This was also exemplified by the fact that in many cases, the 1971 cars with their cut-about regulation wings only just about matched the speeds reached in 1969 when the 'wings' had reached the climax of their exoticism. A more scientific measure of the aerofoils' efficiency is the fact that the coefficient of adhesion of a top-class dry-weather tyre is about 1.4, but that centripetal accelerations as high as 1.7 g were measured in actual cornering conditions (by Matra coming out of the tunnel at Monaco), which means that the cornering force can be raised by as much as over 20 per cent by the down thrust created by the 'wings', even in their present abbreviated form.

But let us go back to tyre developments. The original reason for increasing the width of the rim on which they were mounted was to reduce the slip angle under cornering and thus improve the handling and cornering power, which also benefited from the increased contact area between the tyre and the road. In this connection, it must be remembered that tyres do not follow the law applying to solid objects, which says that the adhesion depends only on the coefficient of adhesion and the force with which the two surfaces are applied against each other: rubber is deformable and conforms to the road surface, gearing itself into the rugosities of the latter, so that the greater the number of 'gears' meshing with each other, the greater the adhesion. The wider the rims and the tyres became without any increase in the overall diameter of the latter, the lower became the profile ratio and the better the lateral stability of the tyre. Above a certain point however, the reduction of the slip angle under a given lateral force becomes very small and would certainly not have warranted a further increase of the rim and tread widths up to the currently used 16 and 17 inches and the consequent drag penalty, had not the much reduced unitary pressure resulting from the increased contact area between tread and road allowed the use of extremely soft and sticky rubber compounds providing an increased coefficient of adhesion. Such compounds would wear away in no time if the contact area were smaller.

Having reached the desired target, a new problem cropped up, when, in rapid succession, the rim diameter was reduced from

15 to 13 inches and tyres with a 30 per cent profile ratio replaced those with a profile ratio of 40-42 per cent. The notably reduced overall diameter of the tyre brought about a reduction of the length of the contact area between the tyre and the road (it is called length, because it is measured parallel to the longitudinal axis of the car though, in actual fact, this 'length' is shorter than the 'width') which somehow, had to be compensated for. The solution to this problem were the current 'slicks' of which the tread has no pattern and of which consequently the entire contact area is really effective, in contrast to sculptured treads, of which the channels are not effective in bringing rubber into contact with the road. Channels are still used for wet road tyres however, when they are essential for draining the water away from the actual contact area and the wear problem is not critical.

There have been no major developments in the suspension systems during the last decade, but their geometry has been progressively adapted to the varying tyre characteristics. Whereas ten years ago, with the relatively narrow tyres featuring a curved tread profile, negative camber was a desirable feature to secure high cornering forces and a quite notable amount of it was used to ensure that the camber was preserved on the more laden outside wheels when the car rolled on a corner, the modern wide, flat-treated tyres must remain as vertical as possible, otherwise the tread does not make full contact with the road over its entire width and the useful contact area is reduced with consequent loss of adhesion and increased temperature and wear. With the very soft, temperature-sensitive rubber used today, temperature is very critical and different dry-weather compounds are made to suit the prevailing temperature conditions. If the tyre runs too cold, its adhesion is reduced; if it runs too warm, the rubber will wear away extremely quickly and, on faster circuits, become detached in lumps from the carcase. In some cases, the temperature range of a modern racing tyre is as narrow as 20-25 degrees C and very often it happens that a certain car uses three tyres of a given mix, while the fourth (usually the front left on clockwise circuits) is made of a mix designed for thes next higher temperature range. There have even been instance when three different mixes were used on the same car.

Design in Excelsis

Though the requirement of keeping the tyres vertical would be best fulfilled by a beam axle, independent suspension is still considered to be the better compromise because of its lower unsprung weight and lesser tendencies to induce undesirable gyroscopic phenomena. But independent suspension is a very delicate compromise. For purely suspension movements when the car is not submitted to lateral forces, parallel action, such as that provided by pure trailing or leading links or wishbones arranged to form a true parallelogram, would be ideal. But such a system is unacceptable because, on corners, the wheels would adopt the same roll angle as the car, whereas we want them to remain as near vertical as possible, specially the outside wheels which take the larger part of the car's weight, as it corners. Moreover, with parallel action suspension, the roll centre is on the ground which, all other factors being equal, increases the undesirable roll. Consequently, we must give the suspension some 'swing axle' characteristic, that is there must be increasing negative camber as the suspension is compressed. To minimise the required swing axle characteristic, which is undesirable on a straight line and specially while braking, when 'dive' causes a considerable deflection of the suspension at a time when maximum-tyre grip is required, one solution consists of using all possible means to reduce roll.

Roughly, the roll angle is proportional to the height of the centre of gravity (h_G) over the roll centre and to the cornering force (F_C), and inversely proportional to the track(T) and to the roll stiffness (R) of the suspension, which we can write:

$$\alpha \div \frac{h_G \cdot F_C}{T \cdot R}$$

There is not much we can do about the height of the centre of gravity above the roll centre. Ferrari claims that his flat-12 engine produces a slightly lower centre of gravity than a V-type engine, but this remains open to discussion, as the crankshaft centre line must be raised, in this configuration, in order to make room for the exhaust system beneath the blocks. As for raising the roll centre, this produces an increased 'swing axle' effect

Move over! Peter Collins (Ferrari) tries to overtake Wolfgang von Trips' similar car in Ancona: 1957 Mille Miglia

Steady as she goes . . .! Manoeuvring aboard Ronald Barker's 1908 Napier

Lotus 49B, 1969 Spanish Grand Prix

'The 1971 cars with their cut-down regulation wings only just about matched the speeds reached in 1969 when wings reached the climax of their exoticism.' (see page 46)

Tyrrell-Ford, 1971 Rothman's International

Le Mans, 1971: 'Porsche 917s took the World's Manufacturers' Championship for both 1970 and 1971' (see page 69)

Heat Wave: 'Colin Chapman came up with a piece of clever thinking in the form of the gas-turbine-powered Lotus 56' (see page 68)

'This was the ultimate, this swift passage poised on the outer edge of disaster. .'
Juan-Manuel Fangio, Maserati 250F (see page 102)

Dawn chorus: Ferraris at early morning practice, French Grand Prix at Rouen.

'The invincibility of Italian-built Grand Prix cars was so unquestionable that . . . well, we didn't question it'. Hawthorn's Ferrari, 1954 Spanish Grand Prix (see page 104)

'In the cutaway cockpit he was clearly visible, arms tensed against the kicking steering wheel, teeth clenched with the sheer effort of controlling this turbulent machine': Baron Emmanuel de Graffenreid, Maserati (see page 103)

'Carlsson would change down, drive hard into the bend and let the tail slide round until it hit the snow bank . . .' (see page 142)

Lateral inversion of '. . . a somewhat insecure individual who likes to have an audience to applaud his finer moments at the wheel and to share with him the agony of his moments of grief?' (see page 135)

Yumping—Swedish Rally, 1969

Another kind of rally—Lagonda Club Night Navigation variety

'The Alfa Romeo Tipo "Monza" seemed the ultimate in sports cars . . .' (see page 155)

Start of the North banking at Monza: Maserati, Vanwall and a pair of Ferraris
(see page 158)

'*Monza has always attracted enormous crowds ... and, to an Italian, Ferrari is racing*' (see pages 159 and 160)

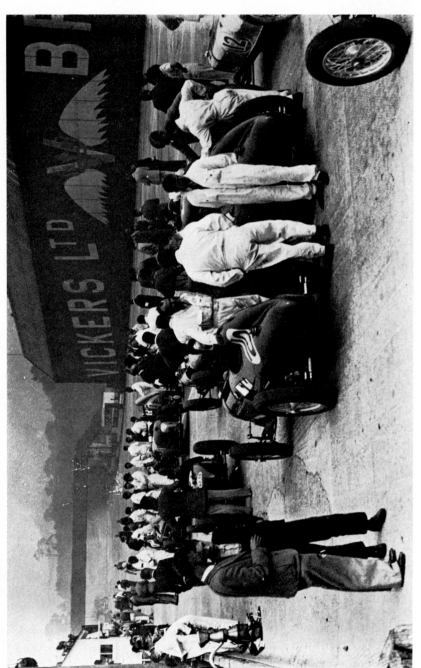

Brooklands 500 start scene: the smaller cars are already in action. Rileys in the foreground (see page 172)

Top: Sammy Davis (left) in the Bentley he had never driven until the 1929 500 had started, and his co-driver Clive Dunfee (see page 173)

Above: R. T. Horton (beret) and co-driver Jack Bartlett after winning the 1932 event in Horton's M.G. Midget at 96.29 m.p.h. (see page 177)

Left: John Cobb, two-time winner of the 500 sharing his 24-litre Napier-Railton with other drivers (see page 177)

1928 Trophée National at Boulogne: seconds after the start, Malcolm Campbell's 1.5-litre GP Delage is in the lead (see page 204)

'Despite its aroma of rotting fish, Boulogne can be quite an attractive place' (see page 192)

Atmospheric: an Hispano-Suiza in one of the early Boulogne races

'Valcourt' in his Type 43 Bugatti on the line for the sprint in the sports car class. He crashed his Type 35C Bugatti in the racing car class (see page 203)

Swan song: Mrs. Ruth Urquhart Dykes' 12/50 Alvis at the St. Martin hairpin in the 1928 Boillot Cup (see page 205)

Right from the start José Froilán González led the 1954 British Grand Prix. Be[hind] him are Fangio and Kling (Mercedes) and Moss (Maserati) on the right (see page [2])

How González and his 4.5-litre Ferrari took most of the corners while winning the 1951 British GP (see page 221)

Master of Silverstone, 1954

The 'Pampas Bull' in his usual stance—sideways-on in the 4.5-litre Ferrari, French GP, Reims, 1951 (see page 220)

'Pepe', with his father and his wife, after winning the 1951 Coppa Acerbo at Pescara

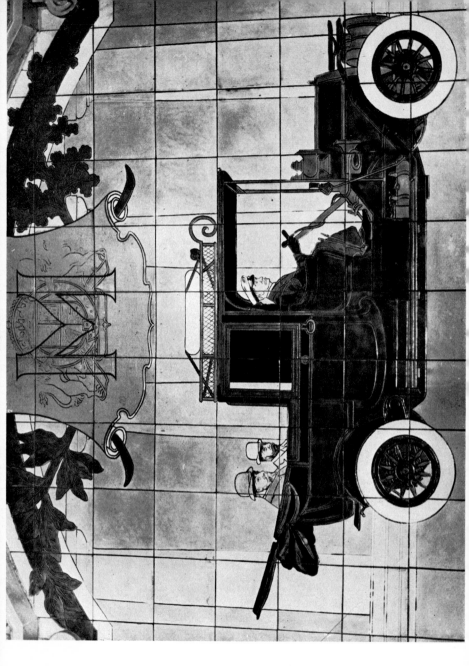

'Where did you get that tile?' Millionaires . . . Mercedes Sixty landaulette . . . Michelin ceramics (see page 108)

(increased camber variations) which we set out to reduce to the minimum possible in the first place. So the only two variables we can really work on are the track and the roll stiffness. Though relatively soft springs produce a more constant wheel grip on less than perfect road surfaces, modern racing cars use stiffer springs than they used to. This provides not only higher roll stiffness, but is called for by the relatively heavy wheels and tyres and by the necessity to reduce dive on braking and squat on acceleration which better gripping tyres and increased power have made really critical as these phenomena also produce camber changes and require an increased ground clearance. Traditional anti-dive and anti-squat expedients have failed to effect a cure without introducing even less desirable evils. Roll stiffness is further increased by the use of relatively strong anti-roll bars front and rear. Much more striking however is the extremely wide track of most current Formula I cars which can be as wide as 64.5 inches (Matra MS120B) which, with the current wide tyres, makes the car about 80 inches wide.

In a Formula car especially, widening the track is quite an attractive proposition, as with the outrigged wheels, the frontal area is hardly changed at all and there may even be a benefit of reduced drag thanks to the fact that the flow of air along the body is less disturbed by the proximity of the wheels. Even if the CSI does not intervene on the grounds that the increase in car width to unrealistic figures could, in the end, make overtaking rather difficult, there is a factor which could well put an end to the trend towards increased tracks: this is the instability introduced under severe braking by unequal brake performance or road grip on the different wheels. Any difference in braking between the right and left wheels produces a torque aiming at deviating the car from its line, which increases with the track.★ This can only be compensated by lengthening the wheelbase, which in the end increases the weight in an undesirable measure. In 1971, the Tyrrell-Ford had its wheelbase increased for some races by using a longer bell-housing and longer rear radius rods.

★ Meanwhile the CSI have introduced a rule limiting the width of any racing car to 82.7 in.

D

In the case of Sports Cars, the situation is slightly different, because any increase in track introduces a proportional increase in the frontal area, as the wheels must remain covered by the body. This is one reason why the trend towards greater width, though existing, has been less marked on that type of car. Also with a full width body, the increased body width tends to make the car feel unwieldy for the driver.

Whereas all the more highly developed single-seater racing cars have a monocoque structure, their shape lending itself very well to that sort of construction, the problem facing the designer is different in the case of two-seater cars. Basically, monocoque single-seater racing cars can be of two different configurations:

(*a*) the bath tub or open monocoque of which the upper part is closed by a plastic 'lid' with an opening over the driver's seat;

(*b*) the closed monocoque of elliptical cross section, except for the opening over the driver's seat.

Both have hollow side walls containing the bag-type fuel tanks, a strong rear bulkhead to which the entire engine and transmission unit is bolted as an integral part of the structure and taking the rear suspension, a strong front cross member or bulkhead to which the steering and the front suspension are attached, and appropriate cross members. One of these is the structure of the driver's seat which provides some very strong bracing and assists torsional stiffness, the hollow space between the sharply inclined seat back and the rear bulkhead also incorporating an additional fuel tank.

Two seat bodies are a less obvious proposition for the monocoque construction, especially as, even with a closed car, the roof is never integrated into the structure, a light fibreglass top saving weight, even with the regulation roll bars. For such cars, Ferrari have, for many years, been using a composite construction of steel tubes and sheet metal, while Porsche have always stuck to tubes to which a very light fibreglass body is bonded. In recent years, the tubes have been of aluminium, a complete frame for the closed 917 weighing only 47 kg, while the frame of the ultra light (less than 550 kg or 1,100 lbs) 908/03 3-litre of 1970–71 vintage weighs only 35 kg (78 lbs). Experiments have even been made with magnesium tube frames which save another 15 kg (35 lbs) on the 917. With the present minimum weight limit of 650 kg imposed on 3-litre sports cars, there is little point in going to such extremes, but they should certainly pay dividends in Can-Am type racing where both the weight and engine capacity are free from restrictions.

The failure of four-wheel drive and the beginning of the 'wing' era. The 3-litre Formula I quickly brought about cars with a power-to-weight ratio of the 650 HP ton order in average racing conditions and wheel spin when accelerating in the lower gears became a problem and performance-limiting factor, specially in the wet. The outcome of this were more or less experimental four-wheel-drive cars, some of which, like the McLaren and the Cosworth were never actually seen on the starting line of a race, while the Matra-Ford and Lotus-Ford were never really competitive (they might have been if they had been raced in the wet, but 1969 was a particularly dry year, as far as Grand Prix racing is concerned). The main problem was very severe understeer, which, putting it very simply, can be explained by the fact that the front wheels, which tend to be pushed straight forward by the driving force of the rear wheels (specially if a limited slip differential is fitted, which is essential on a racing car) are less able to resist side forces if they are driven. As a consequence, their slip angle is higher under any given conditions and they might even lose grip altogether. It is quite significant that the only manufacturer who could not be bothered with the design of a 4-wheel-drive Grand Prix car was BRM who had had previous experience of this type of car. Neither could the weight penalty of well over 100 lbs—probably nearer 150 lbs—be disregarded, while two other factors contributed to the fact that 4-wheel-drive cars disappeared even before they had been properly sorted out: the tremendous progress made in the development of racing tyres providing ever better grip and the advent of aerofoils.

Even though the CSI quickly put a limit to the height and

dimension of the 'wings' or aerofoils and ruled that they must be
part of the sprung masses (i.e. the body), the 'aerodynamic aids'
have become an essential part of the modern racing car. Their
effect on race averages has been shown earlier in this essay and as
mobile 'wings' are forbidden, a lot of thought has gone into
aerofoil configurations that will produce the greatest down thrust
for the lowest drag penalty. As mentioned earlier, thanks to the
help of aerofoils, lateral accelerations up to 1.7 g have been
registered on accelerometers experimentally fitted to Grand Prix
cars and, as the coefficient of adhesion of the best modern racing
tyres is of the order of $\mu = 1.4$ at a right-angle to the plane of the
wheel, the implication is that the down thrust produced by the
aerofoils increases the cornering force by some 20 per cent in
bends that can be taken sufficiently fast for the 'wings' to be
really effective.

As tyres grew wider, thus making up an enormous part of a
Grand Prix car's total drag, and as the ever-increasing power of
the 3-litre engines called for ever larger tanks, manufacturers
tended to pay less and less attention to the shape of their cars,
'wings' becoming their major aerodynamic concern, until once
more Colin Chapman came up with a piece of clever thinking
in the form of the gas-turbine-powered Lotus 56, designed for
Indianapolis, followed by the Formula I Lotus 72, both featuring
a wedge-shaped body. It is improbable that this shape reduces the
drag of the car itself, not being in itself a good aerodynamic
shape, while it is also unlikely that, with the turbulent flow of air
around the body of a racing car having external wheels, within
reasonable limits the body shape makes any noticeable difference
at all to the drag. But by giving the body a shape that will, in
itself, create a down thrust, at least the drag is made to serve some
useful purpose and the aerofoils themselves can be given a lesser
angle of incidence, their drag being thereby reduced and providing an overall reduction of the vehicle's drag. The latest
development is now to give the body a down-thrust-creating,
wedge-like form and to use the lateral extensions of the car's
'nose', which may have a maximum width of 1.50 m (38 inches)
as long as this width is measured below the height of the front
wheel rim (otherwise the maximum width allowed is 1.10 m or

43.3 inches)* to form a partial cowl for the front wheels and improve the air flow over them.

Engines. Though the 3-litre Formula I and Prototype capacity limit seemed to favour engines with 12 or even 16 cylinders, it is significant that, since the introduction of the current Formula I, every one of the six world championships was won by a V-8 (twice Repco and four times Ford-Cosworth) while among the Proto-types too, up to 1972 the twelves never managed to beat the eights, though they were supreme among the 5-litre Sports Cars. This seems to point to the fact that comparative simplicity is still a major asset and that a good torque spread is just as important as a very high power output. Relatively, the torque characteristics and general tractability become more important and the absolute power output less so, as the engine capacity is increased, for there are very few tracks on which the real maximum speed of a large capacity racing car can be reached and consequently acceleration is at a premium. This explains why Porsche took the World's Manufacturers' Championship for both 1970 and 1971 with the 917 which has only two valves per cylinder and a specific output of 124 HP/lit., while all Formula I engines have 4 valves per cylinder and a power output nearer or even above 150 HP/lit.

There has not been any great single breakthrough in engine design in recent years, neither is one likely in the near future, specially as the development of the NSU-Wankel type of engine has not proceeded far enough to make it competitive under the present rules.

At first sight, there does not appear to be any close relationship between the progress in tyre design, aerofoils, and racing engine development, but in fact, the very high lateral forces produced when modern racing cars are cornered at the limit have caused a lot of headaches to the engine designers. Dry sump lubrication has, for decades, been a feature of racing engines, originally because a separate oil tank could be given a larger capacity than the engine sump and because it made it possible to drop the engine a few inches nearer the ground. But even with a dry sump, some oil accumulates in the sump before it is sucked in by

* Increased to 1.40m or 59.5 inches for 1973.

the scavenge pump and returned to the main tank, and under the current very high cornering forces, oil surge becomes a vital problem. Just remember that, when a car is cornered at 1.7 lateral g, the level of the liquids contained in the vehicle, instead of being horizontal, forms an angle of no less than 70 degrees to the horizontal, which means it is much nearer vertical than horizontal! In order that the scavenge pump or pumps still drain the oil from the sump, rather than suck in air, a complicated combination of suction lines and inertia valves is necessary. Otherwise the oil will accumulate in the sump and splash will occur with consequent severe loss of power (due to oil drag) and overheating and aeration of the oil. A similar problem must be faced with the fuel tanks, made even more complicated by the fact that with the universally adopted fuel injection systems, the slightest trace of air in the fuel will cause the engine to cut out: catch tanks with non-return valves preventing the fuel centrifugated into them from returning to the main tanks are the answer to this problem, but many races have been lost because practice did not quite work out as theory would have it.

Racing cars of tomorrow. Racing car design cannot be dissociated from the rules to which the cars are built. The trend in regulations today obviously is towards increased safety in racing and several amendments have already been made with this object in mind to the original 3-litre Formula I of 1966 as well as to the rules governing sports car racing. The compulsory general cut-out switch, easily accessible from in and outside the car, more severe roll-bar specifications, bag tanks and the compulsory fire extinguishing installation spraying its liquid into the cockpit and onto the engine at the push of a button at the driver's reach, are outstanding examples of this trend. Meanwhile the minimum weight requirement went up in steps from 500 to 530 kg in order to cope with these rules and has been increased to 550 kg for 1972 in view of the heavier outer layer of sheet metal imposed to give better protection to the tanks.

The Pininfarina-Ferrari 'Sigma Grand Prix' 'Safety Grand Prix Car' built in 1969 has undoubtedly had a considerable influence on the official trend of thought, and self-sealing tank fillers and fuel lines and better fuel tank protection through widened bodies providing a crush area protecting the fuel tanks are likely developments within the next few years. If the trend to increased body width on Grand Prix cars is brought to its logical conclusion —i.e. if the regulations allow the body to be extended to the full width of the car—then the day might come, when there will be very little difference left between a Sports car and a Grand Prix car, except for the fact that the latter is a single-seater, and I personally would welcome a merger between the two groups at the expense of today's so-called sports cars which hardly serve any useful purpose as a full-width parallel line to the Grand Prix cars, while it seems highly illogical to restrict the latter to their present functionally entirely unjustified, drag-producing shape. Highly-modified Touring and Grand Touring cars could with advantage replace the current Group 5 Sports cars, while a group for high-powered racing two-seaters already exists in the shape of the current Group 7 cars of unlimited capacity and no minimum weight ruling.

In view of the all too obvious fire hazard to which current racing cars are subject, several interesting safety tank designs have been proposed and it seems most likely that the CSI will enforce the use of some much more efficient design of safety tank than hereto. In addition to this measure, the international Body considers it desirable to limit the tank capacity to a volume less than the current 230-250 litres carried by most Grand Prix cars. Not that the driver would have any better chance to survive say, a 100-litre fire than a 250-litre fire, but because a smaller tank could be accommodated in a position where it would be much better protected from any outside impact than the current large side tanks. According to the most recent information, the capacity is likely to be limited to some 160 litres, which would mean that refuelling stops would have to be made in the course of a Grand Prix, but the risk of a fire while refuelling would be considerably minimized by the self-sealing fillers to be made compulsory by 1973. And in any case, provided the fuel supply installation is properly designed, the danger of a fire to human life is much less in the case of a car blazing in front of the pits, when the driver can jump out and firemen are at hand, than in the case of a fire breaking out while the car is still on the move, following an accident out on the track. In my opinion however, the capacity limit proposed is a very half-hearted measure, because it would still require side tanks, and the fact that they would be smaller is of little importance. My personal opinion is that it would be quite satisfactory to use efficient safety tanks with an adequate additional side protection, without enforcing any capacity limit.

The inclusion of refuelling stops in Grand Prix racing is certain to provide additional drama for the spectators however and should make it possible to increase the race distances in such a manner that the race duration, that has been much reduced in recent times, gives the public some more adequate return for its money and its often tiresome journey to and from the track. In the light of the latest developments, however, and with the prospect of cars darting in and out of the crowded pit area, it is unlikely to contribute much to safety in Grand Prix racing.

This, gentlemen, is the safest car ever built, providing *it doesn't meet another just like it, of course.'*

COOLING AUNTIE

A misprint of the better kind informs us that Boots the chemists sell auntifreeze.

If your old aunty is properly on the boil, and when reprimanded for furious driving, has struck a policeman over the head with her umbrella, do not pour ethylene glycol BS 3150 into her. It is not fit for human consumption

'Autocar'

A BORE

In the absence of a printed form or card, there was an extempore, hand-written one at a French airport. It said, "Persons making a declaration raught with inexactitude expose themselves to the severest ennui."

'Autocar'

(From *The Daily Leveller*, 24 September 2112)

SMITH GETS THREE YEARS

Giant electronics plotter pleads guilty on all counts

by Michael Scarlett (of *Autocar*)
State Crimes Reporter

John Hamelin Smith, the self-confessed man behind the recent destruction of the nation's transport system was yesterday sentenced in the State High Court to three years' hard labour. Telling Smith, 42, that he was 'a most dangerous enemy of society with a mind as pervertedly individual as your bizarre physique' Mr Justice Mediocran said that the leniency of the sentence took account of Smith's obvious unsoundness of mind, even though Smith declared himself sane.

The crimes against the State and the people perpetrated by this giant (5 feet 10 inches) of undoubted but misapplied genius have affected every citizen of the State. We therefore make no apology for devoting the entire issue of *The Daily Leveller* to the judge's final summing-up of this extraordinary case.

Mr Justice Mediocran

'This case is very unusual. It is perhaps the strangest case in British legal history for centuries.

On his own admission before this Court, one man has defied the State. One man has defied the entire police force. One man has denied his fellow countrymen of their means of transport. One man has destroyed every motor vehicle in the country—in one night.

You have now heard each side, the prosecution in great length, the defence in less. The offences with which the accused is charged, and to which he cheerfully confesses, are very serious. To understand them, and to understand if you can the actions of the accused, you must understand a smattering of the mechanics of the motor car. So must I. Therefore, for our mutual enlightenment, I shall rehearse to you the principal points of the case, as I understand them, before directing you to consider what the Court shall require of the accused.

John Hamelin Smith, of 71 Jeremiah Grove, London sw93, is charged with obstructing the public highways, obstructing police officers in the course of their duty, causing wilful damage to the property of the State, minor assault on persons enumerated in Appendix A (consisting of sixteen folios), minor assault on persons unknown, high treason, using wireless transmitting equipment without a Post Office licence, trespass on a factory, and walking on a public highway.

The prosecution began by reminding the Court of the recent history of the motor vehicle.

Motor cars were, in the first 80 years of their existence among us, horrifically lethal. Drawing a veil over the evil early days of antideluvian anarchy seen on this island before the introduction of overall speed limits, the first so-called 'safe' cars were in production by 1980. It had for some time been accepted that human beings in sole control of moving vehicles would have accidents. No government amongst the free nations would dream of restricting driving licences to persons mentally and physically best equipped to drive. Better driver education for everyone would only improve the driving of persons with natural aptitude for driving. Either solution was obnoxiously élitist and there-fore morally unacceptable.

The only democratic answer was to make it difficult if not impossible for people to hurt themselves in cars. The first

move was to decree an overall maximum speed limit of
45 m.p.h. The second was to provide a totally safe car for
everyone. The third was to allow no one to own or drive
any other sort of car on our roads.

What its designers called 'the crush-crash-proof (CCP) car'
was accordingly evolved. The actual passenger, motive-
power and road-wheel-carrying box was only 12 feet long,
5 feet wide, and 5 feet high. With 3-inch thick padding over
all surfaces—rubber over metal and clear transparent foam
over glass—this 'occupant capsule' was built strongly enough
to withstand the detonation of a small tactical nuclear
weapon 10 feet away. So that an occupant would survive
unscathed the shock of driving at 45 m.p.h. into another such
vehicle, or a lamp-post, bridge support, wall, motorway
crash-barrier or building, extra bodywork was added app-
ropriately to the front, back, sides and roof. There was 20
feet of bonnet, 20 feet of boot, and 5 feet extra thickness of
side and roof. If any such collision occurred, the extra bodywork crushed progressively, absorbing the shock and pre-
serving all inside.

This certainly cut down injury to car occupants. But
there were disadvantages. Cars 52 feet long and 15ft wide,
even with an 8 feet wheelbase, imposed parking problems.
They were also difficult to drive in a straight line or round
corners. An early production modification was the provision of small castor wheels under the four corners of the
car to avoid unnecessary damage to overhanging parts on
bumps. Any road with a dip in it had to be closed for
alteration, owing to CCP cars becoming immobile at the
bottom of such dips as the driving and steering wheels
were raised clear of the road when both nose and tail
castors became the car's only contact with the road on each
side of the depression.

Although car-occupant injury statistics improved most
encouragingly, collision figures went up tenfold. The
number of pedestrians injured by cars also increased
alarmingly. There was a tendency for the irresponsible
younger driver to run his car deliberately into another

in order to see if the attacked car's driver noticed.

No action was taken by the authorities until it was realised that unemployment was rising in one small but important export industry. Ingenious small engineering firms in Italy, Switzerland and Sweden were finding it easy to adapt CCP cars to the specialised needs of militant groups in the Middle East and what used to be Northern Ireland, and this was bankrupting many armoured-car and light-tank manufacturers.

The problem was universal. A 57-nation engineering study group was formed—the Multi-lateral Exploratory Design and Development Logic Executive Committee, MEDDLECOM for short. With the help of advances in car battery design, micro-circuitry, electronics, hydraulics, pneumatics and legislation, the Goodbreath Polymorph Universal Offender was constructed and immediately put into world-wide mass production.

In fact, the legislation came first. Here was perhaps the most far-seeing and fatherly example of world policy that Man had so far provided. The United Nations, in an unanimous resolution, acknowledged the criminal inequity of attempting only to preserve motorists from hurting themselves whilst motoring. Pedestrians had to be protected with as much certainty. So must those in the home; accidents in homes had always up till that time been much higher than on the roads.

The pedestrian question was easy to deal with. Walking anywhere outside a building was forbidden. (Robot agriculture had some time before taken the farmer off his hazardous field).

Home safety needed a little more determination. All places of human habitation more than one storey high were pulled down; people could no longer fall down stairs. So were all buildings constructed in non-shock-absorbent materials. One storey high only, all housing was rebuilt entirely in rubber, and lined inside with cotton wool. That eliminated at one felt swoop the problems of insulating people against shocks physical and electrical.

For transport, every household owned a Goodbreath Polymorph Offender, as they still do to this day. To enable Offender users to walk legally from their car to their front door, shopping centre, place of work or public building, extended all-enclosed rubber porches were provided from doorway to roadside—Personnel Injury Protection Entries, or PIPES. So that everyone could afford an Offender, its price was United-Nations subsidised. It cost only the equivalent of £50 everywhere—which was then no more than the average price of a man's haircut—wonderfully cheap. Adjustments made to each country's personal taxation naturally covered the cost; in Britain income tax for everybody was re-introduced at the rate of 97p in the £.

The Goodbreath Polymorph Universal Corporation was financed by the combined funds of hurriedly diversifying motor insurance groups, and formed by the united-nationalisation of the world's major car makers, electrical firms, environmental engineering concerns, and toothpaste and deodorant manufacturers. In most places the Corporation traded under the Goodbreath Polymorph Universal name, but there were some local divergencies. For instance, in Japan you will still find only cars made by the 'Nipponese National Organisation for Normal Production of Neutralising Gadabout'—as that is rather a mouthful to write on the bonnet, they shorten it to the initials again, Nipponese NONPONG Offender.

Even to laymen like ourselves, now so familiar with the Offender, there is much that fascinates about the design of the car, which has not altered to this day.

It was and still remains the first successful electric car. Insignificant advances in battery design were met on their way up by the fall of the overall speed limit as it came down to 40 m.p.h. The range of the electric car at this level of performance was entirely adequate. Thus the air pollution caused by the internal combustion engine was removed.

No longer did you have to 'steer' the car yourself. You pressed the destination button, and told the computer in front of you where you wished to be taken to. Assuming that you spoke clearly enough, and that the desired destination was Government-approved, the computer selected the shortest route and gave the necessary commands to the electronic guidance system, which then drove you there at the correct maximum speed for the conditions.

When you arrived, the Offender stopped by your destination's PIPE, to which it locked itself. It then slid back both car and PIPE door, and moved each occupied seat to the door by means of the car's revolving floor, helping each passenger into the PIPE. Shutting both doors, it afterwards drove itself away to park and await your spoken request for the return journey.

Just as today however, the Offender's designers realised that electronic systems were never completely reliable, In case one Offender's guidance system went wrong during a journey, provision had to be made against collisions as before.

Here was great ingenuity applied. You may have wondered why such an ideally passive motor car was given such an ostensibly aggressive name. It is not so. 'Offender car' is merely a convenient re-arrangement of 'Fend-off car'.

The full name was originally 'Extendable fend-off car.' The old crush-crash-proof car needed its 52 feet of overall length, 15 feet of overall width, and 10 feet of overall height in order to absorb the deceleration of any sort of a collision before it seriously disturbed those in the car. If any progress was to be maintained, the new car must provide at least the same protection—and therefore shock-softening length, width and height.

But it did not need it all the time. It needed it only when about to have an accident.

The great strides made in pneumatic engineering and the cheapening and miniaturisation of radar provided the ideal means. One of MEDDLECOM's first objectives was to reduce the dimensions of the car to a minimum. They eventually went back roughly 50 years, selecting the old British Motor Corporation's Mini as the basic car shape and size. Its interior space, which history tells us was just adequate for four average adults of its time in spite of their ungainly overdeveloped length of leg, was then and is now more than enough for today's generations. Evolution, accelerated by Man's ever-powerful progress, has been kinder to us, removing at least ten redundant inches from our lower limbs.

The space this gained made room for the electronics and the fend-off rams. It is with the fend-off arrangements that we are here concerned. Considering the basic car as a simple rectangular box, there are five upper surfaces—front, back, two sides and roof. Extra panels, moulded in rubber and mounted on stout frames were made, fitting the original body shell closely like covers, the side ones covering only from body sill to just below the windows, so that one could see out. The frames for these false rubber panels were attached to the ends of very powerful telescopic pneumatic plungers or rams, a pair to each panel. If any pair was actuated, it expanded in the twinkling of an eye to its full 60 feet, thrusting the pseudo-bonnet, boot, side or roof 20 yards away from the car.

A compact and specialised radar system was devised to decide electronically if and when any pair of rams and their panel should be extended. In simple terms which we may all comprehend, the radar sensed any tendency for the Offender to in any way approach any solid object that might harm it. The phrase 'any solid object' embraces a wall, building or lamp-post, a falling brick, roof-tile or meteorite, and, if the car had for some reason begun to overturn, the ground.

In the curiously mountain-to-Mahomet thinking of the safety engineer, if an Offender 'was approached' by a threatening object, the radar sensed such an approach at a predetermined distance, and took protective action. Here the prosecution were good enough to explain some technical terms to you. In the jargon beloved of those MEDDLECOM engineers, it was the Potential Approach of Notional Insecurity Computation radar system—PANIC—which detected any infringement of the Optimum Uncertainty Closing Hazard distance—the OUCH distance.

The acronyms drew their metaphor from Nature; if you or I approach within ten yards of a sparrow—ten yards being its OUCH distance—the bird PANICS, protecting itself by flying away. The Offender's OUCH distance was set at 70 feet. When the radar system 'PANICked', it protected the car by immediately extending the rubber panel on the threatened face. The panel then met the obstruction 20 yards before the car did.

If the obstruction was lighter than the car, it was simply brushed aside. If of equal or greater weight, then what would have been the shock of the Offender's encounter with it was absorbed by the progressive compression of the rams. To avoid an unseemly spectacle resembling a sort of robot boxing match between two errant collision-bent Offenders, the PANIC system was programmed to extend the rubber panels on each obliquely to one another instead of squarely, so that each fended-off the other.

Of course, there were some practical difficulties at first. Ways had to be found of preventing two Offenders travelling in opposite directions along the few old roads left less than 140 feet wide from bristling at each other sideways as they passed. Some other unfortunate accidents under bridges, arches, tunnels and multi-storey car parks with less than 70 feet headroom meant that all such places had to be protected with radar de-sensitizing cable—officially Sense of Obstruction to Hazard Erasing (SOOTHE) wire. Admittedly, deaths of Offender occupants did at first occur in a few cases, owing to the susceptibility of passengers with weak hearts to heart failure produced by the explosive abruptness with which a $2\frac{1}{2}$ foot Mini bonnet became a $62\frac{1}{2}$ foot one during any OUCH infringement.

After a decade or so, such teething problems were completely overcome. In company with the World-State-provided improvement of Man's lot in general, State-approved men and women went about their State-approved ways in State-approved transport in total State-approved security. From State-controlled birth to the penultimate second of his or her State-approved life, every State-

E

approved citizen lived in the overall protection and fatherly guidance of the State. Accidents of any sort were outlawed by the State and prevented by the State. This is so unto this day, for which we must be very grateful. Death is to date the only accident not approved or controlled by the State, but we are working on that.

In the picturesque submission of the prosecution, we harboured in the midst of this latter-day garden of techno-logical Eden a serpent. I like the metaphor, for it seems apt enough. Progress has made Adam and Eve of us all, innocent and almost defenceless against the wickedness of selfish individualism. You have heard the prosecution submit that that wickedness is personified by the serpent of Jeremiah Grove, sw93—John Hamelin Smith.

Smith is a self-declared eccentric. He is well-endowed with intelligence in some respects, being by training an exceptional electronics engineer. He is also a man who has somehow defied evolution, having the grossly over-developed legs typical of our forefathers of 150 years ago; it is said that he is able to *walk with no outside assistance distances of up to ten miles in one day*. You have heard evidence that in fact he has walked considerably more than that. He is a biological freak, standing 5 feet 10 inches tall, which is of course nearly 1 foot more than the State-approved maximum. The means by which he has continued to de-velop himself thus *and survive* are still under investigation by a distinguished team of doctors and psychologists.

Smith first came to the notice of the State by his public refusal to stop the habitual ignition of the illegal plant tobacco in an archaic device once known as a 'pipe' (not to be confused with today's Personnel Injury Protection Entry). This habit, a favourite of our forefathers, flourished from the 17th century until 1987 when it was finally out-lawed in this country under the Air Pollution (Theatres and Homes) Act; the accused, an obstinate and reactionary man, considered the confiscation of his tobacco and the associated apparatus for its consumption as an 'infringement of personal liberty', whatever that may be. It is clear from the evidence you have heard from that time he developed a grudge against society.

The disorders with which this case is concerned began a month later. The accused 'went for a walk'. That expression will not be familiar to all of you; it was used in former times to describe the practice of deliberately walking *outside buildings*. In this instance the accused submitted that he walked only six yards. That is the distance from the hole he cut with kitchen scissors in the side of his home's PIPE—itself another offence against the State—to his rainwater butt, to collect untreated water—a further offence—to feed to his indoor collection of former roadside trees. (The prosecution has chosen to ignore the fact that all roadside trees have for many years been proscribed because of the risk of injury to motor cars.)

A car was passing. Naturally, its PANIC radar sensed the presence of a strange body within the car's OUCH radius, and accordingly thrust out the side panel nearest the accused. It threw him back against the wall of his house and passed on.

The defendant sustained a broken collar bone and a buckled watering can. He sued the Goodbreath Polymorph Corporation for personal damages and a new watering can, but of course lost. A counter prosecution by the State ensued, charging Smith with walking on unprotected State property, and he was imprisoned for one month. The incident appears to have been the seed of the accused's subsequent behaviour.

Like a medieval warlock reincarnated in this twenty-second century and armed with a good working acquaintance with the ways of the electron, he set to work. Using all the tools of his trade, not least our recent acquaintance the acronym, he devised the first of his infernal machines. It was a form of radar-dislocation device which he called SHUNT—Short-range Upset Neutralisation of Traffic System. Having no Offender himself, he first of all used SHUNT to actuate the rams of his near-neighbours' garaged Offenders on the evening of January the 4th. This caused the destruction of eight nearby dwellings. Although Smith's residence was conspicuous by its preservation amidst its demolished environs, the cause of the incident remained a mystery until later.

SHUNT was small and portable. Its inventor concealed it in his clothing and paid stealthy visits to various public places. A previously orderly 25 m.p.h. queue of traffic in Oxford Street on the subsequent Saturday morning was seriously and suddenly disordered when sixteen Offenders began what appeared to be a mechanical fist fight between themselves and with surrounding shops. In the afternoon of the same day in Grosvenor Square a line of Offenders parked nose to tail expanded. Cars adopted all manner of attitudes; two erected themselves on their rams upside down twenty feet in mid-air, while the one at the western end of the line was punched straight through the American embassy. Diplomatic notes were exchanged, but after a personal apology from the Home Secretary our relationship with the United States survived this bruising.

A month later the Hyde Park underground car park was enlarged by approximately 150 per cent as fifty Offenders expanded simultaneously. Unfortunately the roof fell in owing to lack of support for the increased span, bringing with it the Marble Arch at one end and the Hilton Hotel at the other.

Smith has unashamedly told the Court how the Hyde Park disruption was the first work of his second machine, the Beam Universal Nudge Generator system—BUNG. His aim now was to be able to guide a large number of Offenders into attacking specific objects of which he did not approve. BUNG had longer range than SHUNT, could be used with more discrimination where desired, but was still portable.

Smith tells us that he does not approve of what was, before he turned his diabolical attentions to it, our magnificent motorway system. He says that motorways obstruct his (illegal) practice of walking, and that they spoil the countryside. It need not now surprise us as it did on February the 9th that a fifty-mile stretch of M1 should be rendered

useless, laid waste in ten minutes by pathetically de-
mented Offenders. Cars simultaneously thrust all rams.
They swept each other off opposing carriageways, split and
threw aside bridges, short-circuited high-voltage pylons,
tossed service area cafeterias into the fields. The chaos on
this section included fusing the SOOTHE wires over the
adjoining 100 miles of motorway north and south, with
consequent damage to bridges due to Offenders erecting
their roof panels.

He does not approve of our splendid State offices. Before
February the 17th, the 8,437 civil servants needed for the
efficient running of the Ministry of Computer Programming were housed in the very fine Mincomprog
House. Being a State building it was among the few tall
buildings permitted; built over its own car park, it was
400 feet high. Smith had the grace to make an anonymous
telephone call declaring his intention and giving the staff
just enough time to get clear of the building. He then
operated BUNG. This was the first occasion when any large
number of witnesses were able to watch a BUNG operation.
Using only their roof panel rams, the two subterranean
storeys of parked Offenders together gently raised Mincomprog House to a precarious 520 feet before carefully
toppling it into the Thames. The ensuing tidal wave demolished most of the State office buildings (whose staff
had been similarly warned) lining the river for two miles
up and down stream.

Smith's final exploit with the BUNG system was to disguise himself as a worker and gain entry to the Goodbreath Polymorph Universal Corporation's factory. A
large plant, this occupied the entire county of Warwickshire.
He deposited a BUNG set coupled to a modified eight-day
alarm clock in one of the washroom ventilators, then
walked back to his London home. Two days later, after he
had anonymously telephoned again to make sure that the
factory was completely evacuated, the alarm went off,
actuating the rams of all finished and half-finished Offenders,
lifting the entire factory roof off and scattering machinery,

jigs, tools, fixtures, Offenders and the factory walls over the neighbouring shires of Derby, Leicester, Northampton, Oxford, Gloucester, Worcester and Stafford.

He had achieved one of his objects—to prevent the manufacture in Britain of Offenders. Even that was not enough.

Although the police and a team of scientists were doing everything in their power to try and uncover the cause of these motor-car malignancies, Smith was still undiscovered. For three months he resumed an outwardly normal life. In fact he was working on the biggest, most powerful and most cruel of his machines. It was ready by the beginning of June, and he named it the Long-range Elimination Master Motor car Inertial Guidance system— LEMMING. At 3 a.m. on Midsummer Day—a dreadful morning that no one who experienced it will ever forget— he threw the switch that set LEMMING in action. Every Offender in Great Britain, not to mention many on the nearer parts of Ireland, France, Belgium, and Holland carefully ejected anyone it was carrying, expanded its way out of any garage housing it, and drove carefully, deliberately and neatly into the nearest sea.

The country was immobilised. No one could move. Smith was immediately conspicuous because of his abnormal and illegal ability to walk, which he exercised with careless abandon. The police were suspicious and wished to question him. But they could not catch him. No officer was able to walk, let alone 'run'—the old word used to describe high-velocity walking—fast enough to apprehend him. His ability enabled him to hide even from police helicopters, or at any rate evade capture whenever a helicopter crew abandoned their machine in order to arrest him.

Finally one very resourceful policeman found the answer. Commandeering a 170-year-old motor bicycle—described in its day as a 'moped'—from the Science Museum, he contrived to lower the saddle by a foot to enable him to reach the pedals and the ground, and taught himself to ride it. By this means, he eventually caught Smith. This officer, by his very brave conduct, receives the highest commendation of this Court.

The account of the arrest of the accused saw the end of the prosecution's lengthy case. In the face of the evidence, the defence could do little in their client's favour but plead that at no time did the accused's actions injure anyone seriously, and that in any case he is insane. The accused himself has indignantly denied any trace of insanity, fully admits the charges and explains that he was bored. In the circumstances, gentlemen of the jury, I do not see how you can return a verdict other than guilty; boredom is in any case not approved by the State.'

(Taking account of medical reports, Mr Justice Mediocran sentenced Smith to three years' hard labour in the State Science Museum, where it is understood that in between regular psychiatric re-conditioning treatment periods, Smith will be set to work cleaning and repairing the ancient transport exhibits.

When asked had he anything to say, the prisoner replied 'No thank you' and was led from the dock smiling.)

SHANKS'S PONY

The car, as every reader of Hansard knows, is a lethal weapon. So is a pair of feet. So—and more than doubly so—are two pairs of feet joined by a temperamental animal.—'Motor'

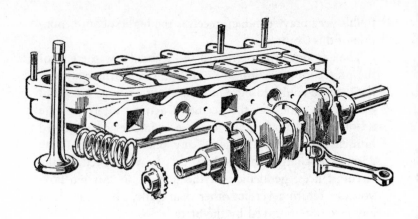

Summat fer Nowt

W. G. S. WIKE

'See all, hear all, say nowt
Eat all, sup all, pay nowt,
And if tha ivver does owt fer nowt
Allus do it for thisen!'
(Old Yorkshire Saying)

This wise old saw, on which many North-country fortunes have been founded, is as good advice today as ever it was (in case you are puzzled, 'thisen' is Yorkshire for 'thyself'). Throughout the course of motoring history, motorists have worried about the cost of their pleasure, and have sought means to reduce this cost.

The first cars were small and economical, simply because the engines then available were incapable of propelling a heavy vehicle. The first car to be sold in any quantity—indeed, the first car to be made with this idea in mind—was probably the Benz, of which several examples still survive in this country.

This was not designed as an 'economy' car, but as a substitute for the horse and trap, and while a Benz is not really at its best in the rush-hour on the M4, it is still a practical means of occasional transport, and the small size of its petrol-tank indicates that it was not intended to visit the local chemist too often for replenishment, as it was economical.

Cars soon became faster and more powerful, but small cars were still made, particularly the De Dion Bouton and the numerous competitors of varying degrees of success which used its engine. These were sold as horse-and-trap substitutes; at a time when £75 a year was quite a good wage, economy as such did not enter into the motoring scale of things.

However, with the increasing speed of cars it was necessary to go sufficiently quickly to keep up with the Jones's, and the cyclecar was born. This was an attempt to persuade the motor-cyclist that he had got a motor-car. Only the Morgan, which had three wheels, and the G.N., which had four, were well enough made to survive, and even these were really of more interest to the enthusiast than to the struggling motoring neophyte. You can get much dirtier in a Morgan than you ever did on a motor-cycle, because you have to dress-up properly to ride a motor-cycle in wet weather, while a Morgan is, in theory, a car.

After World War I everybody who was anybody wanted a car, and few could afford them. Cyclecars were re-born and died with appalling suddenness, although the Morgan and G.N. struggled on, the latter eventually becoming the fast, sporting, but hardly 'economy' Frazer Nash; Morgan three-wheelers were made until 1939, because they were taxed less heavily than four-wheeled cars, and this appealed to the economy-minded motorist; also, they were notably light on petrol and could be repaired by any moderately mechanically-minded owner. A few attempts were made to produce really cheap cars; in about 1925 a firm in Grimsby tried to sell the Lloyd, which consisted of a plywood box with two axles bolted to it, without the intervention of springs, whose place was taken by large-section 'balloon' tyres; a very small air-cooled engine drove one back wheel. Economy in this case had o'er-stretched itself, and the Lloyd was no more.

After the 1930 financial crisis, cars could only be sold if the price was kept as low as possible, which is why so many of the cars made after that date were so terribly bad. The first Ford Eight was announced as a '£100' car, and was certainly of simple design, but it was made of Ford's usual good materials, and the price soon rose to £112.50. This, even in the 'thirties, was quite a good annual wage, but of course there was a simply wonderful selection of second-hand cars at prices which are just not conceivable today. In an *Autocar* of 1931 a 40–50 h.p. Rolls-Royce, ten years old, was advertised by a respectable firm for £95. In 1934 our motoring was done very much with economy in mind, and we bought a 37.2 h.p. Hispano-Suiza for £15, which had six brand new 7.00–21 tyres—but it was not an economy car: about 14 m.p.g. The other £100 car was the Morris Minor, with an open two-seater body and the chromium-plated radiator-shell painted black to show that it really was an economy car. The trouble with all these very cheap cars was that one could get a decidedly better car by spending very little more money, and this seems to be the case today, when the 'Super' model is better and holds its resale value more successfully than the 'De Luxe' (i.e. basic utility) model.

After World War II followed a period of financial stringency, and petrol was severely rationed, in some cases more so than during the actual war itself. This scarcity, or the price demanded by the parallel Black Market, produced not a second crop of cycle-cars, but that curious manifestation, the Bubble Car. This was an attempt to enclose the driver and one passenger in a largely transparent casing, usually spherical (hence the name); the most successful of these was the Isetta, an Italian design quickly taken up and made by the German B.M.W. firm. This was a three-wheeler with two wheels at the front, and was entered by a front door, to which the steering-column was attached, and which folded away as the door opened. It was better than nothing, but just as it began to become popular in England, some careless politician abolished petrol rationing, and the bubble burst.

It had several competitors, including the Heinkel, which had two wheels in front and two more very close together at the back; here the British tax system, under which three-wheelers were taxed at a reduced rate, started furious arguments as to whether this 'counted' as a three-wheeler; luckily it did! Another German aircraft firm, which was also not *very* busily occupied with its original products, was Messerschmitt, who made the 'kabinenroller' which was really a three-wheeled scooter with an aircraft cockpit-canopy on top, which hinged to one side for entry. Not to be outdone, the British firm of Hunslet made a similar scooter, but entered by a normal side door, which made it very tall and reminiscent of a comic-strip horse called Moomin.

The other British effort was the Bond, which was the most serious attempt so far at a real economy car. This had three wheels, one at the front, which steered and also bore the weight of the engine, which drove it. The original Bond was intended to be known as the 'Minicar', perhaps the first use of this term, and had a very small and feeble engine, but it was said to have carried two grown men from Preston to St Albans on one gallon of petrol. A larger engine was later fitted, and eventually it even had a door—then followed first a van, then a saloon, and it had grown out of the original economy concept. So it faded way.

Having bought our car, new or second hand, we still have to run it, and the thing we most often have to buy is petrol. As a result, this is the first thing on which we try to economise, and many and wondrous have been the devices offered to a gullible public with this aim in view. A petrol engine runs on a mixture of air and petrol, and it is a fact that the ratio of the one to the other is fixed within quite narrow limits by the laws of Nature. As petrol costs good money, and air was free and plentiful (and as most of the early small cars were open, this was only too obvious) why not try to feed the engine on more air? Extra-air valves, some of quite ingenious complexity, were offered to the earlier motorists, and as the carburetters of those days were not always as successful in giving a correct mixture as they have since become, some extra air at speed was acceptable and did reduce petrol consumption to some extent. Unfortunately a weak mixture burns more slowly, and was sometimes still burning when the exhaust-valve opened; this component was not always made of very good steel, and the result was that it became burnt by the still-burning gas, and suffered as a result.

The opposite idea attracted a few inventors. As the car does not need any fuel when it is running downhill, or coasting, why not give it a weaker mixture on these occasions? A valve was therefore provided which was sucked open on the over-run, providing more air and reducing the suction on the jet, and a more refined version of this is incorporated in some carburettors, notably the Zenith.

We have described the supply of petrol and air as a 'mixture'. This is what it is: a lot of little drops of petrol being carried along in a stream of air; it is not a gas. So why not ensure that as much of this fuel remains mixed together and gets carried into the engine, instead of some of the heavier petrol being allowed to fall out of suspension and lie idly in puddles inside the induction-pipe? Obviously something was needed to stir the petrol up, and along came the inventors again.

One device, which fitted (like all such devices) between the carburetter and the induction-pipe, had a little windmill in it, the idea being that the mixture would drive the windmill round, and this in turn would mix the petrol with the air passing through the windmill. On second thoughts, this begins to sound suspiciously like perpetual motion, i.e. the petrol drives the windmill, which in turn stirs-up the petrol, but let this pass; if we had perpetual motion we should have no need of petrol anyway! Another device had as its object the straightening-out of the confused mixture, and was made of a series of concentric coils of corrugated metal; in the middle was an ordinary round hole, which was quite big enough for all normal running! At part throttle, the actual throttle valve, which is a disc as big as the hole it works in, causes quite enough obstruction anyway, but not so at full speed, and here is where part of the 'economy' of these devices comes in. They all caused some actual obstruction of the induction-pipe, which was therefore prevented from passing its full volume of mixture. The maximum power of the engine was thus reduced, and as proportionately more fuel is used at full power, the engine was made more economical by being prevented from using its full quota of mixture! Another gadget of this type was simply a small cone of fine copper gauze (again, with the necessary hole in the middle!) and the idea here was to collect any surplus globules of petrol in the gauze, and then to release them when the speed of the passing air demanded them. We doubt whether this had any effect on 'economy' as such but many cars ran much more smoothly with this device fitted, and as they could spend more time in top gear, we had an indirect economy benefit.

As the actual throttle, being pivoted in the middle, acts as a sort of movable dam, the mixture is diverted to one side, on which petrol droplets tend to be deposited. Quite a clever gadget of the basic type which we have been discussing, simply consists of a metal ring which is curved in the direction of the flow of gas, which scoops up this surplus petrol and throws it back into the air-stream; this is still in production. We have tried this device, and on some cars it gives better flexibility and slow-running (like the wire gauze just mentioned) but we remain sceptical about any real 'economy' resulting from its use!

Having thoroughly messed-up the petrol and air mixture, we now compress it in the cylinder, which should do its part in mixing it up anyway, and ignite it. This needs a spark. Now, say the inventors, if we had a really hot spark, surely this would burn the mixture better and we might even be able to use a weaker brew. Devices continue to be offered with this aim in view, but as they usually consist of an additional gap in the high-tension side of the ignition system, and as there is one already inside the distributor, it is hard to see how the extraction of money from the pocket of the purchaser for no benefit (to him, at least) can be regarded as 'economy'. One of these devices used to be advertised as 'Tested and approved by the RAC' Then, in very *very* small letters 'South Africa'.

If petrol is so expensive, why not try something a little cheaper? The snag here is that the greater part of the cost of petrol is the tax on it, and if you try to use a tax-free fuel, the only petrol you are likely to be using will be in the motor-mower in the Governor's garden. This was not always so. There used to be a firm in the North of England by the name of Binks, who made carburetters. In 1916 petrol was rationed and in short supply anyway, owing to the War. Messrs. Binks advertised:

'Run your car at HALF the usual cost by having a Binks' Vaporising Carburetter. Uses common paraffin oil, white spirit, sugar spirit (and of course, Petrol or Benzole), without alteration.'

We like the appeal to the reader's innate snobbery ('common' paraffin oil, forsooth); we do like to think of Mr. B. pulling up outside the Waggon & Horses, parking his Belsize, and striding up to the bar. 'Good morning, sir, what can I get you?' 'A pint of Boddingtons' for me and a large rum for my motor'.

Lubricating oil seems nowadays to be a difficult thing on which to economise; it is very much more expensive than it used to be, but the modern car uses very little, and the recommended periods at which the engine oil should be changed are much greater than of old. Nevertheless, we had an Austin A.90 Westminster in the writer's small works fleet, which had a very fussy driver, who insisted on his oil being changed every 1,500 miles, and Castrol at that (instead of the quite satisfactory but cheaper oil which we were then using). This car covered no less than 93,000 miles in our hands, the head was never removed, and at the end of this time the oil consumption was still negligible. This is true economy far outweighing the extra cost of the oil. Oil does not wear out, and if we had perfect filtration, we should never need to change it. Large stationary diesel engines, which have most elaborate filtering systems, run for months on end without an oil change; and Rolls-Royce certainly quite recently advised oil-changing only every 10,000 miles. For the ordinary car, with an ordinary paper filter, it is very false economy to try to make the oil last for ever—particularly as it does not get 'topped-up' with much fresh oil in the meantime.

This was not always so. In 1932 we had a 24 h.p. Minerva which, although second-hand, was in very good condition. One day we went up to London, about 200 miles, and found we had used a gallon of oil! As we were near the Minerva service-station, we went and asked for advice. A gentleman in a white coat came out, listened to our tale of woe, listened to the engine (which, like most sleeve-valve engines, was almost silent) and then told us that this was the normal oil-consumption for a brand-new car, and weren't we lucky? So for the rest of this car's life in our hands, we bought an oil, which is still on the market, which consists of other peoples' old sump oil which has been cleaned. Many commercial vehicles use it without any complaint!

Tyres are expensive. We remember reading an account of a year's motoring in a book written in about 1906 by a retired Indian army officer, who had bought a small car (make unknown) which had full-elliptic springs and solid tyres (thus exactly reversing the recipe of the Lloyd 'economy' car previously mentioned). He said that this was all that was needed, and quoted an instance of a wealthy acquaintance who had spent £500 on pneumatic tyres in the last year, simply because he wanted to drive at over 40 m.p.h. 'There is no future' he said 'in pneumatic tyres. They are only a whim, and are only needed by rich cads!'

Even today, however, when the law looks askance at the worn tyre of the economy-minded motorist, we can save money on tyres. If we can afford new ones, the modern radial tyre has so much longer a life than the usual cross-ply tyre that it is a 'must' for anyone who covers a fairly large mileage; we have proved this again and again, on all sorts and sizes of cars. The low-mileage motorist with no desire to travel at very high speed is well advised to consult his local tyre factor about remoulded tyres. Where these are made by the tyre makers themselves, or the better-known retreaders, they are perfectly satisfactory, and thousands of buses run on them without any trouble at all. If trade is bad, a factor will sometimes offer 'remould quality' tyres, which are simply brand-new tyres which he can't sell!

Repairs are a difficult subject to discuss under the heading of 'economy'. If you have a good small local garage, with a good mechanic, make of him a bosom friend. Go even to the extent of giving him a Christmas present. He can save you a lot of money. He can advise you what to do to your car in the way of preventive maintenance, always a true economy.

Not many motorists really know how much it costs them to run a car, and this is not necessarily a bad thing; if we costed all our pleasures we might have very few! Occasionally pedestrians in Pall Mall pass a large and ornate building on the south side, and hear a high-pitched plaintive squeaking sound emerging; this is the officials of the RAC emitting their periodic estimate of how much it costs to run a car. They never seem to subtract the cost of travel by public transport if you hadn't got a car. They add the interest on the money you would not have spent if you didn't buy a car, but never deduct the Income Tax you would have had to pay on this. A rich friend of ours (but a North-countryman, and thrifty!) once calculated that the loss of interest on his investments, if he sold sufficient to buy a brand new Rolls-Royce instead, would have paid for one, repeat one, bottle of gin per week. Instead of signing the pledge, he bought the Rolls.

We are not all in quite this fortunate financial position. Yet we can still motor and enjoy it if we count the true expenses of motoring, and set these against the utility and enjoyment which we get from our car. Tax and insurance? Here we cannot economise very much, although with an old or 'difficult' car we can carry some of the insurance ourselves, by insuring for third-party, fire and theft only, and some brokers will find policies for small-mileage users, respectable people, teetotallers and other special categories of motorists. Taxing four-monthly instead of annually is a false economy. The biggest cost of all is depreciation, which cannot be avoided, but as this is at its worst in the first year of a car's life, a good car a year old is often a wise buy. Some foreign cars suffer very heavy depreciation, and are even difficult to sell when the time comes for a change, whatever their other attractions. If you have a wife and six children, a very small car is definitely not an 'economy' car; indeed, if one has to buy a car a few years old, a larger vehicle, which will usually have had an easier life, may be the best buy. A little car driven flat-out may use more fuel than a larger and 'lazier' vehicle, and it will wear itself and its driver out more quickly, and we don't want to wear *him* out, do we? Town-work and local running are hard on motor-cars; under these conditions they use far more petrol (some of which is in any case used in heating the water which the radiator has only to cool again!), and if you are only going down to the shops or the local, why not leave the car at home? This is true economy, and the exercise may even do you good! During the 1957 petrol rationing, we had a friend who lived about a mile and a half from his work, in which distance there were two 'Halt' signs (remember them?). His car was one of the 'old' 1½-litre Rileys, a very good car, which could be relied on to do over

30 m.p.g. on a normal run. He fitted up a small spare petrol tank, and used this; he found, to his surprise and dismay, that he was actually, on his home-to-work run, doing 14 m.p.g. Economy?

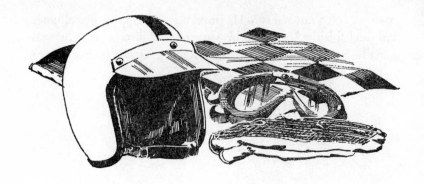

Short Back and Sighs
A tonsorially-induced lament

F. WILSON McCOMB

'See Charlie Bloggs has sold his accessory shop in Bognor, then,'
remarked Colin, expertly wielding a comb in one hand and that
blowlamp-thing in the other. With these two instruments he can
make my hair stay tidy almost right up to the very moment I get
back home again.

'Huh?'

'Charlie Bloggs. Sold that shop of his, he has.'

I looked at him blankly in the big mirror, and he gazed fixedly
back at me. Colin is normally a polite lad, but this time he
couldn't restrain himself any longer. 'You don't know who he is,
do you?', he burst out accusingly. 'Cor, you really *are* out of
touch!'

Colin is in his early twenties, cuts my hair (at somewhat more
frequent intervals than his own), and lives for motor racing. On

one of my first visits to his establishment he spotted the Guild of Motoring Writers pass in my wallet, and for a time I basked in a most satisfying aura of veneration. Unfortunately it didn't last very long. He began to notice that his enthusiastic babblings over the cars and drivers of today were greeted with non-committal grunts—even when I *wasn't* face-down over the basin. And then he started asking awkward questions. Did I write for *Warm Automobile* or *Cardicing?* No, not for either of those. Did I attend most of the Grands Prix? No, not any more. Well, the major British races, then? Uh, no, you couldn't really say that. Just the odd Club event or vintage meeting, these days.

I tried to keep my end up by a policy of sustained name-dropping, mentioning in the most casual way imaginable that Stirling Moss had once tried to sell me his Standard Eight, Mike Hawthorn had once made a pass at my wife, and one delirious day at Rheims I had actually spoken to Juan Manuel Fangio. I told of the time I asked Jean Behra why his smoking Gordini had just stopped motoring round the Le Mans circuit, and was answered with a whole lot of words our French master never taught us. I may have remarked that I had the autographs of Hans Stuck *and* Rudi Caracciola on the same piece of paper. Or that a V.16 B.R.M. had once blown half-a-pint of beer clean out of my tankard when I got too close to its exhaust in the paddock at Snetterton.

But it wasn't any good. The names that I dropped fell with a resounding thud on the floor, down among the hair-clippings. It was pretty obvious that Colin didn't much want to hear about them; he didn't even seem to know who they were. Which I thought very odd, for nothing would please *me* more than the opportunity of chatting to somebody who had actually met the Chevalier de Knyff or Felice Nazzaro.

The last vestige of respect disappeared when Colin realised I hadn't heard of Charlie Bloggs (that wasn't really the name, but it was closer to that genre than you'd think possible). Master Bloggs, it seems, is a famous racing driver of today. More, he is a Grand Prix driver.

I never would have believed it. In my day, nobody with a name like that would have been *allowed* to become a Grand Prix driver, and if in some incredible way it had come to pass, the fellow would at least have had the common decency not to run an accessory shop in Bognor. A high-class brothel in Casablanca, maybe, but not an accessory shop in Bognor.

How far a hairdresser should reveal natural contempt for his customers' shortcomings is a nice point in etiquette, like whether to use a steel knife when eating fish fingers, but I have to admit that Colin's remark rankled with me for several days afterwards. It came as such a shock, for never before had my enthusiasm for the sport been questioned in any way. Dammit, I was still at prep-school when I first cut pictures out of *Speed* to hang on the bedroom wall. At Colin's age I could have told you Villoresi's size in socks or reeled off the winners of the British Grand Prix, all three of them. I had loved motor racing all my life, and was confident that it would still be my surpassing joy when at last I became permanently horizontal.

Of course it does rather depend on what you mean by motor racing. For me, the mental picture that it conjured up was absolutely clear, exact and—I now realised—completely immutable. Motor racing was a sport. Was *the* sport. Was the most thrilling sport in the world. Its protagonists were swashbuckling individuals with foreign names who drove large and magnificently-shaped cars that made a perfectly ear-splitting noise. Most of these cars were red, but sometimes there were blue or white ones to add a touch of variety to the starting-grid. No racing car worth its salt had less than three syllables to its name, and some had as many as five.

The racing drivers—those gods, those supermen—met eight or ten times a year at some famous circuit like Monza or Monaco, Bremgarten or Nürburgring. Their dress was unusual but by no means outlandish, untainted by any hint of circus or music-hall, for its wearer's own reputation was distinction enough. Indeed, there was something almost austere about the plain white, belted overalls and the close-fitting helmets of soft leather or cloth. When driving they wore one pair of goggles and had a spare pair around the neck. They had strange, backless gloves of a type that no ordinary motorist could buy—or, if he could, would have had the colossal impertinence to wear.

Before a race they stood around in groups chatting easily to each other in a mixture of tongues, smoking carelessly and laughing a great deal with a flash of white teeth in brown faces. You knew every one of them by sight. You knew their names, the teams they drove for and the races they had won, but would scarcely have dared to address such beings if unimaginable luck had brought you close enough. If such a chance *did* come your way, the only possible course was to thrust out a race programme and stammer a request for an autograph. For who would aspire to converse with the immortals? Satisfaction enough to see your humble fountain-pen grasped by the same strong hand that held a famous steering-wheel.

Their cars were unloaded from big, dust-covered lorries with unfamiliar names and exotic registration plates by mechanics who were only a little less awe-inspiring than the drivers. They, too, wore white overalls, though not so clean or so smartly cut, and they jabbered away in incomprehensible languages with much arm-waving and occasional displays of bad temper. When the bonnets were lifted off to reveal a labyrinth of machinery, the mechanics would casually break open boxes and boxes and boxes of sparking-plugs—more sparking-plugs than you had ever owned in your whole life—and spin them into the cylinder-heads with incredibly deft fingers. The fuel tanks would be filled from great churns of mysterious liquid that tingled in your nostrils, and made your eyes water, and peeled the paint straight off the pointed tails of the cars. Many more of these churns would be stacked up in the pits along with the mammoth spare wheels that were rolled into position, for all the world like a small boy playing with a hoop, and you noticed that the mechanics scarcely had to stoop at all because these wheels were so big. There were special jacks, too, and rows of gleaming spanners all laid out along the pit-counters.

The cars were so familiar by their shape that you identified them immediately without recourse to the symbols that they bore; the indignity of an actual maker's name painted on them would have been as unthinkable as to see Nuvolari with *his* name emblazoned on his overalls. There was something particularly intriguing about those cars because they were essentially the same as your own, and yet wonderfully different. The components bore the same relationship to each other but they had been refined in the cauldron of competition; they were a functional development of the same bits and pieces that made up your car. You, too, had wire-spoked wheels on your sports car, but what sports car ever boasted such massive wheels as these, devoid of mudguards and proudly exposed to all? Or brake-drums the size of dustbin lids and bristling with cooling fins? Or an engine with 12 or even 16 cylinders, and two superchargers, or a forest of carburetters big enough to bath the baby in? And yet the whole weight of motoring history asserted that what you saw here today might form a part of your own car tomorrow.

But naturally they scorned such mundane appendages as a starter motor, so the mechanics would push them until the engines —the hackneyed phrase is the only one that fits—burst into life. Andrmerciful heavens, what a noise they made! It assaulted the eard ums and numbed the senses, it flattened the grass and raised the paddock dust in swirling clouds. It was a trumpet-call from Valhalla, a defiant raspberry at the Road Traffic Act. It proclaimed for all the world to hear that the myriad components of that engine were doing exactly what their designer had intended them to do, and at exactly the right moment.

The noise, the colour and the smells all played their part in the almost unbearable build-up of tension on race day as the starting time approached. At flag-fall would come the shattering tumult of the massed start. Then, at intervals in the long grind of a full-length Grand Prix, the brilliant expertise of high-speed pitwork to refuel the cars or change their wheels. Perhaps the sight of a less exalted driver's car being called in as a replacement for the team's Number One, who would leap into the cockpit in a heart-stopping endeavour to make up lost ground.

Your chosen vantage-point might be one of the faster corners, to see those big cars weave and twitch under braking, and then the full-blooded four-wheel drift through the bend, smoke rising from the smouldering tyres. This was the ultimate, this swift passage poised on the outer edge of disaster, this superb blend of savagery and finesse. From the driver it demanded perfection, nothing less, as he balanced one force against another with needle-sharp judgment. In the cutaway cockpit he was clearly visible, arms tensed against the kicking steering-wheel, teeth clenched with the sheer effort of controlling this turbulent machine. And you knew as you watched that this was something beyond the reach of ordinary men.

This, to me, was motor racing.

It embodied technology, of course, for the cars were the product of applied technology, specifically designed and built to achieve a certain performance. But the master driver, by the exercise of his unrivalled skill and daring, achieved still more. It was always the human factor that predominated.

And therein, I think, lay the irresistible attraction that turned me into a motoring journalist at a time when—fortunately for me—motoring journalists didn't have to know very much about anything. Technically we were perhaps a little better-informed than our pre-war predecessors, who had an arts degree and a vague idea which end of a car to pour the petrol in, but we couldn't hold a candle to the typical motoring scribe of today (undoubtedly an honours graduate in mechanical engineering, as a glance at his syntax will reveal). No, we were largely indistinguishable from the rest of the flat-'atted, duffel-coated maniacs who thronged the paddock at Goodwood. The quantitative analysis of suspension behaviour under cornering stress was not our scene at all, our writings were a happy mixture of ignorance and unquenchable enthusiasm, and many of us nursed a private conviction that the road springs should be bound with stout cord. Even those who laid claim to expert knowledge were sometimes so misguided as to praise production cars with such abysmal road-holding that inverted examples littered the countryside at the drop of the first snowflake.

We were immensely loyal to our own racing drivers, always ready to wave a truculent tankard and declare, 'Ah, give Bob Gerard a Type 158, laddie, and then you'll see what's what.' But in our heart of hearts we knew there was little hope for any man whose parents had lacked the foresight to christen him Alberto or Guiseppe, Tazio or Achille—or at best, Jean or Louis, Manfred or Rudolf. And so far as the cars were concerned, we didn't pretend for a moment that British ones were the slightest use in Grand Prix racing. It would have been faintly absurd to do so at a time when no British car had won a major Grand Prix in more than a quarter of a century.

When I was roughly the age of my hair-chopping chum, the V.12 Ferrari and 4.CLT Maserati had just appeared on the scene to challenge the 10-year-old Alfa Romeo, with noises off by the 4½-litre Lago Talbot. Drivers whose careers went 'way back to 'way back, like Varzi, Wimille and Trossi, were not only still competing in Grands Prix, but winning them. The Silverstone and Goodwood circuits had just been opened, mainly as convenient playgrounds for our own drivers. Colin Chapman was a young aeronautical engineer who drove Austin Seven specials in mud-plugging trials, and a teenage Mike Hawthorn was still scaring the hell out of other road-users down in Surrey. A certain retired taxi-driver from Buenos Aires had just paid his first visit to Europe, but nobody noticed him.

The invincibility of Italian-built Grand Prix cars was so unquestionable that . . . well, we didn't question it. We didn't even resent it, since it was one of the basic facts of life in motor racing. We might tell ourselves that Reg Parnell dinarfgo in the Thinwall Special, but we knew all the time it was a 4½-litre Ferrari in disguise. A few youngsters like Collins and Moss began to figure in minor speed events with their little Coopers, but dammit, even the Cooper was really the fore-ends of two Fiat Topolinos nailed together. As for the B.R.M., when at last it reached the starting grid its performance suggested a part-refurbished pre-war E.R.A. that hadn't had the benefit of proper maintenance.

And when eventually Ascari and the rest were displaced by Fangio, Gonzalez and Marimon, one couldn't help feeling that these three were just Iberianesque Italians who happened to eat beef instead of spaghetti bolognese. It seemed only right and proper that their cars were painted red.

Then, as time went on, we saw with incredulous delight that our own young drivers had begun to figure in Grand Prix results. If the supremacy of Italian cars merely gave way to that of German cars, at least we had chaps like Hawthorn, Collins and Moss level-pegging with the best that other nations could produce. Admittedly, the sport lost a little of its glamorous remoteness when some of its participants might share a drink with you at the Steering Wheel Club or carve you up at the next traffic-lights. But then, one expected British drivers to approach the game in a decently amateurish way. We noted with approval that they drank beer and chased the girls and obviously enjoyed themselves. Only one of them employed a business manager and encouraged personal publicity, which was considered rather bad form.

With the passing years the Grand Prix scene continued to change, but we didn't realise how much it had changed until that sunny Sunday in Sicily when 50,000 open-mouthed spectators saw Tony Brooks and his Connaught run rings around the entire works Maserati team to win the Syracuse Grand Prix. It was fantastic. After that, we agreed, anything could happen, and a couple of years later we did see further successes by British cars and drivers. Slowly we digested the impossible truth that a British-built car *might* prove a worthy mount for a World Champion—and before very long, even that came to pass. Yet the car that achieved that notable distinction was a funny little thing with a fire-pump engine mounted at the wrong end of a chassis emanating from suburban Surbiton. Not exactly glamorous. It was difficult to avoid the sneaking suspicion that it might be magnificent, but it wasn't war.

Something, somehow, had been lost from Grand Prix racing. The big cars had disappeared from the circuits, and with them the big-hearted men who drove them. However satisfying it might be to have reached the top at last, we looked around and saw with regret that the Italians had gone, the Argentinians had gone, all but one of the French drivers, all but one of the Germans, all the more devil-may-care British drivers. Many had gone the hard way, some had merely crept into retirement, but we would not see their like again. The new type of Grand Prix driver was of a totally different breed, taking himself very seriously, very quick to seize commercial advantage, very ready to exploit the value of publicity, very concerned about personal safety. Just how different he was came into startling prominence in 1960, when a number of them *went on strike* before the European Grand Prix.

A world in which this could happen was not the world we knew and loved.

Thus it is that, for some of us, real motor racing seems to have ended more than ten years ago. What, are today's drivers not skilful and courageous, you may ask? Yes, of course they are, for no man can survive in Grand Prix racing without his full share of those qualities—but merciful heavens, what a dismal bunch of nonentities by comparison with their predecessors! You couldn't make one José Froilan Gonzalez out of the whole lot put together, personality-wise. And that pantomime garb they have adopted! With their face-masks and vizors and bulbous coloured helmets, their stripey fireproof overalls scrawled with advertising slogans, they look like the cast of a spaceship series on children's television.

And the cars they drive—shades of Gioacchino Colombo, have you seen their cars? The purposeful beauty of yore has given way to ugly angularity, a selection of flat surfaces whereon the sign-writer may more conveniently ply his trade. They bear as much resemblance to any motor vehicle—past, present or future—as a block of council flats, complete with four dustbins and a collection of *graffiti* that makes a bingo hall seem the last word in old-fashioned dignity. Don't tell me how fast they go—I don't want to know. By any standards they are a Cubist nightmare on wheels. Did I say *wheels?*

Antonio and Luigi, Juan Manuel and Onofre, have been re-placed by Chris and Dave and Vic and Denny and Jackie and Jacky and even the humble Clay (fancy substituting *that* for a splendid name like Gianclaudio!). After Alfa Romeo and Maserati, Lago Talbot and Bugatti, Mercedes-Benz, Connaught and Vanwall, who wants to see a Buggins-Ford race against a Juggins-Ford and a Muggins-Ford and others equally undis-tinguished and indistinguishable? Even with the added attraction of knowing—as, alas, we cannot escape knowing—that they are backed by Pongo Perfume and Stinko Cigarettes and Slobbo Oil and McNamara's Added-Calcium Super-Crunchy-Flavor Wowf-Wowf Dog Biscuits?

This is motor racing, the great and glorious endeavour that has stirred our hearts since motoring began?

I think not. Me, I'd rather stay at home and read old magazines. And maybe I'd better start looking for somewhere else to get my hair cut.

WOT! NO ARMCO?

. . . from the driving point of view, however, the whole thing was rather stupid. Just a blind along the 10-kilometre straights, which is quite easy when you get used to it though the speeds sound very spectacular, and then a funereal business at each corner, everybody driving as though their boots were made of paper."

Dick Seaman, on his drive in the 1937 Avus G.P., won by Lang (Mercedes) at an average speed of 162.62 m.p.h. Fastest lap by Rosemeyer (Auto Union) at 172.75 m.p.h.

Jackie Stewart tells a story against himself and his preoccupation with racing safety. A stranger steps off the plane at Geneva Airport and asked the way to Stewart's house. "Just follow the Armco barriers," he was told . . .

Eoin Young in 'Autocar'

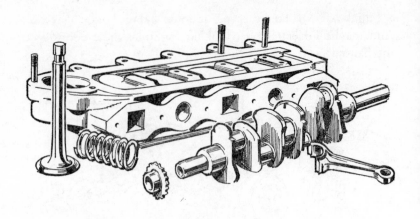

Motors for Millionaires

WILLIAM BODDY

Rolls-Royces have been sold to millionaires, Heads of State, industrial tycoons, show-biz stars, Indian maharajas, and other legendary, improbable people—the Gettys and Gulbenkians of this world—in greater numbers than any other make. The prevailing financial climate scarcely causes millionaires to flourish but, when they do, the makers of the Silver Shadow usually benefit. In any case, today's choice of top cars is very limited. France does not encourage wealth but there is the Citroen SM for its top people. Russia has no problem of this magnitude. German marksmen are catered for by the Mercedes-Benz 600, a great lump of Teutonic thoroughness overshadowed by its multitude of cousins—300SEL, 300SEL3.5, 280SE3.5, 280SE, 250 and 220. Top Britons go for the Rolls-Royce, which is the more distinguished since it casts but one shadow. Rich Americans used to toss a dollar to decide between Cadillac, Lincoln and

Buick, after exotics such as the V.16 Marmon, front-drive Cord, Duesenberg and Packard ceased to be. Now they tend to be deflected by Lamborghini, Ferrari and Maserati, which also serve Italy's first-class citizens.

Today's choice is comparatively easy. It wasn't always so. Towards the close of what we term the Vintage decade (1919–1930) the Rolls-Royce Phantom II was at the mercy of the great 100 m.p.h. 8-litre Bentley, which is maybe why Rolls-Royce Ltd bought the Cricklewood firm with cloak-and-dagger tactics. At this period of motoring history the 50 h.p. Daimler Double-Six loomed very large invariably engulfed in a hazy blue smoke-screen of its own contriving. Even bigger was the Golden Bugatti. But that was an automobile for Kings, not mere millionaires.

Move on half-a-decade and you have the Rolls-Royce Phantom III rubbing hubs with the 54–220 Hispano-Suiza (annual tax £75), competitors in the elegance, performance, hush stakes, each imposing bonnet covering a V.12 power plant. The Hispano could be had with an 11.3-litre engine, but Ettore Bugatti had had the last word on that score, with his 12.7-litre Royale.

Go back instead of forward in motoring time to 1919 and what do you find? A world licking wounds inflicted by a devastating war. A war which brought poverty and riches in its wake, which had trained countless men in the art of driving motor vehicles. After the Armistice the ex-Servicemen hoped to motor at tram-fare, the munitions profiteers wanted the most luxurious motor-carriages money could buy.

They had different decisions to make. The poor had to take what they could afford, when it became available. The wealthy, not wishing to waste a penny, as is the way of the Very Rich, did their shopping with extreme care. The latter's choice ranged wide; let us go with them as they showroom-shopped or walked round the Olympia Motor Show of 1919.

Manufacturers returning to peace-time production had likewise to make decisions; whether to cater for the motoring for the million movement or make motors for millionaires. Some took a middle course. But the better-class companies, companies which had built quality cars before the war, and had in some cases gained a great reputation in war-time with Staff-cars and aero-engines, could hardly contemplate making anything cheap and nasty afterwards; if some of them turned out expensive and nasty cars, it was obviously inadvertently. . . .

As the war clouds rolled away in the tracks of the tanks, the roads and leafy lanes of our green and pleasant land became open again to private cars. Chauffeurs were two a penny (almost) and the munitions profiteers, those nobles who had not been slaughtered, and country gents who were not quite impoverished, all wanted to get out and about in the finest cars available. What should they buy?

The choice, as I have said, was a wide one. Rolls-Royce, for all their aeroplane engine excellence during the hostilities, were content to re-offer the 40/50 Silver Ghost, with an impeccable reputation extending over thirteen years. Daimler smugly went on making its 45 h.p. sleeve-valve confections, which merited the Royal Warrant. Lanchester, whose suppley-sprung, scienti-fically-conceived motor carriages had attained near perfection of individual format prior to the battle, now tantalised with an entirely new overhead-camshaft 40 h.p. with epicyclic trans-mission. Napier, too, who had built up a high reputation before the Kaiser affair, and had this proclaimed loud and long by S. F. Edge, also offered a new model, the technically-advanced 40/50 using an aluminium overhead-camshaft engine, reminder of the sound engineering in its 'Lion' 12-cylinder aeroplane motor. These fine British luxury cars made things difficult enough. But it didn't stop at that. Straker-Squire likewise offered their 'Aeroplane of the Road', and a similar theme was set by the new British Ensign. Across the Channel Marc Birkigt had pro-duced a brilliant motor-car in the form of his 37.2 h.p. Hispano-Suiza, the personification of his talented war-time aviation engine exploits, a chassis which had mechanical-servo four-wheel-brakes and, symbol of its promising performance, proudly wore the Bazin-sculpted Guynemer stork on its radiator cap. In France, too, the Farman brothers were also staking their reputation on a car with a scaled-down aero motor beneath its bonnet, also of 37.2 h.p., a vehicle of massive build. From France also came other

fine cars, with powerful front-wheel anchors: Delage, Hotchkiss
and the Talbot-Darracq with its V.8 engine. Better, perhaps, to
buy British and go for well-established makes but, regrettably,
Louis Coatalen, for all that he was hypnotised by motor-racing,
retained side-by-side valves for his 24 h.p. Sunbeam gentleman's
carriage.

For well-to-do squires rather than millionaires there was a
lesser breed of luxury car, such as the much-discussed new Austin
Twenty from Longbridge, if you overlooked its habit of vibrating
its windows (you could cure this with little screw-down pads),
the 20 h.p. six-cylinder Wolseley, Vickers backed it is true, but
rather 'dated' with its paired cylinders, that battleship creation
the 30 h.p. Armstrong-Siddeley which, however, HRH the Duke
of York was prepared to stomach, and the 25 h.p. Vauxhall,
recent darling of the Staff Officers, but sluggish against a 30/98
which it so closely resembled.*

How to decide? Today's fortunate owners of Silver Shadows
are unlikely to know the bore and stroke of their engine, let
alone have knowledge of its developed horse-power. Fifty years
ago the luxury-car stakes were more intense. The motor-car was
still a fascinating new plaything. Whether racer or status symbol,
it aroused excitement in the bowels of its users. They read everything in the weekly motor papers before getting the maids to take
these magazines out to the garage, in the hope that their chauffeurs might become interested and explain the technicalities to
them. In spite of a limited knowledge of cars, they were apt to
compile long and often verbose letters to the motoring Press, in
which they sought to discuss all manner of petrol topics, from
what tyres, plugs and oils to use, to whether tipsy occupants of

* A fair idea of the high cost of these cars may be gained from the following
1919/20 chassis prices. The figures in parentheses are for the car with an open
body, to which about 15 per cent should be added to arrive at the price of an
average quality closed-bodied version: 40/50 Rolls-Royce £1,575, later
£1,850 (£2,800); 40/50 Napier £2,100 (£2,865); Lanchester 40 £1,875
(£2,933); 37.2 h.p. Hispano-Suiza £2,350 (£3,000); Leyland Eight £2,500
(£2,812); Sunbeam 24 h.p. £965 (£1,510); Austin Twenty £550 (£695–
£875); Armstrong Siddeley 30 h.p. £830 (£1,094); Vauxhall 25 h.p. £950
(£1,300). These totals have to be multiplied at least eight times for comparison with 1972 £s, of course, thus giving a figure of around £25,760
in today's money for a saloon-bodied 40/50 Rolls-Royce!

chars-à-banc should be allowed to fling bottles at them as they
drove past. (*The Autocar* discouraged the latter sort of letter, on the
grounds that it was highly unlikely that the sort of persons who
rode in char-à-bancs would see a copy of that journal. . . .)

It was in this frame of mind, under the circumstances of those
days, that a decision had to be reached as to which quality chassis
to invest in. Once it had been ordered, if it was ever delivered,
there were coach-builders like Barker, Cunard, Hooper,
Windovers, Mulliner, Vincent, Thrupp & Maberly or Grosvenor
who would put quite a decent body on it, don't you know, or,
to speed-up delivery, standard bodywork could be specified.

Perhaps the choice was narrowed by suspicion of those makers
who had contrived to get only a chassis to the 1919 Motor Show.
Bentley was in this predicament, with an *uncompleted* sporting
3-litre, and so were Farman and Ensign. But however you
regarded it, the decision was difficult in the extreme. The would-
be purchasers read about cars, discussed cars, listened to other's
opinions. Before the war long-distance tours on the Continent
had been quite the vogue amongst those with suitable cars and
a month or more to spare but in this turmoil of 1919 experiences
were apt to be cramped. The motor journals were quite excited
if they were allowed to take a new car away for a week-end
instead of just driving it 'round the houses' but Louis Delage,
accompanied by the late W. F. Bradley, had been much more
ambitious, testing his six-cylinder touring car by driving without
relief round France, for more than 3,000 miles in six days,
packing 626 miles into one of them. But he was accompanied
by a mechanic and broke a portion of one of the ¾-elliptic back
springs.

Such feats stood out as exceptional, although by 1921 Napier
had submitted their 40/50 tourer to an RAC-observed Alpine trial
of more than 2,100 miles, rather as they had their pre-war 30 h.p.
six-cylinder side-valve model. The overhead-camshaft Napier
averaged a running time of 20.7 m.p.h. and 18.69 m.p.g. of
petrol. It required no oil or water on the road but afterwards took
one gallon and 4 pints 10 ounces of these fluids, before being
timed over the Brooklands' half-mile at 72.38 m.p.h., which
gives a measure of luxury-car ability fifty years ago.

However, Brooklands had not been re-opened at the time of our showroom-gazing but it is likely, had we still been undecided how to invest our car-purchasing capital a couple of years later, that we would have been influenced by a remarkable correspondence which was then published in *The Autocar*, on the subject of which really was the World's Best Car. It commenced in May 1921, with a letter from the flamboyant Mr F. Lionel Rapson, who was trying to join the millionaires' ranks with his invention of a so-called unpuncturable tyre. On the pretext of being upset by the number of foreign cars on our roads, Mr Rapson claimed that after driving the Hispano-Suiza, Delage and Locomobile he placed an order for a new 40/50 Napier, not after persuasions at the Motor Show but, he explained, by making tests on the road. There followed lengthy praise of the new Napier, its speed, its acceleration, its top-gear hill climbing prowess. Not for Mr Rapson, evidently, foreign cars, on foreign tyres!

This letter sparked off a veritable bonfire. *The Autocar* billed it as an important part of its contents. Rapson's paean of praise for the Napier was followed immediately by a letter from a Mr Henry Lewis who had owned one of these cars for five months and also wrote enthusiastically of it—4 to 60 m.p.h. in a few hundred yards, no labouring or vibration, and every run taken in top gear. Then the spate began. Someone wanted to know why, if Mr Rapson was so keen on the Napier, all his patented gadgets were demonstrated on a Rolls-Royce? Phil Paddon, claiming three years' more driving experience than the instigator of this lively correspondence (from 1898), and ownership of 203 cars, who had also sampled the 1921 Napier, suggested that it required at least ten years before a car's real quality can be judged. Paddon concluded his letter by saying that an Alpine Eagle Rolls-Royce open car would do 17 m.p.g. always on a long run, and that he had driven a 1921 Rolls-Royce 3,000 miles in France without a chauffeur, using but two spanners on it: one for the petrol cap, one for the detachable wheels (he had two punctures), and had averaged 15 m.p.g.

A Yorkshire owner of four fast cars, a 27/80 Prince Henry Austro-Daimler, a 1911 45/50 Mercedes and a 1908/9 38–90 h.p.

G

Mercedes, said 'give me a Rolls-Royce all the time.' He remarked that with a heavy body it would still do 60 m.p.h.
with ease ('the speedometer only records up to 60'). It was the
cheapest car of any he had run, not having cost a penny since it
was delivered in September 1914—it was laid up throughout
the war. Tyres were praised for looking like going 12,000 miles
and 15½ m.p.g. was obtained on a 160-mile run. This correspondent rather ambiguously stated that a car had to be proved by
years, like 1910, 1911 and earlier Rolls which were still going
well, but that when next in London he would have a trial run in a
Napier and, if it came up to the claims made for it, he would
buy one straightaway. A Shrewsbury reader also weighed in on
behalf of the 1920 Rolls-Royce. From Holland came a thorn
in the flesh for advocates of British luxury cars. The owner of a
new six-cylinder Hispano-Suiza cabriolet recorded that it would
do 4 to 90 m.p.h. ('the chassis did 100 m.p.h.!') with the greatest
of ease and without any noise or vibration. The acceleration was
described as almost unbelievable, the braking system formidable,
petrol and oil consumption exceptionally low, tyres as lasting for
7,000 to 8,000 miles, the suspension perfect and the ride an
exquisite joy!

In the meantime Mr Rapson was trying to cope with his
critics. He explained that he had already written a warm testi-
monial about his 1914 Rolls-Royce which had covered 100,000
satisfactory miles and that he was fully aware of the excellence
of the Daimler, having been in charge of the Royal fleet at
Kensington Palace, looking after fourteen such cars during the
Coronation, when Prince Henry of Prussia (no less) told him:
'Rapson, that Daimler is the finest car I have ever been in'. He
now had five Rolls-Royces and many other good makes in his
fleet but still considered the Napier the best. As to how the Acton
cars lasted, he quoted the happy experience of a taxi driver who
had bought their old 1912 15 h.p. model and driven it to 90,000
miles. Oscar Harmer, who was of a mathematical frame of mind
and perhaps biased after 20 years' ownership of Daimlers, sought
to show that if you multiplied chassis price per RAC-h.p. by
actual h.p. the Daimler 45 proved itself the best, having a minus
figure of £466, whereas a Rolls-Royce worked out at plus £43,

the Lanchester at plus £551. Anyway, his Daimler 45 Special gave better than 16 m.p.g. . . . .

Another writer taking part in this unique discussion voted for the latest Lanchester Forty, remarking that the pre-war 28s and 38s were highly thought of, especially in respect of low weight per h.p. and their splendid suspension, and having tried the new model this correspondent considered it streets ahead of the old one. G. R. N. Minchin reminded readers that the new aero-style engines had yet to be proved, whereas Rolls-Royce controls, steering, etc. remained as light as a feather, with no play in them, after ten years. An 'Owner-driver for 21 years' vouched for the Mercedes, saying that in Switzerland British cars were only mentioned for purposes of criticism, but Captain T. W. Mays weighed in with more praise of the Napier, which in 10,000 miles had cost him only two new tyres and a 4d pressure spring, and W. H. Johnson, after going from London to Cannes in one, was also most enthusiastic, saying this 40/50 kept up an effortless average speed without exceeding 68 m.p.h. and noting the quietness of its engine. Finally, for that week, came a most interesting letter from J. G. Parry Thomas, Chief Engineer of Leyland Motors, saying that although his Leyland Eight would not reach the public until 1922 it was the intention to make it the most perfect car it was possible to design and manufacture. But as far as the 'Best Car' was concerned, Parry Thomas regarded his only sparring partner to be the Rolls-Royce —praise indeed from the Welshman who was to produce the overhead camshaft straight-eight Leyland luxury car with its leaf valve springs, torsion-bar suspension, vacuum-servo brakes and other technical marvels.

Thomas also cleverly pretended that he did not know who had started the correspondence but that he thought the letter might have been inspired by *pique*, because no other car would hold a candle to a Rolls-Royce. This did the trick, causing Mr Rapson to write a very long letter in which he explained that his 1920 Rolls-Royce had been delivered in poor running condition and so he reflected that it was not as good as the 1914 model (a Monday morning Rolls?). Since then the trouble had been rectified and now Mr Rapson was full of enthusiasm for this make. As someone else observed, Rolls-Royce Ltd now had Mr Rowledge, who had designed the 40/50 Napier, on their staff, so the next Rolls-Royce should be quite exceptional—as the New Phantom was to prove, but not for another five years.

After this the notable argument ran down, with other makes at lower prices being introduced, but not before D. Napier & Son had seen fit to advertise their own product and Parry Thomas, for his pains, had been told that Leyland was a lorry maker and a car from such a stable was like expecting a race-horse from a cart-horse breeder. (One wonders what the writer of this letter thought, if he saw the Leyland-Thomas break the lap record at Brooklands some time afterwards?) Before the thing finally died a Mr F. W. Taylor told *The Autocar* that you spend £3,000 rather carefully but, after trying most of the top new cars, he had bought another Lanchester.

It is easier, with hindsight, to think where one's own order would have been placed. We know that the Napier only achieved satisfactory smoothness by having the compression pressure dropped in one cylinder, that the Lanchester inherited a faint whine from its new-found sun-and-planet gearing and that engineering complexities never really cured Daimlers of their smoking habits. The only cars under discussion which did anything at Brooklands were the Leyland Eight and the Lanchester Forty. A 40/50 Napier appeared there much later, under a disguised name, and got nowhere.

I think you would probably have spent your money on a Silver Ghost, for all the Christmas-tree appearance of its big, not particularly efficient, side-valve engine for which no developed power was ever disclosed. The Hispano-Suiza had far better brakes, until Rolls borrowed from them in 1924, but was hampered in English motoring by its three-speed gearbox. As you would have employed a chauffeur, whether or not a Ghost's gear change came easy to you would scarcely arise. And the allure of a motor-car built almost throughout of steel forgings instead of iron and steel castings, with a chassis frame bolted instead of rivetted together, in which everything was so meticulously tested and the timing gears were stoned by hand and lapped for quiet running, would surely have won you over? The provision of a separate starting carburetter, hydraulic testing of the fuel reservoir, parts plated in Sheffield nickel silver instead of nickel plate, these and countless other matters of extreme attention to detail, made the Rolls-Royce the World's Best Car in most people's eyes—and think how many have survived!

'A perfect example, I'd say, of the money getting in the wrong hands.'

HIGHLY PLEASED

Writing about his nearly new car in the current issue of Motor, a Macclesfield man says that during the first 500 miles a gearbox bearing collapsed with severe loss of oil; the wiper motor is faulty; the body interior strikes him as poor; the metal sill under the rear window has fallen off and window handles drop off regularly; the transmission gives "horrible whirring and grinding noises"; and the steering is "terrifying", the car handling "about as well as a raft".

He adds: "Generally I have to admit that I am highly pleased with the car."—Peter Simple in 'Daily Telegraph'

In Vintage Veritas

RODNEY L. WALKERLEY

Beginners Start Here

Did you see only the other day where this American neurologis
bought this other American's Bugatti 57SC Atlantique for near
enough £20,000 at auction—and that's not a song but a grand
opera. The event was judged to be so striking, even in America,
that it was featured twice on TV that very night. The Englishman
who was bidding against him (and, I think, had been a previous
owner of the vehicle) gave up at the last thousand dollars. Not
having seen the TV exposition I am left wondering if he was
relieved or raving; in either case I have no doubt he sought the
professional aid of the ultimate buyer.

Americans, of course, when having the stuff in sackfuls, are apt
to be goers and getters, hence the present whereabouts of the
Queen liner, the London Bridge and a plurality of Old Masters
both authentic and forged. They love to gratify a whim. Like the

enthusiast who took home from Europe two of those majestic pre-war luxury automobiles with the Swiss-Spanish name which were built in France. This merely because he wanted to label them Hispano and Herspano. Let Jones follow that.

It is natural that the cult of the Vintage car and its even more valuable forerunner, the Veteran, should have begun in England and then spread throughout the world, catching on in a big way among our cousins across the Atlantic Ocean. Our cults do indeed tend to spread, like cricket, but the Vintage cult has ramified in a quite remarkable manner, even in countries like France, where they have always been convinced that the Englishman's devotion to old cars was because he could not afford new ones after two world wars.

There is a close affinity between the mystique of vintage in cars and the same thing in wines, if only because both come expensive and have appeal only to the knowledgeable, and in both there are pitfalls for the inexperienced palate. The cad who prefers a sweet Cyprus Barsac above all wines is also apt to guffaw at a '12 Bull-nosed Morris Oxford. Me, I just smile.

As with wines mere age does not betoken 'vintage' in auto-mobiles. We must learn to distinguish between the antique, the rare and the authentic vintage product. Years ago, my father's old friend, bluff and bearded chairman and No. 1 Driver of the Panhard-Levassor firm, the Chevalier René (Mac) de Knyff declared: 'There were no vintage products before 1905. The summers were all too wet except for our Panhards, Lou Renault's produce and the old Clos de Cauville, all from the Ile de France on sandy soil.' I mentioned other marques, now much fancied, but he brushed them aside with a single snort of 'Pouf!' I fell back, abashed, spilling half my glass.

In the world of wine the label does not always precisely identify the contents, especially in a poor year when the producer is nervous about having his name mentioned. Hence the vagueness of things like 'Beaujolais', 'Macon' and 'Beaune Supérieur'. This same anxiety afflicted early autoculturists. Thus Papa Daimler suddenly labelled his produce 'Mercedes', after a Bal Tabourin actress. Makers of the Turcat-Méry replied with 'Lorraine Dietrich', then appearing at the Concert Mayol and a great-aunt of the later Marlene, a film actress. In England Durkopp turned up as 'Watsonia', Clément-Panhard as 'Stirling' and Mr H. J. Lawson's companies sold various French imports under fancy names and got sued for doing it, these appelations being strictly controlled.

It was to end this cheerful confusion that the A.C. de France appointed their Comité des Appelations Controlées, to list, in the manner of the wine growers, the homologated Grandes Marques (Resources Regionales) which all men of taste know by heart. The RAC, bless them, hastily pointed out that products not included might also qualify, on a purely national basis, of course.

TABLE A

FRENCH (Burgundy, Médoc, Champagne, Gnome-et-Rhône)

Abbaye de la Haye	Hermitage de Lage
Chateau Panhard	Léon Bollinger
Clos de Peugeot	Pol Roger Benzedrine
De Dion Mouton Rothschild	Riley Fuissé
Entre deux Mors	Veuve Clyno
Georges Irat	Vino de Guingand

GERMAN (Mosel, Rhine, Solitude)

Bernkastler Duesenberg Domtal
Daimler Gottliebfraumilch Auslese
Kreisler Kron Prinz Riesling
Napier Nurburg Nochein
Offenhauser Vogelsang Auspuff

ITALIAN (Orvieto, Soave, Sundry)

Ansaldo Ruffino	Gancia Lambda
Aston Spumante*	Isotta Frascati
Ceirano di Bergerac	Itala Grappa di Monza
Chianti Alfaromeo	Marsala Vaccarella (Sicilian)

Let us now turn to the case of the most famous of all French

*Grand Prix and Medaille d'Or, Brussels Exhibition, 1908.

labels, originated by an Italian in Germany and omitted from the above table by jealous chauvinists. At the age of 20, the Italian E. Bugatti started experimenting and prudently disposed of his produce to French *negociants* to see what happened. Encouraged by results he planted his modest plant on a hired plot in German Alsace (later returned to French hegemony), among the fertile valleys where the Pinot vines do grow and, aged 29, put on sale his first produce under his own label in 1910.

With impish humour he identified his produce by bin numbers, as 'Types' (much as today we have 'Sherry Type' and 'Port Type' wines) and, what has confused connoisseurs ever since, used no numerical sequence but the numbers of whichever bins came readily to hand. His first offering was Bin 13, for a start.

After that the sequence was completely haphazard. By 1927 and the seventh vintage he was already up to '37' and '40' followed a year later. The next year he had a prolific harvest and was back among the '35's. However, that year, 1927, for the first and last time, he allowed natural pride to name a vintage. This was the legendary, revered and very rare methuselah (almost 13 litres) of which only six were for sale, under the label: Konigliche Molsheimer Spezial (Reserve du Roi) VSOP—Very Superior Outrageously Priced—with Bin Number 41. Understandably there was no great rush of purchasers but, in any case, the autocratic *proprietaire* insisted on screening each one personally during a week-end at his chateau where hesitation among the knives and forks or in distinguishing a Montrachet from a Meursault had the prospective customer's taxi at the door before the meal was ended, no matter how he brandished a banker's draft. It is comforting to know that one who passed all tests and became an owner was an Englishman who already had everything.

In all there were 38 vintages—some more vintage than others—in the 29 years of production, Bins 13 to 59. The old Patron had nothing to do with the last of the line, the '251' of '56 which purists prefer to forget.

It is well known that the climate of these islands is not favourable to the cultivation of vines or almost anything else, and mere age too often is substituted for quality. Among the few finding favour is the vintage produce of Maison Bentley, Chateauneuf Soupape, of which the labels arouse reverential awe among the devotees of the old-fangled. The first Première Cuvée (Red or Green Label) was followed by the heavier, more potent 'Four-and-a-Half Grand Brut', some of which were fortified under pressure. Next came the 'Six Speciale Reserve' and finally, the magnificence of the rare 8-litre jeroboam 'Crus Exceptionel'. This had a very rich appearance, even more nose than the others and, when warmed to the right temperature, a faintly oily bouquet of great delicacy and appeal. It was much favoured for galas, banquets and similar routs of those who could afford the finer things and did.

After a change of proprietor in '31 (a poor year) subsequent produce, while still admirable, was much of a muchness and considered by connoisseurs as of secondary class although it was admitted they travelled well. It has been rather like comparing Chambertin with a Gevrey Chambertin—a matter of taste for those with taste.

The question of what are now known comprehensively as 'Veteran' led to long and indeterminate discussion by the Comité who were well aware that, at that date, none could be classed as vintage. The Marquis Chasseloup-Bouton remarked that they might all be regarded as Plonk-de-Plonk Nature but as he had never tasted anything of that sort he suggested all prior to 1904 should be classed as 'Veteran' and left at that. It was left at that while the gentlemen sampled the new consignment of the club sherry, a nutty Fino Barbitone Doloroso, just in from Algeria. The Marquis de Dion, faintly praising it as 'abominable', found himself involved in his second duel of the day behind the Louvre, this time with the affronted club secretary, the Marquis de Beckenham. At their meeting both bowed and fired into the air harmlessly except to a flight of passing pigeons, while a passing motorist got down to inspect his tyres in alarm.

A recent and remarkable development within the Veteran Cult is that more and hitherto unknown examples appear each year at the various assemblies. As is well known, all veterans are discovered being used as hen coops in derelict barns and with small trees growing up through the chassis, or come to light in motor houses where they have stood, untouched, since the decease of their old lady owners upon which their even older chauffeurs left to join the paratroops.

Among so many, two veterans come to mind as typical of astounding craftsmanship. Roger Benz, cousin of old man Karl, opened showrooms in Paris in 1880 in anticipation of the Benz automobile of 1886, filling his empty windows with placards: WATCH THIS SPACE. In due course, avoiding the unpopular German stigma, he sold his cars as 'Pol Roger'—'Pol', of course, after Polly, a well-known actress at the Folies Bergère.

The other was the vehicle fabricated under the railway arches in Le Mans by Léon Bollinger who, in straightened finances, dispensed with the fourth wheel and fitted one at the back, in the middle, near enough. This enabled him to seat the passenger in front, nearer the accident. His original scheme, which he laughingly called his 'design', had been to seat the passenger with his back to the direction of travel, vis-à-vis the driver, but the expression on the passenger's face so unnerved him, who had little control over steering or anything else, that he turned the seat around, giving him a view of a shuddering back instead. The piercing shrieks of the passenger rendered any other audible warning device unnecessary.

It is, perhaps, not altogether surprising that when such as these come to light at the bottom of dry wells the discoverers quickly hide them again under haystacks or wood piles before stealing quietly away determined to be better men and do good unless some innocent with sackfuls starts enquiring.

As a matter of actual fact, I know a large expense account who paid money for a veritable Veteran to a man who said he had found it on a remote Scottish farm doing duty as donkey engine for sawing peat. My friend's idea was to take it home to Bognor Regis (which he did) and restore it (which he didn't). His perplexities began when he discovered the remnants of wheels at the sides as well as one each end. It turned out to be one of those Maddleys made in '01 by John Marston Sunbeam. They are fortunately very rare. There was an S-shaped seat for two on which the occupants sat side by side, with an arm-rest between them, but facing in opposite directions. By leaning forward when asked, they could give the driver at the back a glimpse of the way ahead, often in time for him to stay on the road.

When I last called on him, my friend resembled a veteran himself. His hair had gone snow white, his shoulders stooped with stooping and his hands shook so badly that he spilled as much as he drank. His current idea is to take the thing to pieces, melt them into a lump and use it as a door stop. He had a separate use for the driving chain.

Since the war a rising market has sprung up in rare automobiles, rare paintings and rare wines at prices causing auctioneers to lock their doors after the sales in order to execute little dances of great joy in private. Nor does there appear to be any falling off in the eagerness of chaps with sackfuls to part with shovel-fuls of the stuff, even descending with glad cries on Lots 14 to 44 comprising brass bric-à-brac and boutiquerie of the kind that used to ornament old motor cars for utilitarian purposes.

That now famous Type 57SC in California worked out around £600 the litre. There was a jeroboam of 8 litres of 1806 Chateau Lafite Rothschild that went for just over £100 per litre a few years back. I don't suppose you could pick up 8 litres of 1931 Bentley Crus Exceptionel for as little as that. Costliest bargain seems to have been the sale of a single litre of 1740 Canary dry white which went for £215 in 1967, brewed a good twenty years before the first Cugnot. Many years ago, I remember, over £500 per litre bought a 1902 Chateau Renault when the market was just beginning to cause hypertension. There's gold in them thar wheels.

Outside my window, and gathering a rich bloom as it matures, I have a five-year-old veteran (VOHV) now covered in a finer old crust than any vintage port. Admittedly, it needs loving restoration but it is a nice old gentleman, still far from senility. A certain virility has gone but the wits remain. The nose is very gracious and charming and the colour is lovely. Its body is perhaps a little on the thin side, but it will travel.

My local dealer, a man regrettably of no educated taste, has so far made the best offer of a straight swap for half a doz. bots. of Spanish Chablis which I have declined with a knowing smile. I can do better, in this permissive society. Look for me at the next auction down at the Marquis de Beaulieu's Musée des Arts et Métiers Automobile. I shall be standing nonchalant by my collectors' item wearing a flat cap with a plastic gardenia in my button-hole and open to any near offer and I am prepared to sell the reversing lamp separately.

You, too, can have a nerve like mine. When the band wagon comes along, leap aboard, chums. Even if yours is only a Post-Vintage Thoroughbred '56.

'which of you little perishers has put anti-freeze in your mother's present to me?'

The Walter Mitty of the
Classified Ads

EOIN S. YOUNG

In his Jason Love thrillers James Leasor is fond of picturing the head of the British Secret Service thumbing carefully through the property advertisements in *Country Life* sizing himself up with shooting estates in Scotland that he will never have the time to travel to, or a rambling crumbling Georgian relic in darkest Wales which would cost more in maintenance than the flirtatious purchase price indicates. I have the same trouble with the classifieds in *Motor Sport*.

As each month draws to a close I wait for *Motor Sport* with imagination whetted to drift off into the fantasy world of the classifieds with pipe and glass well charged for the trip.

You didn't know I had a Flying Spur Continental in the motor house, did you? No. You've probably never seen me crunching down the drive for a quiet, graceful swan up through the cuttings and out on to the sweeps over Ranmore Common just before dusk softens the edge on the day's detail. The Bentley has always meant more to me than the added pose value of the Rolls, perhaps only because the cars are both aristocratic sisters behind their radiators but the Bentley still carries the sporting air of its ancestors in the 'twenties and 'thirties.

When I first set foot in England I was very much the raw New Zealander, agog at the traffic, and counting the Rolls-Royces and the Bentleys to tell the folks at home. There had been the 4½ that thumped through Timaru one summer afternoon looking majestic among the Morrises and Austins and Holdens at the traffic lights. The measured throb of the long stroke engine was awesome—it was exactly like the tales of Le Mans that we had read and re-read from the one book in the library about motor racing. And our dismay when we discovered a 3-litre in a service station with the bonnet up and, as we crowded in to marvel at the tall polished and dignified engine, we realised that some vandal had replaced it with a common-or-garden Ford V.8.

In those days our *Motor Sport* ads told us about a 3-litre speed model with a 2-seater boat tail body that Mr C. J. Bendall would let us have for £250. If we had it, and if we could get to England to buy it. Or a 1930 4½ with a D box, a Bentley service history, vague apologies for the 'small estate type body' and what we reckoned to be a very reasonable price of £185.

Every now and then a neighbour drops by with either his replica 1922 bob-tailed TT 3-litre painted what I consider to be rather razzamatazz shrieking yellow, or a 1937 4¼ with an open body built to his specifications. He bought the rolling chassis with radiator and planned to build his personal open Bentley for around £1,000. At last pained reference he was talking about squeezing out of it for £2,500. I am grateful for his visits because it keeps reminding me that this is the sort of car I don't really require. A fast run up over the common also convinced me that the rich enjoy part of the road, leaving the rest for the poor. The only problem being that in this case the rich own the middle half and the poor are consigned to the hedges or verges as we

scythe through the Sunday morning calm in Wodehouse in-
difference.

A friend with an S Type re-stirs my urge to drive behind
the B, and I rearrange my longing from the fastback R Type
Continental conveniently to the more opulent, still modern-
looking S Type Flying Spur. My eagerness for an R Type
stemmed mainly from the thousands of miles clocked by Mike
Hailwood's dad in an R, but I subsequently learned that by comparison with the later S, the R is clumsy and a chore to conduct
and betrays its pre-war design in every turn of the road.

The reason you haven't seen me with my Spur is that I haven't
actually bought it yet, but I'm waiting for *Motor Sport* at the end
of the month because they will most likely be displaying one
that I can't resist.

> **1954 Jaguar XK120.** White drophead; New
> hood and wheel-arches, engine A1, good RAC
> report; collector's item. About £600.

I just *know* that I should have bought an XK120 five years ago
when maybe someone would have paid *me* to take it away instead
of the changed circumstances surrounding these beauties of line
today as they climb the market. At one stage pre-Bentley, the
XK120 was the love of my life and from time to time I suffered
lengthy periods of naked desire, openly coveting the rare im-
maculate 120 that would be advertised sans rust. I know that I
eventually won't buy one, and I know just as well that twenty
years from now the XK120s that have survived will be commanding prices now reserved for vintage Bentleys. The reason
being that they are wildly handsome motorcars, they have a
competition image, and their rate of decay has been such that in
twenty years their numbers—modest to begin with—will be
decimated. I travelled thousands of miles as passenger in a 120
drophead, a car that I adored as though it was my own, and it was
this sleek dark green Jag that captured my enthusiasm for the
marque. Since I never drove it, the brakeless aspect was not
allowed to sully my fond memories. That particular car was
replaced by a genuine C-type sports-racing car which we also
drove to races. The exhaust barked out directly beneath my left
ear, and we always had to make allowances for being deaf at

least an hour after we had arrived at our destination. The risk of losing our hearing did nothing to dilute the bliss of open-road motoring in a racing car.

The XK140, the XK150 or the E Type have never stirred me as much as the original XK120, although I can appreciate engineer Harry Mundy's retort that I must be out of my mind to fancy a 120 in preference to a 150 since the latter model had all the less good features of the 120 designed out of it.

> **Lagonda 1928,** 2-litre speed model; rolling chassis only; rebuilt to high standard; bills for £500. Serious enquiries only, etc.

He obviously doesn't want me ringing up to reminisce about the 2-litre low-chassis Speed Model that almost became mine for £200 but the thought of a duff second gear filled me with dread, and I avoided the issue. It was a fine car, but I fancy I wanted it for the wrong reasons. I really wanted it because it looked a lot like my beloved vintage Bentleys and it was priced within my impecunious grasp. So maybe it was only right and proper that fate didn't allow me to buy it. I may have been drummed out of the Lagonda Register had they known.

A measure of Teachers, a splash from the tap, thumb in another charge of Amphora, and continue down the page.

> **1935 MG PB** two-seater. Sound and 95% original order. £275 o.n.o.

Hmmm. The PB and the TF1500 have always been my favourites, although the only MG I owned was a B of which I was never particularly fond. The PB was for years my ideal MG, small, nippy, with the slab tank and spare that spelled out what sports cars were all about to someone who was desperately trying to graduate from an Austin Seven. From my viewpoint the TF was the last of the classic line and the marque started its drift into obscurity with the unlovely A and then the B. The TF had flared wings, cutaway doors, and of course the slab tank and rear-mounted spare wheel; you could fold the screen down and enjoy open-air motoring for a modest outlay. I make the point eloquently now but my mother could never be persuaded to see the obvious advantages of the TF over our family A35.

H

1928 Austin 7 'Chummy', completely restored; magneto engine; re-upholstered; new hood and side screens; chassis and engine entirely restored; new tyres. Offers over £400—with spares, including blocks, gearbox, back axle, chassis, brakes, etc.

Herbert Austin might have been aware that he was putting his part of the world on wheels when he brought out the little Seven, but I'm sure he never imagined how long those little cars would continue to teach legions of motorists the art of driving and basic mechanics. You had to be something of a basic mechanic to continue being a motorist with the sort of Sevens I owned. The first was a 1929 saloon that had been converted by some previous owner into a two-seater sports that would have looked marvellous in low-chassis form; in its high-chassis form it looked faintly ridiculous. One of the extras was a Ford Model T trembler coil connected to a spark plug in the expansion box of the exhaust pipe, with a triggering button on the dashboard. This odd contraption enabled me, at moments opportune, to back off the accelerator, allow the over-run gases to build up in the expansion box, press the button, and the resulting spark would ignite the mixture in a most impressive BANG! The expansion box was constructed of some light form of boiler plate presumably in anticipation of the side-splitting explosion that never actually happened. Despite continued provocation, the spidery little special never turned over. From time to time flames would issue from under the louvered strapped-down bonnet, but this fire was always extinguished by the simple means of turning off the ignition.

I bought the special from a mechanic who had despaired of continually fitting new axle keys only to have them chew themselves out inside a week, and had finally welded the keys into the axle—a cure that worked so well that I had no key-shearing trouble, and in fact never learned of his problems until the Austin had passed on to yet another owner.

Porsche 911 T Targa, 1968. Tangerine, sporto-matic; S-Type mags; stereo radio/tape deck; special seat; airhorns; beautiful condition; mechanically A1. £2,400.

My sort of motorcar at almost my sort of price but tact apparently prompts him not to mention the mileage or the fact that it's left-hand drive. I drove a stickshift 911T Targa from the factory near Stuttgart through to the first 1,000 kilometre race on the Osterreichring, and every kilometre brought the car and I closer together. By the time I had arrived in Austria I had resolved to buy the Porsche the lhd and the colour notwithstanding. It was painted a sort of violent puke green. I felt that the Porsche engineers had made the car exactly to my measurements, tailoring it to my every whim. It performed like a thoroughbred and tempted me into averaging speeds that I seldom touched in England. Everything about the car was perfect. The handling, the brakes and the engine performance combined to whisk me out of trouble if ever it so much as looked like happening. The trip across Germany and into Austria took something like six hours and I stepped out of the Targa feeling actually refreshed instead of whacked.

There were several thousand reasons why I didn't buy a Porsche, every one of them a £. I considered that the GTV1750 Alfa Romeo was the next best thing I had driven although it didn't approach the lofty Porsche plateau, so I revised my ambitions and bought the Alfa instead.

1939 Railton Straight 8 Sandown Saloon; taxed, M.O.T., £300 o.n.o.

Nobody really seems to love Railtons these days and vintage men will argue with you that nobody ever did, except perhaps the people that built them and a few of those that bought the Anglo-American bastard. The idea was simple. Take a Hudson rolling chassis, fit it with a stylish British body and there you were with an instant high performance motorcar. Reid Railton gave the company his name, and if several of the models failed to live up to the efforts of other more exotic Railtons designed by the famous man, the theory of effortless American power still remains valid in the Jensens of today. The first Railton I ever saw was laid up in a garage in Christchurch, New Zealand, and I was taken in as a little lad to see this sports car. Somehow I was given to understand that this was the very car that had set the lap record at Brooklands, although this feat had, of course, been performed by the Napier-Railton. It turned out, however, as I discovered some years later, that this Railton which had so impressed me was an extremely rare bird—one of the two or three Light Sports models in existence. These were built in 1935 to make the most of the straight-8 Hudson engine and a lightweight body. The car accelerated to 60 in under 10 seconds and had performance figures in the order of the XK120 when it was announced some 15 years later.

The first car I ever owned was a 1928 Model A Ford roadster that I probably saved from the breaker's yard by happening along with a cheque for £45, a sum which represented much more money than I had in the world. The Model A was chosen as a hypothetical base for a hot rod. My next-door neighbour had a 1936 Ford V.8 coupé into which he had fitted a 1948 Mercury V.8 engine and he was the reason for my being converted to American-style hot-rodding. It mattered not that he was a garage mechanic and I was a bank clerk. When I announced my intentions to become a hot-rodder by building up my own rod, we decided that I should buy a distinctly cold rod in the form of the dilapidated Model A, and warm it to the point of becoming hot.

To its credit, the old Ford started after two or three swings on the crank, and while my neighbour and instigator into this hot-rod programme disappeared down the road in a blue haze, I teetered along learning the odd habits of my strange steed as I went. This first five mile journey was also to be the last time I ever drove it.

The hand-throttle in a quadrant on the steering wheel appeared to be something of a novelty since I was able to set my pace and cruise feet-off, as it were. Unlike modern American cruise-control systems, however, the Model A possessed no over-ride on the accelerator, but this point was lost to me as I started the swing into our front gate. The Model A literally swung into the front gate, taking the post and gate out by the roots, before I managed to stop by stalling in a panic.

Since our double garage had an inspection pit, the Ford was rolled over it, and armed with written instructions on a grubby

envelope from next door, I set about laboriously renewing the
king pins. I wasn't exactly sure what king pins were or what
purpose they performed, but I was given to understand that their
being worn contributed to the spooky steering characteristics
I had mentioned after my maiden run. You have to know that
the Model A has a transverse leaf spring at the front to appreciate
the developments as I worked my way through the instructions.
It appeared that a sort of tension was building up throughout the
front end of the car as I undid bolt after bolt, and nut after nut,
but I was blissfully unaware that I was actually releasing the
spring until the very last nut sheared its threads, spronging down
into the pit as the rest of the front suspension seemed to explode
before my terrified gaze. I fell to the floor of the pit, choking
in the grime and dust of ages as the Model A sagged to its tired
knees above me like a wounded elephant. A quick count of
fingers, arms and legs revealed that I was unhurt apart from a
badly damaged pride and the resolve never, but never, to
meddle with things mechanical. With written instructions, or
without.

The Model A left in a rather less spectacular manner than it
had arrived, swinging on the back of a wrecker's tow rope
with the front suspension bound up by Number 8 fencing
wire. . . .

My first motoring experience had lasted five miles, just on
a week, and the total transaction had resulted in a loss of £35.
A fiver a day for a vital course in engineering.

I was to tempt technical fate just one more time in my career
and the results were no more successful than they had been
originally. Seven years before he became World Champion, I
accompanied Denny Hulme around the Formula Junior races in
Europe. Prior to the first event Denny was performing some
internal repairs to the engine, and he suggested that I might like
to change his gear ratios on the Cooper. He would, of course,
give me instructions. It wasn't difficult, he said. Nor was it. I had
tightened the last bolt as he completed his work on the engine,
and when he came to inspect my handiwork I had to admit that
everything had gone together splendidly and that I even had
some washers, and nuts and bolts left over which he might like

to toss in his spares box. He gave me a very strange look, a mirthless titter followed by an expletive and then set about taking the transmission apart again. His instructions hadn't called for leaving bits out.

The cheering thing about being an armchair Mitty motorist is that you can afford to indulge in wild flights of automotive fancy without it actually costing an arm and a leg. Fifteen years ago we were able to indulge ourselves to an even greater degree in the *Motor Sport* small ads, and looking back at issues of 1957, the imagination chokes. There was a Riley Imp for £365, a delightful 2½-litre two-door Delage sportsman's saloon for £145, an S.S.100 for £340 o.n.o., a 1934 2.3 supercharged 8-cylinder Alfa Romeo roadster for £350, and an Ulster Austin for £150.

Now I can speculate on buying my '59 S Type Bentley Continental for around £2,500 for a serene trip up to London without the insistence to try hard that I always seem to feel coming over me at the wheel of the Alfa. There would be a good XK120, a C Type with a history, a Chummy Austin Seven, and probably a TF MG.

It all depends, of course, whether I can muster the necessary £9,000 to cover a stable like that, in addition to a sizeable motorhouse in which to store them. Some months I have trouble raising 15p to buy *Motor Sport*. . . .

THE BEST EMBALMING IN THE WORLD
1928 Rolls-Royce hearse with original body in excellent condition. . . .

"Well... The Road Must Go Somewhere!"

GRAHAM GAULD

As a some-time rally driver I have often wondered, in times of great stress or impending accident, just what makes the rally driver tick. Does he, for instance, see himself as a present-day reincarnation of the pioneer racing driver who drove on an event in a car equipped with the bare necessities over rough unkept roads with a friend alongside him? Or is it just that the average rally driver is a somewhat insecure individual who likes to have an audience to applaud his finer hours at the wheel and to share with him the agony of his moments of grief?

The racing driver, on the other hand, is easier to understand. He is alone in his car going as fast as he is able on a track he knows, because he has practised on it for the past few days, and in the ultimate sense is only responsible to himself for his actions and success.

Racing drivers can't understand rally drivers, and, occasionally, rally drivers can't understand racing drivers. Andrew Cowan, the London-Sydney Marathon winner, for instance, was given a trial by Team Lotus in their Formula III racing cars some years ago. After two races Andrew turned down the offer of a place on the team because he felt he was just not in the groove for racing. 'I remember at Goodwood having a good start in the Lotus and then missing a gear going into the first corner; in that moment half the field shot past me and I got nowhere,' said Andrew.

On a rally special stage the same Cowan would be quicker than nearly all his fellow racing drivers because, for him, driving fast on loose surfaces, or over roads he has perhaps never seen before, has become instinctive. So rallying develops in a driver a whole new range of skills that the racing driver does not require in his own sphere.

To come first on a rally the driver must have the fundamental ability to drive fast on a variety of road surfaces, from mud and rocks to snow and ice. By the very nature of special stages and their length he must anticipate corners coming up and set his car up in such a way that, if the corner suddenly tightens on him, he has room to break the tail away and still get round it. As Eric Carlsson, the great Swedish driver, once said when asked what he did when he drove over a blind hump in the road at high speed without knowing what was coming, 'Well . . ., the road must go *somewhere*'.

Rally drivers are funny people and their activities get mixed up sometimes. Take the case of the club rally driver who arrived at the start of a Rally with his beat-up old Volkswagen and a new co-driver. Shortly after the event started, they shot round a corner and rolled the Beetle on to its roof. You can imagine the scene, the two of them kneeling on the roof listening to the pencils dropping out of their pockets with the engine still running and the ominous drip of hot oil on the exhaust pipes. The co-driver panicked and started to kick at the door to get it open, only to be howled down by the driver: 'Hey . . . mind the upholstery!' You see; the priorities are wrong. Had it been Jackie Stewart they would have been half a mile away and to hell with the upholstery!

I can think of few racing drivers who have ever become rally drivers, but occasionally you get rally drivers turning to racing, the most successful being Vic Elford, the late Lucien Bianchi and the Belgian driver, Olivier Gendebien. They all came to the fore in rallying before turning to racing but the main stumbling block for the opposite conversion—racing driver to rally driver— is the racing driver's genuine fear of being driven by someone else.

Though he started off in small club rallies the late Jim Clark was sensitive about taking part in any events where someone else would have to share the driving with him. Indeed, just before he was killed in 1968, he and Graham Hill drove a Ford Taunus on a Ford-organised trans-European promotional trip and Jimmy spent most of the time whilst Graham was driving biting his nails in the passenger's seat. When, however, in 1966, he was persuaded to compete in the RAC Rally driving a Ford Lotus Cortina, he went quite happily with Brian Melia who was one of Britain's most experienced co-drivers. During the event he confided in me that in his opinion Melia would have driven some of the stages quicker than he (Clark) could. What this par- ticular exercise proved, however, was that a top racing driver like Clark, with very little practice, could be just as fast as the top rally drivers and he somewhat bruised the myth of infallibility which the rally drivers had woven around their own craft.

Of the hundreds of men who start rallying at club level every year, there are few who do not aspire to becoming International rally drivers with factory backing. In Britain the chances of reaching the top and of attaining this enviable position are even fewer now than they were ten years ago when British manu- facturers gave a lot more support to International events. But rallying is a growing sport and the role of private sponsors is now becoming important so that the top people at club level look for sponsorship to take them out into the International rally scene, and this trend is likely to increase, particularly as it was estimated that some two million people watched the RAC Rally in 1971.

To my mind International rallying is one of the friendliest sports open to anyone, and good performances are respected by the top people as well as by the novices. What is more, it is a sport where everyone seems to wallow in dramas and yet always sees the funny side of it.

Take, for instance, the case of the Scottish rally driver—and being Scottish most of my tales concern Scottish rally drivers—who was asked to be third man in a crew setting off from Glasgow in the Monte Carlo Rally. This was in the great days of the Monte, when the British entry formed the largest proportion of the field and yet the majority of the drivers were out purely for the 'prestige' of having taken part in the Rally. Today we are more honest with ourselves which is why the Monte entry from Britain is so small. But back in those days there was one particular Scot who used to take part with a big burly friend and, usually, a third man. The burly one sat in the back seat of the car, said nothing, and was along purely for the ride and to pull the car out of the snow drifts. In this particular year the entrant approached one of Scotland's more serious rally drivers as he had been told this fellow was good. So the bond was made and our rally expert joined the motley crew.

When it came to the rally, however, the entrant joined the strong silent one in the back seat and told the rally driver to get on with it. On the A1 from the Glasgow start heading towards London the screen-washers packed up. The driver bemoaned the fact that he couldn't see so the big fella in the back took his pipe out of his mouth and ordered the driver to wind his window down. At this he leaned forward and threw a flask of tea over the windscreen and remarked '. . . now wipe the bloody screen'. They went on like this surviving all sorts of dramas—such as when the entrant saw snow on the ground as the ship sailed into Boulogne and had to be persuaded not to immediately return to Britain on the next ship. Meanwhile our rally ace was still at the wheel and wilting visibly. Eventually the entrant decided he would drive but he was so slow that the rally driver took over again and, 1,500 miles after leaving Glasgow, they eventually arrived in Monte Carlo. As if this wasn't enough, the driver was so tired he only realised as he was being dragged to his hotel that he had left his false teeth in the Parc Ferme and then spent a fruitless half hour trying to persuade the marshal to let him into the car to retrieve his pots!

There was also the case of the Scottish doctor who probably holds the record for the shortest Monte Carlo Rally: he hit a bus

150 yards from the start when everyone was still cheering him off. But don't laugh, the young French driver Piot set off on one of his early Montes from Paris without his route control card and collected a taxi on his way back to the start!

Rallying is filled with characters who are larger than life. People like Johnstone Syer, who in real life is a professional photographer, but who spends most of his time on International rallies with Brian Culcheth. It was with Culcheth that he finished second on the World Cup Rally in a Triumph 2.5PI. Some time earlier, however, he was out on a reconnaissance for the Monte Carlo Rally with Culcheth and the other members of the B.M.C. team at that time: Timo Makinen, Paddy Hopkirk and Rauno Aaltonen. On this particular event Tony Fall had been brought into the team for the first time and was being shown the ropes.

They arrived at a stage south of Gap, in the high Alps north of Monaco, and Fall was sent off first, followed by Culcheth and Syer in their B.M.C. 1800 and then by Makinen in a Mini. Near the summit of the narrow mountain road, Fall went off on the outside of a corner and buried his Mini up to the tail lights in a snowdrift. By the time Culcheth had stopped to find out what was wrong they could all hear Makinen roaring up the stage behind them. They quickly ran down the road to stop him before he arrived on the scene.

'What's the matter?' said Makinen. 'Tony's stuck in a snow-drift', they replied, so everyone went up to have a look. As soon as he saw what had happened, Makinen remarked: 'Why you stuck in snowdrift, Tony? . . . You should be pulling 6,000 revs. and you go right through'. Then, to demonstrate, they removed the Mini, Makinen jumped into the 1800 which, incidentally, was the team manager's own car, backed off down the road and took a run at the snowdrift and barged clean through it. The trouble was he took the petrol pump off the 1800 but he had proved his point! Unfortunately the 1800 only just made it to the top of the Col before expiring, so Syer climbed in with Makinen and Paul Easter, whilst Culcheth went in the other Mini with Fall and Mike Wood. On the downhill part of the route there were only two pieces of straight joined by a fast right-hand bend and the stage was like a bobsleigh run. Syer recalls Makinen catching Fall and doing a 'wall of death' on the snowbank to get round on the fast right-hander before heading off down the pass.

These memories still stick in Syer's mind, and I know how he feels for, until you have driven with one of the top Scandinavian drivers on a snowy special stage, the whole impact of what rallying is all about cannot be fully grasped.

The Scandinavian domination of the sport for the past ten years has a lot to do with the fact that many of the special stages which decide International events are now being run on loose-surfaced roads or else, in winter, on snow and ice. In these conditions, the Scandinavians have few peers. Like French and Austrian skiers, they live with these conditions all the year round and they become atuned to them and adjust their driving styles accordingly. At the same time rallying is a major sport in both Sweden and Finland and it is said that over 40,000 competition licences are issued in Sweden, a country of only eight million people, or one-sixth of the population of Britain!

The Scandinavians have a different approach to rallying. We in Britain tend to cling to the old maxim 'to win you must finish', but generally speaking a Scandinavian will suggest that their motto is 'if you aren't going to win, why finish?' The result is an approach to driving on stages which at times looks like the last rush of the lemmings before falling over the cliff, or perhaps a fledgling Kamikaze squadron in training. Stuart Turner, Ford's director of motor sports, has described their determination in terms of percentages. The up-and-coming Scandinavian will drive at 110 per cent of his ability and, if he survives the pace and can keep up with the cost of the car repairs, might subdue his enthusiasm and reach a consistent 100 per cent. In Britain we will start out at 80 per cent and struggle up to 95 per cent. Naturally, these are generalisations for there are a few, but only a few, British drivers who can compete on level terms with the Swedes in their own kind of conditions. I never tire of watching the Swedes and Finns in action every year during the Swedish Rally in February, when the snow lies thick on the ground and the rivers and lakes freeze over. It is an event with none of the glamour of the Monte, for who would say that Karlstad in the Swedish Lake district can compare with Monte Carlo? But out in the forests you can see drivers at work really practising their art.

But what is it like driving with the really top Scandinavians? A man who is acknowledged as one of the greatest rally drivers of all time, the Fangio of the rallying world, is bear-like Erik Carlsson, who now lives quietly in the South of France with his wife, Pat Moss, and their family. As a part-time member of Saab's public relations staff, Erik still commutes between Nice and Stockholm but freely admits that he is too old for rallying now. I had the opportunity to drive with him in a factory Saab 96 V4 through one of Sweden's snowy forest special stages the week after the 1971 International Swedish Rally. Picture the scene—a bright sunny day with the snow sparkling and the patches of ice glistening on the road. On the opening stretches of the stage, where Billerud, the forest company, had chopped down the trees, you could hardly pick out the route in the blinding light but, in the trees, it was darker so the undulations, the twists and the dips were harder to see.

The stage itself runs from Grasmark to Barnarna in the Swedish lake district just south of the little village of Torsby. It has the nickname *Soptunnan* which means 'garbage can', because the start line for the stage is marked by one of those big, wire, garbage boxes found in Swedish forests. The Saab 'pace notes' on the stage refer to it as being '. . . wide with a smooth surface but with many curves in the early parts and very fast towards the end.' On the rally itself this 13 mile stage through the forest had been covered at an average speed of 63 m.p.h. by Stig Blomquist in a factory Saab—which gives some idea of the speed these rally drivers can maintain over snow and ice while flitting between the trees.

Right from the start of our run through the stage Carlsson accelerated hard through the gears, the front wheels spinning, and as with all good competition drivers he kept the car on power nearly all the time, changing up and down through the gears without apparently lifting off the throttle. Once he had reached his general average cruising speed of about 80 m.p.h., the true skill of the man came out as he let the car plunge over blind crests and skitter down the other side. With its firm suspension the car tended to buck and leap at every bump in the road, yet each time it came down to earth Carlsson just sat back and calmly steered out of the slide. As with all rally cars running in Sweden the tyres were equipped with rally studs with upwards of 300 to each wheel. These are extremely effective—particularly on braking where you can afford to brake hard in a straight line.

Inevitably we came over the occasional rise only to be faced by a tight downhill slope with a bend. In those situations it appeared impossible to get round the corner but Carlsson would just change down, drive hard into the bend and let the tail slide round until it hit the snowbank, which slowed the car and at the same time cannoned it off in a new direction, just as a snooker player would play a shot off the cushion.

On one particular piece of road which was straight, though bumpy, Carlsson really let fly hitting 7,000 r.p.m. in top gear which is just over 100 m.p.h. for a brief second before plunging over another rise and down, braking hard, into a deep dip and out the other side like a bullet.

'Not bad for an old man,' remarked Carlsson; and I agreed.

I asked him the biggest mistake people make in trying to drive in this way and he remarked that people faced with slippery conditions and a surprise dip or a corner tend to freeze and either brake or do nothing. To a seasoned rally driver there is always something that can be tried right up to the moment when the accident happens.

If you think about it, in the history of post-war rallying very few rally drivers have been killed on special stages in events and there are two reasons for this. I feel they have a great survival instinct and, except in certain circumstances, are travelling much slower than a racing driver on a circuit. Nevertheless, most racing drivers will tell you that rallying is potentially more dangerous than racing. Rally drivers are more philosophical, perhaps. I once asked Peter Riley about the dangers of having accidents in the forest and he came out with a perfect tongue-in-cheek reply: 'If you go off the road you don't need to worry too much as there are always plenty of trees to slow the car down!'

In accidents on rallies you occasionally get amusing situations developing, such as the time on an Alpine Rally when a Citroen had gone over the edge of a cliff and was parked tail first in the trees, the headlights pointing straight up into the sky. One of the crew had broken an arm and was still in the car, whilst the other had climbed back to the top and was literally hanging on by his finger tips with his head showing above the road. A well-known British rally driver came along, slowed and shouted 'What's up?' to which the Frenchman replied something like '*Mon ami est blessé*', to which the British driver replied, 'Sorry, I don't speak French', and drove off. In the same incident another British driver, reporting the state of the Citroen crew to the control marshals, got his feet and metres mixed up, telling the startled marshal that the car was 150 metres down the valley, when in fact he meant 150 feet.

The marshals on rallies have their problems too—for instance the one on the RAC Rally some years back who, like most marshals on International events, was equipped with one of those expensive chronometers hung by a strap round his neck. Rauno Aaltonen and Henry Liddon in their factory Mini-Cooper arrived at the start of the stage where the marshal knelt down, took the strap off his neck and held the watch in his hand. He gave the usual count down but at the 'go' the car shot forward, whipping the watch out of the marshal's hand. By mistake the neck strap had fallen over Aaltonen's door handle and the Mini set off with it banging against the door. Neither the driver nor the co-driver could think what the banging was all about, so half way through the stage, and still at speed, Aaltonen opened the door and the last they saw of the watch was it cartwheeling down the road behind them in the dust!

The rally driver has to have many attributes. He obviously must have skill at the wheel, a skill which is almost telepathic. He has to have a sense of survival which will allow him to keep working at a potential accident situation right up to the moment when he flies off the road into a ditch, which he must surely do on some ocasions during his career, and he must have a great deal of physical stamina. Until you have competed in a two- or three-day event non-stop, you have no idea the boundaries of tiredness you break until you are eventually overcome by a numbing fatigue and the resolution that you will never again do another International rally. I think almost every competitor who has taken part in any of the big European events will admit that on some occasions they wish they had never started and yet within ten minutes of the finish all such thoughts have vanished and someone has pressed a fresh set of regulations for another rally into your hands.

All of which tends to develop a driver who, when compared to a racing driver, can look ragged when he is cornering fast on a stage. Not for him the immaculately precise arm movements of the racing driver with the car in perfect balance. Indeed rally drivers have developed a range of driving techniques, including the reverse flick technique on loose surfaces which calls for a great deal of skill and confidence. Briefly described, it works like this. You arrive at a left-hand bend at speed but, instead of turning into the bend, you flick the car to the right and then immediately left, so inducing an almighty tail slide which you then hold through the bend with the power on. So the driving might look sloppy but the skill and precision is still there.

This brings us finally to co-drivers. To have the nature and inclination to sit beside someone who is doing all these improbable things takes a kind of courage in itself. Unlike the

1937 German Grand Prix at Nürburgring: Caracciola (Mercedes) and Rosemeyer (Auto Union). From a drawing by F. Gordon Crosby

E. Bugatti 1913

Mixing pur-sang cars and horses in carefully posed pictures was something of a
Bugatti speciality. In this 1913 photograph, Le Patron and his mount almost
obscure a delightful Type 13 Berline (see page 238)

Not even the Ghostly glory of its radiator brought British—or French—motorists flocking to invest in a Secqueville-Hoyau (see page 240)

This Lagonda Rapier is almost completely original except for the absence of slats in front of the radiator block (see page 240)

n years after its birth, the little Ogle is still a superb road car' (see page 270)

'*AC 428—good-looking, fast, beautifully-made and typical of its time*' (see page 267)

'*To get the best, the absolute best, out of a Ferrari Dino, you need to be a Driver, not merely a motorist*' (see page 270)

Keith Schellenberg with the Barnato-Hassan Bentley

'Glory shall remain . . .'

Hugh Hunter with the 2.9-litre 8–cyclinder supercharged Alfa Romeo

Jackies: Ickx's Brabham leads Stewart's Matra in practice for the 1969 German Grand Prix (see page 26)

Up aloft: '... a collection of ugly projectiles, rear-engined specials thrown together by a band of mad plumbers.' Jo Siffert's Cooper-Maserati, at Nürburgring (see page 258)

Lotus 72 and Ferrari 312B: power/weight ratios equate today's Formula One Grand Prix cars very closely with these awesome German cars of 1937 (see page 258)

driver, who has the opportunity of doing something in a sticky situation, it is the co-driver who has to sit there and watch it all happen as a kind of third-party voyeur—for a psychologist might well relate it to some form of sexual communion. At the same time, for the doubtful pleasure of sitting there, he has to 'manage' the car. It is the co-driver who sees to it that the car has the right amount of fuel, checks into the controls at the right time and drives when the lord-and-master decides to sleep. His role was aptly summed up by the Finnish driver Esko Keinanen in 1964 when he drove a factory Chrysler Valiant for the first time in the Monte Carlo Rally. His co-driver was told to drive the car from their Stockholm starting place to Chambéry in the South of France whilst Keinanen slept. After this marathon 56-hour drive the co-driver was absolutely exhausted and was then put in the co-driver's seat whilst Keinanen proceeded to throw the big Chrysler round the mountains as fast as he could go. Afterwards Keinanen explained: 'By the time we reached Chambéry he was so tired he hadn't the strength to be frightened'.

International rallying today is a sport which has become very important in terms of publicity and also for its contribution towards making production cars stronger; yet a sport where the competitor sees the lighter side of life in circumstances where most people would take things very seriously. Indeed their acceptance of the risks and their approach to them are summed up in the story of the two British competitors who hit a dry stone dyke on the Circuit of Ireland Rally and literally rolled the car along the top of the dyke before it fell back on the road as a heap of rubble. Both driver and co-driver were so amazed at their escape they burst out laughing and were staggering about the road doubled up with laughter when your actual Irish farm labourer arrived, red-faced and panting in ex-army boots and greatcoat. 'My God' he said, '. . . Oi heard that half a mile away . . . are you not killed?'

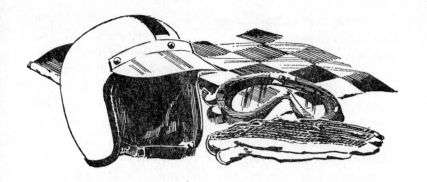

The Autodromo Di Monza

DENIS JENKINSON

The name Monza means different things to different people. To anyone living in Milan it is a suburb to the north-east these days, although it used to be a small town on its own. To motor racing enthusiasts it means the Italian National racing circuit in the Parco di Monza, though to natives of the town the Royal Park means a lot more than just motor racing. It covers an enormous area that caters for all manner of activities, from camping and swimming to horse riding and walking, and the National Auto-dromo is quite a tiny plot of land within the whole park, even though the circuit has a length of 5¾ kilometres. The name Monza first made an impression on me in 1933 when I saw a photograph of an Alfa Romeo Tipo 'Monza', for though it was not in colour in those days, the photograph really captured my imagination and the Tipo 'Monza' seemed the ultimate in sports cars to my schoolboy mind. I soon realized that this fierce sports car was

named after the National racing circuit, just as the Riley Motor
Company had named their low and racy sports car the 'Brooklands' model after our own racing track, so that the name Monza
came to mean to me Italian racing red, noise, speed and excitement and everything that was motor racing. I learnt that the
Monza circuit was something special in that it was a permanent
track and very fast and had been built in 1922, the first Grand Prix
being held there on September 10th of that year. The winner
was Pietro Bordino driving a Fiat, at 86.89 m.p.h. and the name
Monza was synonymous with Fiat and Alfa Romeo in the
Golden Twenties.

Unlike today with air travel making distances no problem or
mountains no obstacle, the mid-thirties were times when even
France seemed a long way from England and Italy was quite
unattainable, so that all I could do was to read about Monza when
the Italian Grand Prix took place each year and to look back on its
history in the motoring books. The war suddenly made travel
available to everyone, even though most people did not want it,
and many saw Italy for the first time from the air with no desire
to land, or from the land when they wished they could fly away!
When sanity and racing returned I was soon travelling about
Europe on the Continental Motor-cycle Circus, racing every
weekend and in 1949 we heard that the Italians had resurrected
the Monza track and that our season was going to end with a
motor-cycle World Championship meeting on the famous track.
Although I had travelled through most of the Western European
countries by this time I had yet to visit Italy, and as we crossed
Switzerland heading for the Gotthard Pass over the Alps I recalled a stirring story I had read many years before. It was written
by Rodney Walkerley, who was 'Grande Vitesse', the Sports
Editor of *The Motor* at the time, and he described a journey back
from Monza in an MG Magnette sports 2-seater at night in
pouring rain, and the crossing of the Gotthard Pass. It was not on
good concrete road, with tunnels and guard rails as it is now,
but in the primitive times of the mid-thirties with a loose gravel
surface and the odd stone to mark the road edge. His graphic
description of the headlights picking out the direction signs
saying 'San Gottardo' as he climbed up the Ticino valley from

Como was memorable, and how once near the summit and into the centre of Switzerland the signs read 'St Gotthard'. My first trip was in the other direction, and also at night but thankfully not in rain, and as I drove our van over the pass, on loose gravel on most of the northern side and part way down the southern side, apart from concrete on the tight hairpins, I relived Walkerley's trip as the signs changed from 'St Gotthard' to 'San Gottardo' and Italy approached. Como and Monza lay ahead and it was with great relief that we ran onto the Lombardy plains south of Como next morning and into Monza.

What a memorable day that was, to see the famous Monza track for the first time. England was racing on disused airfields, France and Belgium were road racing on temporary circuits lined with straw bales and with wooden grandstands, the Swiss circuits were all on public roads closed for the occasion and, though there was plenty of racing, nothing seemed very permanent in those immediate post-war years. Brooklands had crumbled and gone, Montlhéry was very derelict and the Nürburgring was still being rebuilt, so that my first sight of Monza made a lasting impression. The solid concrete grandstand, the concrete pits, the vast concrete towers on each side of the iron gates onto the track itself, the paved paddock and lock-up garages, all put my racing life into true perspective. Racing was here to stay. Monza, the home of speed, noise and excitement was all real and far larger than I ever anticipated. The enormously wide starting area, the height of the great cantilever canopy on top of the grandstand in ferro-concrete was all magnificent and the track was faster than anything we had raced on before. Up went the gear ratios, up went the speed, and we contrived to tuck ourselves in out of the wind as never before. It was a glorious full-throttle blind, with only the two sharp right-hand corners at Lesmo and the double right-hander at the old Curva Sud, or Curva Porfido as it was known with its cobbled surface. While battling for the lead against a 4-cylinder Gilera sidecar outfit our Norton blew its sparking plug out and by the time we had fitted another and ridden like demons we could only regain fifth place. It was enough to win us the 1949 Sidecar World Championship so we were taken up onto the VIP balcony in the grandstand, along with the race winner, and as I looked down on the seething, cheering, waving crowds of Italian enthusiasts I thought Alfa Romeo were absolutely right to name that exciting sports car the Tipo 'Monza'.

Since that memorable day in 1949 I have visited Monza at least once every year, and in some years on numerous occasions, and I still get an enormous thrill every time I drive through the entrance gate. Monza means sheer unadulterated speed above all to me, where engines have to be powerful and strong. Competitors pass the pits virtually at maximum speed and disappear into the distance still 'on full song'. To be walking down the road leading under either of the tunnels that give access to the inside of the track and to hear a racing engine, be it a 4-cylinder motor-cycle or a 12-cylinder motor-car, approaching at peak r.p.m. to pass overhead and continue at its peak until out of earshot going into the Curva Grande, still makes me want to break into a run. Not away from the noise but towards it, not with the hope of catching it, but with the knowledge that 'this is Monza' as I might be in time to hear the car or motorcycle going down the back straight still 'on full song'.

Needless to say I have a thousand memories of Monza culled over twenty-three years, and it is one of the tracks I shall continue to visit for it always produces something memorable. In 1955 it underwent a great rebuilding and a steeply banked speed bowl was incorporated using the main straight and a new back straight, parallel with the existing one, the concrete bankings at the North and South being incredibly steep, and they turned out to be incredibly bumpy as well. Used mainly for record breaking the banked track could be used in conjunction with the road circuit to make a 10-kilometre circuit. The old Curva Porfido was replaced by a new one, as the South Banking took a line through the old corners and the new one was called the Curva Parabolica, being one long fast sweep through 180 degrees from the back straight to the main straight. When I gave up motor-cycle racing in 1952, competing in the Gran Premio di Nazione at Monza for the last time, I took up journalism and moved from the track to a position high above it in the Press Tribune at the top of the huge concrete grandstand and over the years have witnessed some memorable races and events. During practice and training I enjoy watching at the Lesmo corners, the Vialone or the Parabolica, and when the banking was in use to stand at the foot of the North banking. There are many things I shall never forget about Monza, especially the two Indianapolis-type 500-mile races on the banked track in 1957 and 1958, with an all-time high in lap speeds of 177 m.p.h., or the sight of Ricardo Rodriguez on the banking in a Grand Prix Ferrari in 1961, pointing in any direction except forwards, with all wheels off the concrete and his foot hard on the throttle. Monza enjoyed drivers like that. There were races for the Inter-Europa Cup with as many as twelve 250 GT Ferrari coupés battling away, the sound from the 144 cylinders being glorious, or the Supercortemaggiore sports car race in a cloud burst when 60 m.p.h. was about the maximum that anyone could do. Then the classic race in 1957 when the three Vanwall cars of Moss, Brooks and Lewis-Evans drove the Maserati and Ferrari opposition so far into the ground that it was a long time before they got up again, or in 1967 when Jim Clark had a pit stop and made a whole lap on the rest of the field to regain the lead, only to run short of petrol on the last lap and let Surtees and Brabham have a straight fight into the last corner, no holds barred, and Surtees won with the Japanese Honda Grand Prix car. With only three sharp corners to the lap wheel-to-wheel racing is the order of the day no matter whether it is an F3 race, a Grand Prix or a Sports Car race, and I find the sight of as many as six cars lapping at 150 m.p.h. in a tight bunch very exciting to watch.

The Press Tribune at Monza has a particular feature all its own, for the sound of the cars is thrown up between the grandstand and the pits and office buildings opposite, and is trapped by the great overhanging canopy. The sheer physical fatigue experienced during a race when Grand Prix races ran for three hours or more, was remarkable, but I would not want it any other way. The day the Monza Press Tribune is encased in sound-proof glass, like the Press room at the new Paul Ricard circuit in France, I shall go down below and join the milling public, even if there are 120,000 of them. Monza has always attracted enormous crowds; there were 80,000 on that first visit I made in 1949 and in recent years their enthusiasm has become stronger than ever. With racing

in Italy limited to three circuits and no more town-to-town open
road racing, this is not surprising and the scene at the end of the
1970 Gran Premio d'Italia is one that will never be forgotten.
The Ferrari team was on the crest of a wave and everyone loves
a Ferrari, even if they hate old man Enzo himself, and to an
Italian Ferrari *is* racing. When the newcomer Gianclaudio
Regazzoni won that race the circuit nearly burst asunder and the
crowds poured onto the track, even though they had to climb
a fifteen-foot wire mesh fence. The scene was indescribable and
some of the drivers had to give up racing on their last lap as the
track became covered with running, shouting, weeping,
screaming Italians. It was as if a riot had broken out, but everyone
was happy and the tension and excitement had reached bursting
point.

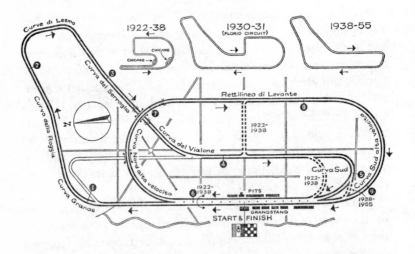

Monza has its tiresome side as well as its joyful one, and it has
its tragic side too like any permanent racing track. In 1933 motor
racing lost three great drivers when Campari, Borzacchini and
Czaykowski all crashed and were killed on the same day. In
recent years the track saw the death of von Trips and in 1970
Jochen Rindt was killed, and there have been many more, some
famous drivers like Alberto Ascari, who was killed in practice,
and some not so well-known like Tommy Spychiger who was

killed in a sports car race. Over the years the track has gone
through some tiresome phases, for example when the military
police were used for control in the pits area, and as few of them
enjoyed the job they were very short-tempered and a fracas with
someone who did not understand Italian would soon flare up.
I recall one motor-cycle friend of mine in 1951 being uncere-
moniously thrown in Monza gaol for flattening a military policeman. We went to the gaol to try and get him out but were too
late, the paperwork had been filled in and sent to Milan and
justice had to take its course, which took ten days. The Commandant of the gaol was very sympathetic and explained that
had we been ten minutes earlier with a fist full of money we
could have stopped the forms being filled in and could have
'done a deal' to get our friend out. Now it was too late, official-
dom in Milan knew there was a prisoner in cell number two and
nothing could be done. We offered to replace our friend with
another prisoner, the six of us reckoned we could soon snatch
a passing Italian off his bicycle or scooter, but the Commandant
would not hear of it; our friend was destined to stay in the
Monza gaol for at least ten days. As some consolation the Commandant showed us round the gaol trying to convince us that
our friend would be comfortable, and proudly showed us the
new neon lighting and told us about the film shows on Friday
nights.

Like many permanent circuits there are rules and regulations,
and you can only enter by this gate or that gate, and this ticket
does not let you go there and that one will not let you on the
track, and the one marked 'Pits' does not mean that at all. At
times it can get very frustrating but rather than throw an apop-
lectic fit like some people do it is better to go somewhere else and
say 'oh well, its Monza'. There are plenty of amusing memories
of Monza as well, such as the Vanwall transporter that went
through the tunnel to the paddock alright fully laden, but when it
was being used to go back to the hotel unladen it fouled the
roof of the tunnel and stuck. The resourceful driver saw a squad
of military police about to go home so got them to stand in the
back of the van and compress the springs enabling him to drive
out of the tunnel with a cigarette paper clearance. About the

same time the Maserati mechanics took the top off their van as they completely forgot about it being unladen and belted into the tunnel without slowing up!

Some circuits leave no impression over the years, but Monza always leaves something, from excitement to frustration, but never boredom, for the name itself conjures up action. 'Monza', with the accent on the 'Mon'. Apart from that Alfa Romeo sports car many things have been named after it, from petrol filler caps, and tyres to sidecars, and only recently I saw a television set named 'Monza'. How it was going to live up to the name I could not imagine, unless it exploded after a particularly good programme. Over the years the circuit has had its ups and downs: people have boycotted it because it was too fast, or too dangerous, or too frightening; other have complained that it was boring, or stupid; many think the slip-streaming that goes on spoils racing. But whatever they all think Monza lives on and is still the home of Italian motor racing and the one place where you can guarantee to see close and very fast racing, and where the racing car needs a strong engine and a brave driver.

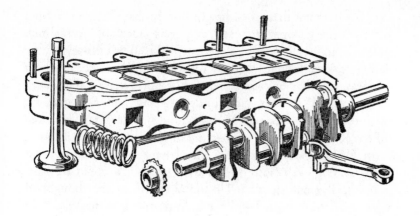

'If you can handle a screwdriver ...'

RICHARD O'HAGAN

I wonder if the chap who invented the wheel ever got, from his contemporaries, even a fraction of the kudos he deserved? If he did, that was the only accolade he received for his name is long lost in the mists of time. We know, of course, that the wheel played a vital part in the Bronze Age economy and that the wheeled car was known, in Mesopotamia, *circa* 3000 B.C. but there isn't as much as a hieroglyph about the man who first thought of it. In view of the way in which it caught on and has retained its popularity throughout the subsequent millenia, this seems to me the classic case of human ingratitude for men have had monuments erected to them, and honours showered upon them for much, much less.

Archimedes, to take but one example, is remembered for

ever for noticing that when he got into his bath, the water rose; from whence he went on, firstly, to give a loud cry of 'Eureka' and, secondly, to invent his famous screw. But I submit that even if he hadn't noticed this phenomenon we would still have been bathing whereas, had our unknown benefactor not invented the wheel, where would Detroit, Longbridge, Turin and Stuttgart, to mention but a few, be now? How would Boadicea have knocked off the Romans without wheels to which to attach those monster razor blades? How would Ben Hur have won his chariot race? And, coming even closer to our own time, how could we have had wheelers and dealers? The mind recoils at the thought of what we'd have missed and the industrial and cultural desert in which we would now be living.

But, whatever about the original inventor, I am prepared to bet that his prototype wheels had not been trundling around for very long before some restless minds began to wonder if a few, quick bronze shekels could not be picked up by improving on the basic design. And so, within a comparatively short time, some other operator was offering the spoked wheel which was lighter and thus gave more miles to the gallon of sweat. And then someone else the wooden, spoked wheel. And then a further someone the iron tyre for the wooden spoked wheel—a tyre which, as an additional benefit, you could fit yourself.

And that, of course, was the beginning of the great DIY cult which has still to reach its apogee and is now a part of the very fabric of our lives. One—anyone—can now essay such disparate tasks as, for instance, curing rising damp or building one's own electronic home organ. More. Not only can one astonish one's friends by unveiling this music maker—which is also, to coin a phrase, a lovely piece of furniture—but with the assistance of yet another instruction kit one can sit down at the keyboard, smiling quietly, and tear off a piece of the old Toccata and Fugue by Johann Sebastian or one of his mates.

But, of course, nowhere has this flowering attained such Royal Horticultural Society heights as in the case of the motor car for the embellishment of which you can buy almost anything including, even, a set of parts with which you can construct your own transport from the rubber up. There is, seemingly, no end to the things that can be purchased to stick on; adapt; supplement; improve or beautify the heap. We live, in short, in a highly-coloured; chrome-embellished; plastic-packaged; self-tapping-screwed; wonderful world of DIY accessories.

I think of such accessories frequently; indeed, it would be difficult for me, or any other motoring correspondent, to forget them since it is a dull mail that does not contain at least one glossy leaflet advising us of the materialisation of yet another brilliant conception which, besides enhancing any chariot, can be fitted in a trice or even quicker. But I wonder, uneasily, from time to time if these gadgets are ever bought as presents by some kindly-motivated, but misguided, donor who over-estimates the intelligence or dexterity of the presentee. In the perspective of the vast cornucopia of DIY bits and pieces, can one deny that this is a very real danger? If one can, let us illustrate my apprehension by means of a simple example.

A famous British electrical company markets a set of ignition points which come in one piece and thereby supersede the conventional six-piece device that took some expertise to instal. This new one, the makers claim, is simplicity itself to fit and I can warmly endorse that statement. Indeed, having used it once I would use no other and it is scarcely an exaggeration to say that I could fit this replacement set whilst clad in my immaculately-tailored dinner jacket, with two inches of snowy cuff protruding from each sleeve, and soil neither my hands nor said cuffs in the process. So, too, could thousands of others, for this device has been ingeniously designed with the maladroit very much in mind and the maker's slogan: *If you can handle a screwdriver, you can fit these points* is as near the absolute truth as makes no odds.

But if it is an axiom of the entertainment business that you can't please everyone, it is equally true that no gadget, however simple, can be simple enough for every possible permutation of human intelligence. Let us, therefore, consider the case of Fred.

Whilst it is true that Fred can handle a screwdriver, in that he does know which way is up, Fred is by no means what his best friend would describe as dexterous; indeed, it takes Fred some pretty wrapt concentration to get the top off a boiled egg and even deeper devotion to the matter in hand to fathom the *modus operandi* of a clothes peg. Fred has only the haziest notion of what happens under the bonnet of his car and even though he has picked up some of the lingua franca from his more clued-in chums and has been known to drop terms like 'overhead camshaft' into the conversation, Fred wouldn't recognise an overhead camshaft if one were to enter the room and shake him warmly by the hand.

With the onset of Christmas, Fred's offspring are in their usual dither about what to give Daddy by way of a present. The drawers of Fred's chest of are filled with the socks and ties of previous Yules and there they lie, like a surrealist's nightmare, unworn and unused. Even to look at them in the privacy of his bedroom gives Fred a quick, shuddering spasm across the eyeballs and the thought of appearing in them in public brings on a strong weakness. Mum has let the kiddiwinkies know, delicately, that it might be a good idea to think of something rather different on this occasion and much furrowing of tiny brows has broken out. Then Clarence, the eldest and most precocious of a series of repulsive children, sees an advertisement for this one-piece ignition set and, his eyes glittering behind thick, horn-rimmed spectacles, bullies the rest of them into divvying up so they can buy it for Dad. Clarence knows how Fred dotes on his Whizzo '71 and how he will positively love anything that will enhance said Whizzo; further, the fact that this replacement is much cheaper than socks is by no means the least of its attractions for the lad. So, on Christmas morn, Fred finds one gift-wrapped under the tree.

Despite himself he is intrigued, not to say relieved, since he had been bracing himself for another pair of psychedelic hose and had rehearsed the hypocritical cries of appreciation he would utter on opening the parcel. He reads the instructions and is heartened by the assurance that anyone can fit it for, tho' modest to a fault, he does know he can handle a screwdriver. Putting the set carefully to one side, he makes a mental note to have a quiet bash at the first opportunity.

This presents itself much more quickly than he envisaged; in the anti-climax of Boxing Day, he finds himself with absolutely nothing to do but nurse his hangover and sip vintage draughts of bicarbonate of soda. It is a dull, leaden afternoon with troughs of low pressure moving in from all directions to replace those already *in situ*. The children are out dismantling someone else's house under the guise of attending a party; there is nothing on the Telly but a succession of movies which look as though they had been made for 19th-Century Fox with a box camera held by someone as hungover as is Fred himself. Further, it is four hours at least before he and Mrs Fred need begin preparing themselves to go wassailing in some other establishment and, what with one thing and another, the immediate future looks pretty bleak. It is at this moment his eyes fall on the children's gift and there comes, unbidden, to his mind the telling phrase: *If you can handle a screwdriver you can fit these.*

In the garage, under the glare of a 40-watt bulb, the engine stares up at him sinisterly; Fred adjusts the light as best he can but parts of the works still lurk in ominous shadow. After a systematic search he locates the distributor and makes a positive identification by means of the wires sprouting from it to those thingumajigs in their little holes in the cylinder head. So far, so good. He moves under the light and reads the first line of the instructions carefully: *Remove distributor cover and pull off rotor arm.*

After some minutes spent abortively trying to unscrew the cap, it dawns on Fred that there is a little, clip-like spring that must be undone; it is not until considerably later he realises there is another little, clip-like spring hidden in the shadows at the back. This he eventually releases and with it the best part of a fingernail. Flushed with triumph, he hardly notices this injury but moves at once to attack the rotor arm. This proves stubborn, not to say obdurate, so he uses the screwdriver as a lever but with such force that it suddenly comes away like a guided missile, strikes the underside of the bonnet, ricochets off the air cleaner and disappears into the murky depths.

Twenty minutes later, with the aid of one of his offsprings' Christmas torches, Fred finds it nestling coyly between sump and block; the bakelite is somewhat chipped but he is so pleased at having located it that he is scarcely conscious of such trivia. By this time, however, he is very warm indeed and this suggestion of tropical ambience is heightened by the fact that his complexion has darkened appreciably and his hands are black and oily to the elbows.

He puts the rotor arm in his pocket and studies the instructions once more: *Remove nut (B) and insulator, and lift off leads (C) and (D)*. Fred stares closely at the distributor, which stares coldly back, but try as he might he can see no sign of any nut or bolt being marked with the letters indicated in the instructions. He peers at the little picture embellishing them and turns it until it coincides approximately with the real thing. Gingerly he removes what he thinks might be (B) and it comes away easily: so do (C) and (D). Emboldened, he removes contact lever (E) which also slips off unprotestingly. Fred is starting to feel a modest glow of triumph and begins to hum as he sets about unscrewing (F) and lifting off the metal plate and fibre washers. There is really nothing to this sort of thing, he reflects, if only one tackles it methodically and with a certain pragmatic approach. After all. . . .

This happy soliloquy is interrupted by screw (F) slipping from his fingers and rolling across base plate (G) there to fall into some unlettered aperture. Fred has a moment of pure panic as he thinks of the problem of extricating it from the midst of whatever infernal machinery lies beneath said plate. He bends over it, sweating freely, and then sees that it has not, in fact, quite disappeared from sight but is teetering on the very brink. As, indeed, is his reason.

Swallowing convulsively—a montage of screams of wifely rage, as she finds herself transportless for the night's cavorting, sounding in his ears—he tiptoes stealthily into the house and finds a pair of eyebrow tweezers in her handbag. In his relief at not being observed he fails to notice that he has left a trail of greasy fingerprints over practically everything in sight, for which there will be a grim accounting later. Back in the garage he manipulates the tweezers with all the delicacy of a society surgeon removing a splinter from a millionaire's brain and holds his breath until he has (F) lifted clear. As he relaxes, it falls from the jaws.

Eighteen minutes later, flat on his face on the unyielding cement, he discovers it lodged almost underneath the off-side tyre. By this time Fred has visited parts of his garage he never even knew existed and he is using language which is far from edifying and certainly not in keeping with the Spirit of Christmas. But not alone this. He is rapidly conceiving a deadly hatred for his eldest and first-born who brought all this anguish upon him; as he straightens up, his vertebrae snapping like castenets, he thinks almost tearfully of his comfortable armchair and determines that, given the first half-way reasonable excuse, he will break Clarence into a series of very small pieces.

However, his mercurial spirits rise somewhat on reading the next part of the instructions: *Place replacement set in position with hollow pillar over post.* This task he accomplishes in a mere three minutes but his morale nose-dives sharply when he then sees that he must now replace (F). Fred has developed a monstrous psychosis about (F) which unsteadies his hand to the extent that makes holding the screwdriver a major operation. But he eventually manages it and leans against the garage wall, breathing heavily. He feels like Barnard when the transplant has been successfully completed and it is doubtless this association of ideas that causes him to hum, in relief, a few bars of that well-known song: *I left my heart in an English gardener.*

Quickly, for him, he removes nut (H), places lead (D) on the nylon post, followed swiftly by lead (C). He is overjoyed to read: *Your replacement set is now fitted.* Whistling gaily, he is about to put the instructions away when his eyes light on the following, ominous, words: *To set the contact gap.* To set *what?* What the Hell are they on about? Wasn't it supposed to come in one piece completely ready for use? Who do they think they are, anyway? For two pins he'd tear it all out and put back the original . . . at this moment, as from a great distance, he seems to hear the echo of cynical laughter and Fred realises, only too bitterly, that he couldn't put back the old ones if his life depended on it. Glumly, he reads on.

Turn engine slowly until a cam (K) of distributor shaft strikes the heel of the replacement contact and forces the points a maximum distance apart. Fred knows what he would like to strike at that very moment and it isn't the heel of the replacement contact. Could it be short for 'camouflage' or 'camphor' or even 'camera obscura'? He stares fixedly at the distributor but all cams are

K

hidden and silent. And what is this folly about turning the engine *slowly*? How does one turn the engine slowly or, for that matter, quickly? Then, in a flash of inspiration, he has it—the starting handle!

Ten minutes later, after a protracted search, he is convinced that some miscreant has knocked off his starting handle. Baffled, he leans against a wing and begins to go quietly out of his mind. Recovering, with a manful effort, he rubs the grease off his watch face. *He's been at it nearly three hours!* He whimpers on a rising note of hysteria.

At this moment Clarence enters the garage through the house door, his face flushed with half a gallon of lemonade, assorted ices, an infinity of mince pies and the winter air; Fred regards him with near hatred.

'*Have you fitted them, Dad?*, the boy asks, interestedly.

'Shut up', Fred explains.

'*But, Dad, it says you can fit them in a . . .*'

'I know what it flipping well says', Fred roars—and it's a good thing for Clarence that the Whizzo company did not provide a starting handle for Fred to find or it would have encircled Clarence's bonce like a close-fitting halo.

'*Well, why don't you go ahead and start it then?*' the lad enquires, reasonably enough, oblivious to the fact that his parent's eyes are glowing like hot coals. '*Have you adjusted the gap?*'

'No' Fred sneers, 'why don't you do it?'

In a trice, the boy has darted around, made sure the car is out of gear; pressed the starter solenoid under the bonnet, got the cam near a high point and completed the operation with the fan belt; inserted a screwdriver through the 'V' slot on the base plate; used the box flap as a feeler gauge; securely tightened screw (F); replaced the rotor arm and then the distributor cap with two definitive clicks, and climbed into the car. Fred has watched the pudgy fingers fluttering to and fro as one mesmerised and is even more transfixed when the engine starts at once. Clarence triumphantly *vroom, vrooms* the accelerator.

Fred re-asserts himself. 'Switch off', he roars. 'Don't you know those exhaust fumes are poisonous?'

Crestfallen, the lad does as he is told and they walk back into the

house, Clarence manfully trying to pick up his crest. Inside, the
little woman is getting ready for the off.

'What were you doing, Fred?' she asks, biting back a witty
comment about the Black and White minstrels.

'Just changing the ignition points' Fred says, nonchalantly,
washing his hands at the sink.

'*Were you really?*'—she is openly and unwontedly admiring—
'*Isn't that terribly technical?*' Fred gives a careless laugh and shrugs
his shoulders slightly.

Lurking in a corner, Clarence regards his father speculatively,
a dawning awareness in his eyes.

When a truculent toot
   Whistles straight up your boot
It is simply because you inherit the fruit
   Of a peripatetic endeavour.
The driver behind
   Ought to make up his mind
That our traffic arrangements are now of a kind
   That are bound to be with us for ever.
The hope of improvement
   In mimicking movement
Is dismally bleak and remote.
   Your only recourse is
To go back to horses
   Or gallop to work on a goat.

                   Alan Reeve-Jones

Nine Years' Wonder

'S.B.'

Although very few Americans knew it, and those who did know it probably didn't believe it, Britain's indigenous Five-Hundred, staged at Brooklands from 1929 to '37, was a faster race than Indianapolis five times out of a possible nine. This testifies to the *grande talent pour le silence* observed in the English by Carlyle, interacting with the grand talent for trumpet blowing cultivated by Uncle Sam. To gain acceptance of their claim that the Hoosier long-distance event was the world's fastest race of its length, Americans only needed to reiterate it often and loudly enough, and this they did. Counterclaims on behalf of the British Racing Drivers' Club, organisers of the Brooklands 500, on the other hand, were infrequent, *sotto voce*, and never commanded international hearing or credence.

The relative statistics of the two races require qualification in only one particular. The ninth and last in the Brooklands series was docked from 500 miles to 500 kilometres (312 miles), so the

1937 winning speeds by John Cobb's Napier-Railton and Wilbur Shaw's Gilmore Offenhauser—127.05 and 113.58 m.p.h. respectively—aren't directly comparable. On the other hand, Britain's fastest-ever Five-Hundred *Miles* Race, won at 121.28 m.p.h. as far back as 1935, wasn't outspeeded at Indy (and then by a mere fraction of an m.p.h.) until 1949. Brooklands by that time had been defunct as a race track for almost a decade and its hallowed concrete was sprouting trees, factory buildings and perhaps even a few embryo stalactites.

Contrasting with the professionalism of the BRDC's post-war race promotion, there were some aspects of the Five-Hundred's organisation that look curiously amateurish and casual in distant retrospect. A classic example concerns the Speed Six Bentley that the late W. O. Bentley himself entered for the inaugural race in '29. To handle this reputedly rather hostile machine, Mr Bentley nominated two drivers, of whom one was Clive Dunfee and the other wasn't. The one who wasn't (the car had 'scared away most drivers', as William Boddy tells it in his invaluable, three-volume work: *Brooklands*) defected at a late hour and his place was taken by Sammy Davis, *Autocar*'s sports editor.

It's true that Davis was an all-rounder of the highest repute and widest experience, but when one considers that the Speed Six was not only known to be a rogue but was expected to prove the fastest car in the race, it becomes well-nigh incredible that Sammy was permitted to drive it without doing a single qualifying lap. Indeed, he'd never previously driven a Speed Six of any kind, on any road or track, until he took over from Dunfee following the latter's opening spell in the 500. Literally, he taught himself the controls and learned to read his instruments as he went along. In his book, *Motor Racing*, alluding to the gear-lever, he afterwards wrote: 'I had a sense of panic which lasted until I located the blamed thing outside the body'. The other Bentley's he'd raced had had their maulsticks *inside*.

Dunfee/Davis didn't win the 1929 Five-Hundred—the stiff handicap they'd been dealt saw to that—but they did the next best thing by turning the day's fastest overall average, 109.4 m.p.h., and finishing second, headed only by another Bentley.

This baptismal 500, incidentally, established the BRDC event as easily the world's fastest motor race of its distance, for the Speed Six's average topped the Indy race record by no less than 8.27 m.p.h.

This wasn't the only instance in BRDC Five-Hundred annals of a driving partnership of winning potential coming to the start line in a state of total inexperience of their car. In 1935 the late Earl Howe entered a special 3.3-litre Bugatti, which he and Brian Lewis (the present Lord Essendon) were to share. The car reached Brooklands from the factory at Molsheim the day before the race, too late for any practice or qualifying hoopla. It was nevertheless allowed to start. Lewis, doing his homework after leaving home, was holding the overall lead when, well beyond quarter-distance, the Bug was bugged by carburetter flooding. Well, perhaps he hadn't done *all* his homework by this stage, for although he knew there was a button or a switch or something, somewhere, that would abate superfluous air pressure in the fuel tank, he didn't know what it looked like or where it was. While he was finding out he lost the lead to Cobb and the mighty Napier-Railton went through to win.

Although by no means deficient in technical and esoteric interest for insiders, the Five-Hundred was, mainly by reason of its indispensable handicap system, a veritable banquet of boredom for the less-well-informed. You can fairly interpret our title, *Nine-Years' Wonder*, as meaning it's a wonder it lasted nine years. The local standard of showmanship, in the broad sense, was execrable, particularly at the level of communication with the public. The defect was nutshelled in the closing paragraphs of *Autocar's* report of the final 500 in 1937: 'Cobb finished without any spectacular demonstration whatever. The public did not even know the race was over. The scoreboards were not informative and the loudspeakers were inclined to be secretive'.

It was even possible for spectators not to be aware that a 500 had started. For handicap purposes the fields were divided into groups according to engine capacity, based on international classes. Obviously, the smallest and slowest cars were despatched first, and when, as actually happened in 1931 and 1933, the limit-start 'group' comprised a single 750 c.c. car, a solitary MG Midget or Austin Seven would be the sole focus of *soi disant* action for anything up to half an hour.

The Brooklands 500, unlike Indianapolis, was perforcedly a handicap in order to bridge the performance gaps between the available cars, which ranged in displacement from the Midget's and the Seven's 750 c.c. to the Napier-Railton's 24 litres. On the catch-as-catch-can principle, the BRDC happily accepted entries from sports and racing cars alike (the former sometimes predominated); fuel, to quote one commentator, could be 'anything that would burn'; blown or unblown engines were equally welcome. As for driver eligibility, this was in the spirit of St Matthew's line, 'I was a stranger and ye took me in': you'd still have got by if you couldn't have proved you'd ever actually raced in your life before.

Indeed, one of the biggest and theoretically fastest cars ever fielded in a Five-Hundred was shared in the 1929 opener by two young RAF officers, yclept Noel and Pole, neither of whom had raced before. Pooling their scanty service pay, these boys acquired and entered an enormous 17½-litre aeroplane-engined Mercedes, which on paper anyway was capable of nearly 150 m.p.h. Their chances of demonstrating any similarity between the monster's calculated and actual capability was dashed when the Dunlop people pointed out that, even down around a 115 m.p.h. lap speed, the Merc would use up sixteen tyres in 500 miles. Only having the price of two spares between them, Noel/Pole glumly settled for a 100 m.p.h. norm. Also, having noted their car's tendency, during practice, to skitter around like spit on a red-hot stove, they ballasted it with 300 lb. of gravel. They lasted the distance.

As further evidence of the 500's anything-goes character, the decision whether or not to put a riding mechanic aboard was left to the entrant; juxtaphobes made the long haul *à seul*, consenting adults *à deux*, assuming the existence of passenger space. Similarly, the choice was free as between lone and shared drives. Seven out of nine Five-Hundred victories were won by twosome partnerships, the exceptions being Eddie Hall and the late Fred Dixon—Yorkshiremen both, incidentally. Women drivers were barred from the first six Five-Hundreds but thereafter the race was open to them by individual invitation. Acceptance of entries in the early events was subject to an 80 m.p.h. lap speed capability. This was later stiffened to 100 m.p.h.

Considering that American drivers and cars were about as rare as unicorns at Brooklands, and in particular in this totally unAmerican 500, it's strange to relate that a US man/machine combination recorded, during practice for the 1934 race, what was probably the fastest lap ever clocked within the Five-Hundred framework—an unofficial speed of 140-odd m.p.h. This was by Whitney Straight at the wheel of a Duesenberg. It failed to start in the race itself.

As a natural concomitant of the huge speed differentials prevailing, the BRDC Five-Hundred was potentially a hell of a dangerous race; it's one of its minor wonders that it claimed only two lives. First to go was Clive Dunfee, who in 1932 co-drove a hybrid 8-litre Bentley with his brother Jack. In a passing manoeuvre at the top of the Home Banking, Clive apparently misjudged the width available to him. The Bentley went over the edge, cut a swathe through an intervening barrier of young trees and was completely wrecked.

The second and, mercifully, the last death occurred the following year when the MG Midget of M. B. Watson, for reasons that were never satisfactorily explained, overturned and caught fire on the level stretch of track between the Byfleet and Home Bankings.

The prize for the luckiest escape was shared by motor-cycle TT rider Walter Handley and his own lap-scorer-*cum*-signaller in the rain-deluged 1934 Five-Hundred. Handley, jockeying the famous Magic Magnette for Capt. George Eyston, had procured the use of a little look-out shack on the infield flank of the Railway Straight, and installed therein a helper blessed with—fortunately for him—marked athletic prowess. Spin-outs on the drenched and puddled concrete were almost the common lot that day. When the Magnette, in its turn, went into uncontrollable gyrations, it bore down, by a thousands-to-one co-incidence, on Walter's own signalling post. This it smashed to splinters, but not before its occupant had made a VTO evacuation.

Notwithstanding the high, in some cases brilliant, standards of handicapping, the 1932 500 had been, and remained, one of the few races in the series with a close finish. The shock of anything so atypical seems to have been too much for the man at the microphone, who somewhat deflated the climax by naming a car that hadn't even started as a likely contender for first prize. It was in 1935 that all-time's master handicapper, the late A. V. (Ebby) Ebblewhite surpassed himself by misassessing the co-winners' time for the 500 miles by exactly 23 seconds. He'd calculated that Cobb and Rose-Richards would average 121.47 m.p.h. in the former's Napier-Railton. This flattered them. They made it 121.28.

A staple ingredient of the boredom of the duller Five-Hundreds was a system whereby, instead of snapping the action off short when the winner had won, and giving the rest of the survivors placements commensurate with distance covered at that time, cars still mobile after the third-home entry completed the course were required to keep going for a further thirty minutes. If they succeeded in this they ranked as official finishers, and if not, not. The miles-to-kilometres curtailment in 1937 isn't surprising in view of the fact that in '36 there were as few as eighteen starters, of whom only four officially finished. One year (1935), by what seemed a curious interpretation of its own rules, the BRDC awarded the team prize to Fred Dixon as the entrant of three Rileys which by definition had all failed to finish.

Although the Five-Hundred is best remembered for the exploits of John Cobb and his Napier-Railton, if only by reason of the superior speed that scored this 24-litre giant its two victories, its polar opposites—the 750 c.c. mechanical microbes— hold an honourable place in the race's annals. They won twice: an Austin Seven side-valver in 1930 (Sammy Davis and the Earl of March, now the Duke of Richmond), an MG Midget in 1932 (R. T. Horton and Jack Bartlett).

While it's true, of course, that the ham element was never absent from the 500, there were also notable instances of entries from meticulously prepared and professionally organised teams of works cars. It was as members of such a team, with Lord Austin himself behind it, that the Davis/March partners beat their handicap to win at 83.42 m.p.h. in 1930. This speed *per se*, from 747 c.c. and side valves, was creditable enough in that day and age, but more remarkable, in view of the contemporary Seven's gossamer lightness and the roughness of many parts of the track, was the fact that it stayed in one piece for such a distance. Uniquely, in a spirit worthy of Lord (Be Prepared) Baden Powell, the whole team had been put through full 500-mile workouts *in camera* during the race preliminaries. In the decisive closing stages, while lapping at an astonishing 87 m.p.h. Davis doubtless touched wood on behalf of a two-bearing crankshaft that popular jokes likened to a piece of bent wire. . . .

There were poignant aspects too, of the Horton/Bartlett win with another seven-fifty, the former's Midget, in 1932. Short on cash and general resources, Horton was obliged to settle for an irreduceable one-man pit crew: one brain, one pair of hands, to take care of all contingencies: lap scoring, signalling, keeping an eye on how the opposition was doing, changing wheels and/or plugs as required, bodging anything that might need it, exercising what Sammy Davis once called The Worrying That Wins.

He needn't, as it turned out, have worried that much. A rival Midget, entered by George Eyston and driven by Bert Denly, blew a piston while leading the race after three and a half hours. So Eyston, without waiting to be invited and true to the *non Angli sed Angeli* fibre of his being, drew stumps and moved *his* well-trained and numerous crew into the Horton pit. His anxieties gone, Horton raced elatedly on to win at 96.29 m.p.h. This speed, the product of 750 pathetic little cubic centimetres, was a fraction of a mile slower than the previous year's Indianapolis, in which 6-litre engines had been standard.

Two years later, in 1934, another fractional difference between the winners' speeds gave the title of the world's fastest long-distance race to America: Fred Dixon (2-litre Riley) won the Brooklands 500 at 104.80 m.p.h., Cummings in a Miller-engined car averaged 104.86 for his Indy conquest. But there were qualifying circumstances: Dixon did the whole driving stint himself, Cummings used two pairs of hands. Brooklands was awash throughout, Indy was dry. Also, Cummings had a big advantage in engine capacity.

Although run under an international permit, the Brooklands

500 seldom attracted any foreign drivers and those it did attract weren't of the first flight. The best placement by a continental visitor, speaking from memory, was Zanelli's with an Alfa Romeo in 1933—he finished sixth. There were good reasons for this lack of enthusiasm for the 500, in common with other Brooklands races, across the Channel. Foreigners loved the compulsory Brooklands silencers as slugs love brine, on the grounds that they caused overheating and cooked pistons, plugs, etc. Secondly, they were used to being paid to race, not to paying for the privilege, but to the BRDC and the track authorities entry fees were sacrosanct, not lightly to be waived. Above all, continental drivers, reared on straight-up scratch races, where the man in front was the leader and no argy-bargy, either couldn't or wouldn't be bothered to unravel the obscure and so-English handicap arcana.

With no Grand Prix Drivers' Association to fight for speedmen's rights, circuit surfaces both within and without this green and passably pleasant land fell far short of today's standards; and Brooklands, at its worst, could be almost intolerably bumpy, even for the relatively low speeds of the 'twenties and 'thirties. But only once, in the notorious Five-Hundred of 1935, were spectators treated to the sight of a section of the track breaking up before their eyes as the race went on. What happened was this:

From the start, several cars in and around the 2-litres bracket produced lap speeds far above the handicapper's estimates. This had the effect of taking them higher on both the bankings than their normal line, exposing some areas of the concrete to a non-standard pounding. One such patch, on the Home Banking, started going to pieces, slowly at first but faster as a succession of speeding offside wheels hammered away at the deckle edges of the shallow crater that was developing.

The result was an unprecedented epidemic of thrown treads and a coming-apart of cars under the shocks transmitted through their stiff track springs. Shortly before the start, the BRDC weathercocks had forecast rain, precipitating a hurried switch by many drivers to road-racing tyres, which were themselves more vulnerable to the kind of punishment they had to take.

The rubber slaughter began when its victims had done as little as three laps, with offside front tyres almost invariably the hardest hit. The very fast Rileys were high on the casualty list and, as *Autocar*'s report put it, referring to Cyril Paul in one of these cars: 'At about 120 m.p.h. the rubber from his offside front tyre exploded into the air, great chunks hit the Vickers' Shed, others fell all over the track'. Within twenty minutes of each other, other rapid Riley handlers, including such contemporary Jehus of the Brooklands scene as Pat Fairfield, Fred Dixon and Edgar Maclure, were temporarily sidelined by gashed and treadless casings. At the back of the pits, Dunlop artisans worked frenziedly at wheel changing and jettisoned covers were stacked in tottering, head-high towers. 'As each tyre stabbed the hole a fresh gout of debris would spurt up, to roll in a cascade of stones down the slope, until the slower cars had to pass over a miniature beach' (vide *Motor*).

One of these sharp-edged fragments, catapulted by the back wheels of a slower car that John Cobb was about to pass, struck him in the face, drawing blood. True to the legend of Cobb imperturbability, John kept his eyelids unbatted and held his course at 125 m.p.h. Enforcedly planning their tactics to meet the day's crises as they went along, some drivers opted to escalate relatively slow cars above The Hole, bringing their offside wheels to the very lip of the banking, while others, including Cobb and Rose-Richards with the heaviest and fastest car in the act, deliberately warped the huge Napier-Railton *below* the dreaded spot. Metal, like rubber, was meanwhile providing frightening evidence of fatigue: at the far side of the track, on the Byfleet Banking, Tom Clarke felt his Bugatti lurch and slew, and simultaneously he was overtaken by one of his own back wheels a second before it vanished from view into the fringe of firs beyond the banking. Riding on three wheels and a brake drum, Clarke légèrmain'd the car to a slithering standstill in a quarter of a mile.

Twenty-nine cars had started in this, the most gruelling race in the Nine Years' Wonder series. Six of them were officially listed as finishers. The winning Napier-Railton, co-drivers Cobb and Rose-Richards, averaged 121.28 m.p.h. This was a round 15 m.p.h. faster than the same year's Indy winner's speed, so not even the traditional ritual of Memorial Day ballyhoo—the brass bands, knees-upping drum majorettes, nation-wide newspaper headlines, 100 p.s.i. publicity razzamatazz—could rob the low-key British of their World's Fastest 500 title.

FAIR WARNING
Sticker seen on a soberly-driven car the other day: "Support mental health or I'll kill you".—Peterborough in 'Daily Telegraph'

Why Pay More?

JOHN BOLSTER

Are the very expensive cars worth the money? This is, of course, a question to which there is no simple answer. A very expensive car is certainly worth its price to a man who merely wants to show the maximum number of people how rich he is. Even so, it might be argued that he has wasted his money if he gets inferior motoring to that enjoyed by the peasants in their cheap cars. He has wasted his money, too, if the people he thinks he is impressing are laughing behind their hands and saying, 'Good Lord, he's bought one of *those!*' On the other hand, he has spent his money wisely if he gains an inner satisfaction from the way his car goes, looks, and handles—a satisfaction that he could not get from anything less costly.

Let us examine the problem more closely. In the early days of motoring, expensive cars were the best and, if you could raise the money to buy them, they were the cheapest in the end because they needed fewer repairs. All cars were hand-built and if the price was high, the manufacturer could afford to employ more and better craftsmen. He could afford to use the best materials, too, but above all he could afford to spend more time on each individual vehicle. There was no assembly line, no automatic machinery, and the king of the machine shop was the ordinary lathe.

It was only possible to build cars by these methods because men worked long hours for little money. In spite of that, they had a pride in their craftsmanship and a loyalty towards their firm which encouraged them to turn out excellent work by sheer skill. Many a mechanic punched his own private mark on the parts he made, as those of us know who have veteran cars. The point is that, by these methods, a firm producing only a few cars could do it just as efficiently as one building many vehicles, whereas modern production methods are only applicable to vast manufacturing programmes.

We now come to the great difference between the cheap car and the costly one in earlier days. It is also the reason why a man, however rich, gets far less satisfaction from squandering his fortune on a car nowadays than he did in the first thirty years of the century. It was the great coachbuilders who made the owner-ship of a costly car so very well worthwhile.

If you bought a cheap car, you chose a standard body from the catalogue. The man who was buying a quality car invariably ordered a bare chassis. He had it sent to his favourite coach-builder, who prepared drawings incorporating all the pet ideas of his patron. What fun it was and how much we are missing! The client chose the shape and size of the body and all its equip-ment. He picked the upholstery, the carpets, and the paint. Best of all, he made regular visits as the car progressed, usually accom-panied by his friends, who often made suggestions that entailed extra work over and above the estimate, to the secret delight of the coachbuilder. These visits were generally regarded as social occasions and it was all part of the fun of having a new car. King Edward VII adored going to the coachbuilders, where he chatted to his gentlemen in French so that the workmen should not eavesdrop. He may have been discussing matters of State and then, again, he may not.

I used to be taken to the coachbuilders as a boy and it was fascinating. I can still remember the scents of planed wood, glue, and leather. It is curious how rough the best coachbuilding seems until it is almost complete, when suddenly the ugly duckling emerges as a swan. Full size drawings on the wall showed how the complete car was going to look and one could guess the shape as the wooden framework was built, before the panels were put on. The panel beaters had my deepest admiration, because this is a craft which the amateur can never emulate. I can build a car, but if I want a double curve in an aluminium panel I know better than to try to do it myself. The professional takes a large sheet of aluminium, measures it up largely by eye and makes a few chalk marks. He then cuts it up in a most terrifying way, wallops it with various hammers and mallets, often against a sand bag, and eventually the beautiful curved panel fits snugly in place.

The panel beater made a lot of noise and often sang at his work, but the upholsterer was a silent man because he always carried tacks in his mouth. Really large closed bodies of great height consumed an enormous amount of leather or Bedford cord, the upholstery job on a big limousine costing more than a complete small car.

Such was the greatest attraction of the really expensive car and it has gone for ever. After the first war, elaborate coachbuilding continued on a smaller scale but gradually the sports car began to take the fancy of the wealthy man. In Edwardian times, silence and luxury were the major virtues of costly cars and nobody bothered very much about performance. This was because the roads were narrow and winding and the cars only had rear wheel brakes. To drive fast under those conditions was a hair-raising business of which most drivers soon grew tired.

After the war, roads began to get better and front wheel brakes made fast driving much more enjoyable. The better sports cars were very expensive indeed by the standards of those days, but their performance was in a different world from that of the popular family tourers. Indeed when the public started to demand saloons instead of open cars, the extra weight killed any performance which their vehicles might have had. The maximum speed of a Bentley was double that of many popular small saloons, so who cared if it cost more than five times as much? Once again, the costly car was worth every penny of its price.

The very rich man had added a new dimension to his motoring. Instead of sweeping up to the club in his chauffeur-driven limousine, he let everybody know he was there by the deep rumble of the exhaust of his sports car. He then announced loudly in the bar that he had 'touched eighty coming over the Hog's Back, old man'. When he drove up to Scotland for August 12th, he claimed to have 'averaged forty', which was then the target figure. Naturally, the chauffeur followed behind in a more sensible car, carrying the luggage.

It was fun to be rich in the nineteen-twenties but even the cars of poor men were getting better. Mass production created excellent cars for half the price and, for the first time, the big manufacturers could afford improved techniques which were often denied to the small builder of expensive cars. Then came the great depression and even if you had not lost your money, it was considered very bad form indeed to run an expensive car.

In the early nineteen-thirties, the very expensive car was almost dead. The few which were made were pretty bad, because there was not enough money to develop them properly or to design new models. The wealthy turned against the hairy speed model, partly because it was so uncomfortable but mainly owing to the arrival of cheap copies, which vulgarised the sports car. By a sort of inverted snobbery, it became smart to be seen in a Humber or a Chrysler instead of a Bentley or a Bugatti. Much later, the rich and the royals were to take up the Mini for a short time, for the same sort of reasons, no doubt.

That great slump of 1929–31 was the dividing line between the old and the new motoring, as far as the very wealthy were concerned. Before then, almost every rich man had a country estate and was constantly engaged in outdoor pursuits, such as huntin', shootin', and fishin'; motorin' came in the same category. In the redistribution of wealth, a new sort of rich man appeared, who worked in an office and lived in a centrally heated house. When the very expensive car re-emerged, it would need light steering, soft springs, and a heated interior, to suit this flabby fellow. The cars of the nineteen-thirties had none of the character of those of

L

the previous decade, and the last great 'thoroughbred' sports car, the straight-eight supercharged Alfa Romeo, was a total failure commercially in spite of its competition successes.

Afer the second war, any sort of car could be sold at first, but it was not long before the rich wanted something more showy with extra performance and luxury. Wealthy men of earlier times had tremendous responsibilities, and before writing a huge cheque for a personal toy they had to consider all their dependants, such as retired servants, to whom they made an allowance. The rich man, 1945 model, was often a selfish creature with a blow-you-Jack philosophy who looked after nobody and could spend his own money as he liked. It meant that, for the second half of the twentieth century, there would be more men with money burning their pockets and fewer things on which to spend it.

There are so few really worthwhile objects on which the newly rich can spend their money. A pop star, for example, would probably get little pleasure from acquiring artistic treasures, while to endow hospitals and universities might seem altogether too old-fashioned. On the other hand, a rather vulgar car, garishly decorated and frequently photographed, could be just what he needed. For a few years after the war, the motor manufacturers did not realise that they were not charging enough. The demand for the Rolls-Royce rocketed when the price went over £10,000.

In fact, however, the super-luxury car, such as the Rolls-Royce,

It says, "This-is-not-Company-car".

is not typical of the very expensive machines most in demand·
The car for the millionaire must certainly have every sort of
luxury, with air-conditioning as a matter of course, but it is
usually a two-seater coupé with the 200 m.p.h. look and a
maximum speed that few purchasers would ever dare to employ.
Obviously, such a car can never be given its head in England or
the USA, and even on the roads of the continent it would not
get very far ahead of a comparatively cheap car, like the E-Type
Jaguar, under normal traffic conditions.

There are, of course, occasional opportunities to use the tremendous acceleration of these extremely fast cars but immense
power may even be a handicap under difficult conditions,
especially if the driver is, shall we say, a little below Formula I
standards. Some of these specialised cars do not, in any case, have
as good road-holding as certain cheap saloons, and their special
high-speed tyres—essential wear for speeds over 150 m.p.h.—
may grip less well than common rubber.

The motor car, nowadays, is an immensely complicated
machine. In only a few years, it has advanced from absolute
simplicity to extreme intricacy and the cost of designing, developing, and tooling up for a new model will certainly run into
tens of millions of pounds. If a manufacturer is only going to
make a few cars a year, he simply cannot afford this sort of
expenditure, however much he charges for each example. One
has only to consider that Dr Agnelli, with his Fiat and associated
companies, makes more cars before lunch every day than W. O.
Bentley did in ten years. With this sort of output he can afford
laboratories, test tracks, experimental departments, and computers
galore, not to mention the top scientists and technicians. All these
adjuncts of motor manufacture in the nineteen-seventies are
denied to the smaller constructor.

It is thus likely that the very expensive car will be less well
designed than its cheaper sisters and it is certain that it will have
had less testing and development. Too often, the buyer finds that
he is doing the testing himself, which is a bit of an anti-climax
after spending ten grand.

Another difficulty with a very rare car can be that of servicing.
In the past, manufacturers of quality cars had service repre-

sentatives permanently on the road. They called on customers, took their cars out on test, and discussed any mechanical problems with their chauffeurs. All this was done entirely without charge. If work beyond the capacity of the chauffeur was required, an expert mechanic with the necessary spares arrived and did the job in the owner's garage. In my own family, I can remember such service being provided for a Bentley and a Packard, but I don't suppose anybody gets similar attention nowadays, even with a Miura or a Mangusta.

Thus, it is likely that the owner of an exotic car may be obliged to take it to London for service or to rectify faults, which is a bit of a chore if he lives in Inverness or Cornwall. It also means that he must keep a second car for use when the show piece is having its complicated engine checked over by the experts. For a rare foreign car, it would obviously be impossible to set up an effective British dealer network, with factory-trained mechanics.

A foreign car may become something rich and rare when it leaves its own country. Some cars from abroad increase so little in price when they are imported into England that one wonders how the freight and tax can be paid. An excellent example is the Renault, which costs only a little less in Paris than it does in London, and the whole operation obviously depends on very efficient arrangements and large sales. Russian cars actually cost very much less in England than they do in their native land, but this is artificial marketing to get foreign currency, no doubt. However, much though I admire Russian cars for their toughness and reliability, none of them remotely approach the category we are discussing here, for plutocrats are slightly unpopular in the USSR

When expensive foreign cars are considered, it is amazing how much profit the importers make. In some cases, the cars probably sell better because they are expensive, which at once makes them attractive to the very rich. Remember, though, that most millionaires are very mean when it comes to paying out relatively small sums, and will be furious if they get a bill for a set of sparking plugs and a fan belt. It is probably good business to charge an extra thousand pounds in the first place and then to throw in some free service.

Such things as import duties are constantly changing, and for this and other reasons the prices of foreign cars tend to vary. The figures I quote are therefore approximate only and I cannot be held responsible if changes occur after the ink is dry. Some cars, though definitely in the rare and exotic class, have had proper servicing arrangements made for them in Great Britain and this must have cost a bomb. In this category come the Ferrari and the Maserati, which may both cost something like £3,000 more to an Englishman than to an Italian. Curiously enough, the profit on a Lamborghini appears to be much greater than this, but if there is an elaborate service network in the U.K., with works-trained mechanics standing with their spanners at the ready, the secret has been very well kept. The concessionaires probably feel that such a car ought to cost £10,000 if it is to be a plaything of the *richissime*.

A curious case is that of Mercedes-Benz, of which most models appear to cost about half as much again as they do in Germany. In England, the *marque* has been built up until it is almost regarded as an exotic, yet in its country of origin it has no such reputation, the popular 220 costing Herr Braun no more than Mr Brown pays for his Rover 2000 or Ford Zodiac. The more powerful Mercedes are very expensive indeed in England and might therefore be regarded as poor value for money. Yet, they are probably much better cars than most costly, small-production vehicles because this great firm can afford all the research and development that a really advanced new model needs. If Mercedes were sold for less in England they might even lose some of their appeal, but if most of the taxis here carried the three-pointed star, as they do in Germany, a lot of the glamour might rub off.

A beautiful piece of engineering can be just as desirable as a work of art. If one can afford to do so, one probably buys an elaborate and costly watch, though it does the same job as an ordinary one. In the same way, one might buy a Rolls-Royce Corniche because the coachbuilding work of H. J. Mulliner-Park Ward has no equal anywhere. Even this firm, however, cannot build you a one-off body on a Silver Shadow, because the body and chassis are of integral construction.

It is impossible to turn back the clock of course, and the

separate chassis is on the way out, but the combined steel body and chassis has taken away the greatest pleasure of owning a very expensive car. A man who had had a body built to his own ideas possessed a car that was peculiarly his own, as I have already explained. No modern car, however powerful or technically advanced, can inspire quite such a pride of ownership because, except for its colour and a few details of equipment, it had all been thought out by somebody else before the owner came on the scene.

The more I think about this question, the less certain am I which side I am on. Some of the worst cars I have driven have been very expensive and, indeed, I have occasionally breathed a sigh of relief that I am not a rich man. Popular cars are now so good that they can do just about everything that is required of them, and some of them have a world service network behind them which can ensure a rapid return to the road after an accident, anywhere. The 180 m.p.h. car is probably an absurdity and a two-seater costing £10,000 is a ridiculous extravagance. Yet, the thought of having all that horsepower under my foot is a wonderful reverie and, though the tremendous reception that one gets at any grand hotel should not impress me, one is human. Perhaps the very expensive car offers fewer advantages now than it did in the past, but if I were rich beyond the dreams of avarice, would I fall for one myself, in spite of appreciating all the pitfalls? I don't know!

People expect us to test a new car under working conditions before we sell it, and of course we do. Then they complain of assembly faults in the first cars to come off the line for sale to the public. But how can you test the assembly line under working conditions without making cars for sale? Melt the first 10,000 down and start again."

A distinguished engineer reported in 'Motor'

NOVEL SOLUTION

If any State event is paralysing the traffic—say, for instance, that H.M. The Queen is trooping that distinguished visitor, the Omi of Ugg—then you may be sure that I will have a good book in the car. I have been in two-chapter hold-ups.

My tail-panel bears a notice: SCHOLARLY DRIVER—PLEASE HOOT. *Even the longest jam dissolves sooner or later.*—The Scribe in 'Autocar'

SHELSLEY WALSH

What makes it so exciting are all those hairpin corners between the Esses and the Finish. John Bolster

A 1966 MG 1100 was advertised "late property of clergyman, religiously maintained". Sounded like a good buy, as it must have attended regular services.—The Scribe in 'Autocar'

Mr Pickett's Boulogne Races

PETER HULL

'Despite its aroma of rotting fish, Boulogne can be quite an attractive place' wrote an English motoring correspondent in 1925. If the former observation is true, it had not prevented a number of racing motorists, all blessed, perhaps, with an imperfect sense of smell, from making an annual pilgrimage to Boulogne and its environs from 1909 to 1911, and again in 1913, for the celebrated Coupe de l'Auto races. After the war the Boulogne 'Speed Week' or 'Semaine Automobile', which gradually became more and more an Anglo-French affair, was held from 1921 until 1928.

Responsibility for the post-war series of races and speed events lay with a remarkable Englishman called Mr Francis N. Pickett, variously known as 'The King of Boulogne' or 'The Ammo King'. Mr Pickett had made a fortune out of selling shells left over from the Great War for scrap, after devising a safe means of de-fusing them. By 1921 he had acquired not only nine factories with 10,000 workers, his own armed guards to shoot looters on sight and his own prison, but also the Splendid Hotel and Casino at Wimereux and a house on the hills above Boulogne with golden angels on the ceilings and dubious plumbing.

With the idea of increasing his popularity with the French, he organised his first 'Automobile Week' in 1921, in preparation for which he had the roads resurfaced which had formed the 23.22 mile course for the early Coupe de l'Auto races. This circuit, triangular in shape, lay to the east of the town, the start being just before the St Martin hairpin at the '*fourche*' enclosing the St Martin church and cemetery, the bend where Zuccarelli had somersaulted his high Lion-Peugeot on the first lap of the 1911 Coupe le l'Auto race. The next leg of the course followed the main St Omer road to the east through the village of La Capelle to Le Wast and traversing the Forest of Boulogne. This 8-mile stretch was mainly fast and straight, particularly through the forest itself where, however, the road was steeply cambered and resembled a switchback. A sharp and slow right turn in Le Wast led to the twistiest part of the circuit of approximately five miles through Alincthun and Desvres Wood to Desvres itself, where a further sharp right turn led to the 10-mile westerly leg back to the start, through the village of Wirwigne (known to the English competitors as 'Earwigs'), and up a steep hill in Baincthun to the top of Mont Lambert Hill, from where the cars descended to the grandstands and pits and the finishing line. On the left hand side of the road, between the start and St Martin, there was a memorial to Georges Boillot, the great French pre-war racing driver, who had died as a result of being shot down over the Western Front, and had won the last race held on an extended 32-mile Boulogne circuit, going beyond Le Wast, in 1913 on his Peugeot.

Mr Pickett was evidently a G.N. admirer, for he invited the two partners in the firm, Capt. Archie Frazer-Nash and H. R. Godfrey, to bring two competition G.N.s from their Wandsworth, London, works to Boulogne to take part in the 1921 'Week' and stay as his guests. The British G.N.s were not successful, but a team of French G.N.s, built under licence by Salmsons of Paris, won the Pickett Cup for the best team in the 279-mile Light Car

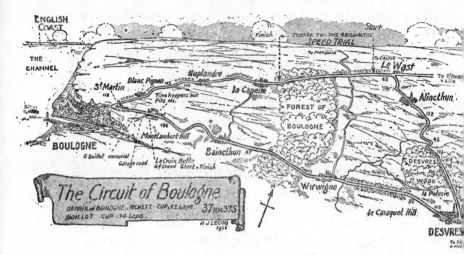

The Circuit of Boulogne

GT PRIX of BOULOGNE.. PICKETT CUP..12 Laps.
BOILLOT CUP ..14 Laps.   37 KM.375

H J LECOQ
1925

and Voiturette Grand Prix, in which Honel's car won the cycle-car section of the race. A 1914 Peugeot and a 1920 Corre La Licorne won the Light Car and Voiturette sections, and André Dubonnet's big 6.8-litre Hispano Suiza was victorious in the 232-mile Georges Boillot Cup race for sports cars. A similar Hispano-Suiza won the race in 1922, when French La Perle and four-cylinder Salmson cars were the respective winners in the Light Car and Voiturette G.P.

It was not until 1923 that the English influence at the Boulogne Automobile Week began to be felt, largely due to the efforts of Capt. Archie Frazer-Nash in attracting drivers, Frazer-Nash by now being involved in Mr Pickett's business projects as general manager for Pickett Construction Ltd in the U.K., whilst Mr Pickett himself was one of the three directors of Frazer Nash Ltd, the new firm established in 1922 by Frazer-Nash after he had left G.N.

The Brooklands driver, J. G. Parry Thomas, was at Boulogne in 1923, having entered his big 8-cylinder, 7.2-litre Leyland-Thomas for the three short distance sprints that opened the Automobile Week. These consisted of a 3 kilometre (1.86 mile) flying start sprint on the switchbacks of the St Omer Road (though in the opposite direction to the racing circuit), a standing start kilometre at the same place, and a hill-climb over half a kilometre in the town. As *The Autocar* pointed out, there was such a multiplicity of classes in the sprint events—25 for 52 competitors—that several drivers had the honour of being first and last in their respective classes. On the aggregate times for the three events Parry Thomas was first in 2 minutes, Louis Rigal on a 4.8-litre, sleeve-valve, sports 4-cylinder Panhard was second (2 minutes 5 seconds) and Frank Clement on a T.T. 3-litre Bentley (2 minutes 12⅘ seconds) was third. De Hane Segrave took 2 minutes 13⅖ seconds in one of the famous French G.P. winning 2-litre Sunbeams with which he had achieved his great victory at Tours earlier in the same month of July, though the car was said to be off form at Boulogne. Parry Thomas fitted smaller wheels to his car for the standing start kilometre and the hill climb, for which he was disqualified after a prompt protest from Rigal.

The sprints took place on the Wednesday, Thursday and Friday, and on the Saturday Segrave in a 1½-litre Talbot-Darracq set the pattern for the first of six consecutive wins by British drivers in the Light Car and Voiturette G.P. for small racing cars which lasted for the whole of the series up to 1928. The cars left in pairs at half minute intervals from 8 a.m. and Mlle Duforest, driving an obscure make of French 750 c.c. cyclecar called a Ready, created attention at the start by wearing a face mask and clenching a whistle between her teeth as a substitute for a hooter. Unfortunately Mlle Duforest missed a corner on her second lap and her car overturned. Happily she was unhurt, nor did her whistle disappear down in the Duforest during the *bouleversement*.

Segrave's Talbot-Darracq won the four-hour race at 67½ m.p.h. by 20 minutes from R. C. Morgan in the side-valve Aston Martin known as 'Green Pea', which also had 'Petit Pois' written on its bonnet for the sake of the Entente Cordiale. The car belonged to a Mrs Agnew, who travelled as its riding mechanic, and a contemporary report said she seemed 'extraordinarily fresh' at the end of the race. It went on to say that 'she was wearing what one might call masculine-type costume, but she said she had enjoyed the show thoroughly and is going to take part in as many similar affairs as she can in the future.' George Eyston was third in the 1½-litre class in the special twin overhead

camshaft Aston Martin which Count Zborowski had driven in
the 1922 French G.P. at Strasbourg. The Pickett Cup was won by
the twin-cylinder Frazer-Nashes (which were really G.N.s)
driven by Frazer-Nash, Cushman and Ringwood, Ringwood
being Mr Pickett's chauffeur. Benoist's Salmson, winner of the
Voiturette 1100 c.c. class at 63 m.p.h., was faster than the Aston
Martins in the 1½-litre Light Car class, and Senechal's 750 c.c.
Senechal won the Cyclecar class at 50 m.p.h. after the works
Austin Sevens had all retired.

Once again the Coupe Boillot sports car race was an entirely
French affair, with Garnier's Hispano-Suiza winning outright
at a record 70.91 m.p.h. average, a winning speed that was never
bettered in the entire Coupe Boillot series.

In 1924 Parry Thomas averaged no less than 127 m.p.h. in the
now fully streamlined Leyland-Thomas over the flying 3 kilometres compared with 110 m.p.h. the year before, and spectators
later witnessed the unusual sight of this big white and blue car,
mainly associated with Brooklands track, ascending the steep
½-kilometre hill from Boulogne up to the suburb of St Martin
in the afternoon's hill-climb—a hill with tramlines to one side of
it and bordered by what one English reporter described as 'sordid
houses'. Great preparations were made before the ascent of the
Leyland-Thomas. 'When the white car comes, stand back if you
value your lives!' the crowd was told, its only protection from
the monster being a thin rope near the edge of the pavement.
Thomas won the sprints on aggregate from Humphrey Cook
(3-litre TT Vauxhall 'Rouge et Noir'), J. A. Joyce (1½-litre racing
A.C.) and Major C. G. Coe (sports 30/98 Vauxhall).

Rain ruined the Concours d'Elegance on the Friday, where
Coe's apple-green Vauxhall won first prize for sports cars, and it
continued raining on both the Saturday and the Sunday, the
start of Saturday's 279-mile Light Car and Voiturette G.P.
being delayed by an hour. Once again R. C. Morgan, accompanied by Mrs Agnew as passenger, drove the Aston Martin
'Green Pea' (transformed into a flower and called 'Sweet Pea' in
The Autocar report), but was delayed by ignition troubles. George
Eyston drove a single-seater Aston Martin ('Green Pea' according
to a confused *Light Car* reporter) which was destined in 1925 to

form the basis of Frank Halford's Halford Special, but Eyston retired when leading the race after an accident involving Marechal's Delfosse with a lath-and-calico body. This allowed the race to go to a black Brescia Bugatti driven by a London motor dealer and amateur driver called B. S. Marshall, who won at 54.46 m.p.h. in mist and rain by 13 minutes from the two surviving cars of the Senechal team which were awarded the Pickett Cup.

The 325-mile Boillot Cup race on the Sunday was run under similar conditions. Coe's Vauxhall was on scratch in this handicap based on weight and engine size, but after 9 laps (207 miles) he retired at Le Wast with a run big-end, his best lap being 21 minutes 45 seconds to the fastest lap in 20 minutes 20 seconds of Leonard's winning 'tank'-bodied 2-litre Chenard-Walcker. The winner averaged 62.1 m.p.h., a similar Chenard finishing second and a Type 30 Bugatti third, the other British hope, Eaton's Aston Martin, retiring through running out of petrol whilst leading on handicap on its fourth lap.

1925 was the first year in which the organization of the 'Semaine Automobile' was shared by the Automobile Club du Nord and the Essex Motor Club with the sponsorship of the magazine *L'Auto*, and it was now the turn of the sprint events on the Thursday to be visited by rain. Parry Thomas crashed the Leyland-Thomas in practice and returned home to England nursing a badly bruised knee before the actual competition took place. As in 1923 when Thomas was disqualified, the best performance on aggregate in the sprints was put up by a sleeve-valve, sports 4.8-litre Panhard, the driver being M. Ortmans who broke the World's Hour Record at 116 m.p.h. in 1925 in this car. He averaged 97 m.p.h. in the wet over the flying 3 kilometres, and was also fastest, amidst clouds of blue smoke, in the newly-instituted Mont Lambert hill-climb over a muddy, steeply cambered macadam road with three awkward bends rising out of Baincthun on the return leg of the racing circuit. The $\frac{1}{2}$-kilometre St Martin hill-climb in the town was less exciting than usual as the road had been resurfaced, and here Joyce's A.C. was fastest in 22⅖ seconds from 'Scrap' Thistlethwayte's ivory-painted and stripped 30/98 Vauxhall (24 seconds) and Ortman's road-equipped

Panhard (24⅕ seconds). Thistlethwayte put up fastest aggregate time in the racing classes with 3 minutes 22⅗ seconds, so the time of 3 minutes 2⅗ seconds by Ortmans' Panhard running in the sports classes was all the more remarkable. Joyce's A.C. (4 minutes 38⅕ seconds) suffered plug troubles in the 3-kilometre sprint.

In addition an acceleration and brake test was held over a ½-kilometre course, the drivers being required to stop astride the finishing line, but with the additional concession that it was also permissible to finish sideways provided the four wheels were divided by the line. Joyce, having no front wheel brakes, failed to stop at all.

For the second year running Bertram Marshall, dressed all in black in his black Brescia Bugatti, was fastest overall in the Light Car and Voiturette GP to win on a sunny day at 64.29 m.p.h.— 10 m.p.h. faster than his 1924 average. He was fortunate to be the overall as well as the Voiturette winner, for Clive Gallop achieved the best performance ever in racing by a chain-driven Frazer Nash, putting up the fastest lap for the race at 67.72 m.p.h., and winning the over-650 kg Light Car class, but failing to beat Marshall due to a 6½-minute pit-stop for plugs. His Boulogne model Frazer Nash belonged to 'Scrap' Thistlethwayte and had an Anzani engine. Frazer Nashes also won the Pickett Cup. R. C. Morgan, still with the indomitable Mrs Agnew as passenger, finished third in the erstwhile 'Green Pea', which now sported a cowl over its Aston Martin radiator, and having been fitted with a Hooker-Thomas engine was entered as a Thomas Special.

The equivalent at Boulogne of Peter Prunty 'czar of the leather-lunged megaphone wielders', to quote the words of Peter Helck, who used to shout 'Car coming!' at the old Vanderbilt Cup races on Long Island, USA, was a certain M. Berretroe who gave details of the races through his gargantuan megaphone. Another Edwardian feature was the blaring of a trumpet at the top of Mont Lambert to herald the arrival of a car approaching the pits and grandstand area.

Robert Senechal, who finished second to Marshall in the Voiturette class, albeit 35 minutes in arrears, protested that the winning Bugatti was overweight, but this was disproved on the weighbridge. The other Senechals had suffered from their steering columns coming adrift, Pisart tying his up with string and wire at his pit, but his team mate Lottin, who was evidently something of a perfectionist, was criticised for 'wasting time' whilst he made up a proper steel bracket.

In contrast to the Saturday, when the spectators had been relatively few, the circuit was black with people turning out to watch the Coupe Boillot handicap for sports cars over 14 laps on the Sunday, a gorgeous sunlit day. This was the only Georges Boillot Cup race in the series in which a British car and driver featured in the first three in the results. The winner at 63.5 m.p.h. was Lagache on one of the remarkable two-seater 1100 c.c. slab-sided Chenard-Walckers, ugly little flat blue sports/racing cars with high trumpet-like exhaust notes that were still competitive in sports-car races ten years later. Second came Robert Laly on a 3-litre Aries at 66.05 m.p.h. and third Major C. M. Harvey's 1½-litre 12/50 Alvis at 59.9 m.p.h., which also won the team award with R. M. V. Sutton's sister car in sixth place. A tragedy occurred during the race when the Bignan driven by a Brussels coachbuilder, Henry Matthys, caught fire when doing 90 m.p.h. downhill in the Forest of Boulogne. The mechanic jumped out at 70 m.p.h., fracturing his skull and later dying in hospital, whilst Matthys brought the car to a standstill and appeared to be all right when he returned to the pits on Lallain's Bignan, though with his shirt charred and burns to his arms and face. Later he died from his burns and a memorial to him and his mechanic Paul Vauthier was erected on the site of the accident, a granite obelisk ornamented with a bronze broken steering wheel with oak leaves entwined in it.

The English journals frequently accused the French of entering thinly disguised racing cars in the Coupe Boillot, but the two Alvises were really Brooklands cars capable of over 90 m.p.h. but fitted with four-seater bodies, and the officials made Harvey change his differential-less back axle for a standard one which had to be borrowed off an English spectator's Alvis before they would let him start in the race.

In 1926 the 3-kilometre sprint with a 1-kilometre run-in was increased to 5 kilometres (with the direction changed between practice and the event) to encourage an attempt on the flying start 5-kilometre World's Record, then standing at 126 m.p.h. Segrave, driving the V.12, supercharged 4-litre Sunbeam Tiger with which he had gained the Land Speed Record at over 150 m.p.h. on Southport Sands earlier in the year, thoroughly frightened himself by going flat out and getting airborne at the crest of one of the switchbacks to record 140.6 m.p.h. overall, with a speed of 148.1 m.p.h. by hand timing for the third kilometre. This was a time of 1 minute 35⅗ seconds, whereas Parry Thomas, an older and perhaps wiser man, was second fastest in the Leyland-Thomas with 1 minute 55⅘ seconds. Ortmans on the sports Panhard did 2 minutes 8⅜ seconds and Archie Frazer-Nash 2 minutes 15⅛ seconds on a supercharged Anzani Frazer Nash. This was the only sprint event in 1926, for R. B. ('Dick') Howey was tragically killed in his 5-litre Indianapolis Ballot after a skid in the Mont Lambert hill climb in which spectators were also involved. The climb was cancelled thereafter, and also the St Martin hill-climb which was to follow.

For the Light Car and Voiturette GP George Eyston had entered an unsupercharged 8-cylinder Type 39 1½-litre Bugatti he had recently acquired from Malcolm Campbell, a linered-down Type 35 and the actual car with which Meo Costantini had won the voiturette class of the 1925 Italian GP at Monza. When Eyston took out the back seat squab one day he had been thrilled to see Costantini's name pencilled on one of the wooden uprights. Due to initial plug bothers, Eyston at first had to give best to a girl driver, Ivy Cummings, in a 4-cylinder supercharged Type 37A GP Bugatti, until the lady had a front and rear brake on opposite sides seize simultaneously and her car went into a ditch. Miss Cummings decided to telephone race control to report her mishap, only to find she had no change for the telephone. She later said that onlookers showered francs on her in such profusion that, in her own words, she would have been quite wealthy if she had accepted them all, and there was much applause when a grey-bearded gentleman insisted on kissing her on both cheeks in front of the small crowd gathered round her damaged car. Thus George Eyston went on to win the race at 64.13 m.p.h. from Capt. J. C. Douglas's Type 37A Bugatti. No sooner was the race over than Violet, who was third in the Light Car class in his unusual flat four supercharged 2-stroke Sima-Violet, put in a protest against the two Bugattis, and Capt. Douglas's car was found to be 6 pounds under the minimum weight and so was disqualified. Bourdon's supercharged 1100 c.c. Salmson, which won the Voiturette category, actually finished second in the overall result at 62.37 m.p.h., 8 minutes behind Eyston and 4 minutes in front of Violet.

Only eight cars took part in the Georges Boillot Cup race on the Sunday. Maurice Harvey had lost second place the previous year through running out of petrol on the penultimate lap, so in 1926 he fitted an auxiliary tank above the rear floorboards in his 12/50 Alvis four-seater, only to be told by officials to remove it before the race. This was again a triumph for the 1100 c.c. Chenard-Walckers 'little beetle-backed racers of a type which infringe the spirit—although perhaps not the letter—of the rules in a most pronounced manner' in the opinion of *The Light Car*. Certainly the average speed of 65.4 m.p.h. of Lagache's winning car over the longer distance was faster than Eyston's average the day before under similar weather conditions. Harvey covered 232 miles at 63.5 m.p.h. before retiring after lying third, and Dr Benjafield crashed what was to become the famous Le Mans 3-litre Bentley 'Old No. 7'. The Chenards filled the first three places.

In 1927 a rally was held finishing at Boulogne in conjunction with the 'Automobile Week' on the lines of the Monte Carlo event, John O'Groats, Berlin and Barcelona being amongst the starting points. At the Concours at Le Touquet on the Wednesday held in bright sunshine, there was 'nothing freakish entered, apart from an Amilcar with a square cut saloon body finished to resemble crumpled silver paper' reported *The Motor*.

Quite different venues from the traditional ones were arranged for the sprint events this year, the most eventful being over three kilometres past the golf links outside Le Touquet towards Stella Plage, which included a right-angled corner covered in sand. Here there were cries of '*Il est mort!*' from the crowd if a car skidded, and boos if it did not. The Hon. Mrs Victor Bruce, who had won the Ladies' Prize in the Rally in her A.C. starting

M

from John O'Groats, was looking down and fiddling with the
floor mat as she came up to the corner, but a quick application
of the handbrake by her mechanic prevented her charging the
crowd. Baron von Wentzel-Mosau did some inadvertent
motoring on the golf links in his supercharged 33/180 Mercédès,
and a young Frenchman called Sauvage ran up a bank in his
Bignan and overturned to cries of *'Il est mort!'*. Far from being
'mort', Sauvage crawled from underneath completely unhurt,
righted his car and continued to the finish with two extra
passengers. Richard Plunkett-Greene, who taught at the same
prep school at Aston Clinton as the novelist Evelyn Waugh,
was the fastest sports-car driver in his Frazer Nash in 1 minute
49 seconds, and Goutte's Salmson was the fastest racing car in
1 minute 37½ seconds.

On the Thursday afternoon there were sprints over a straight
900-metre course along the sea-front with times announced
through M. Berretrot's gigantic megaphone. Goutte's Salmson
was again fastest overall, and Mrs Bruce, the Baron and Sauvage
all figured in the results, now unhindered by the complexities
of cornering.

Fog, rain, mild blizzards and brilliant sunshine formed the
weather picture for the Light Car and Voiturette GP on the
Saturday in which Prince Ghica on a Bugatti provided the main
diversions. So determined was he to get near the front of the
field that he first overturned his car between Le Wast and
Desvres, and shortly afterwards again capsized at Baincthun. On
this second occasion he broke several ribs and had to retire, much
to the disappointment of the crowds in the grandstand for whom
he had been providing the big thrills of the race when he elected
to career past them at 80 m.p.h. or so in a series of wild and
apparently uncontrollable skids. Victory went to Malcolm
Campbell in a Type 37A Bugatti at 67.24 m.p.h. from 'Sabipa'
in a similar car, with George Eyston in a Type 39A Bugatti
third. A mere two-fifths of a second separated the latter pair
after Eyston's pit crew had sportingly lent tools to 'Sabipa' to
make a clutch adjustment, this undoubtedly affecting the result.
Again spectators were sparse out on the circuit when the race
began in the rain, a couple of dozen onlookers at Le Wast, some

gendarmes on the stretch between Le Wast and Desvres, and in the village of Desvres itself a few disconsolate 'natives' stood at their doorways and raised a mild cheer as the first man came through.

The 1927 Coupe Boillot was a farce, the handicaps being based on a secret timing check in an eliminating race of between 10 and 12 laps depending on engine capacity, whilst the final was over a mere three laps. Harvey on a 'beetleback' 12/50 Alvis and Kaye Don, in his first road race, driving a supercharged Hyper Sports Lea-Francis had a great duel in the wet in the eliminator until the Lea-Francis eliminated itself with magneto trouble. Harvey was the first competitor to finish his allotted laps in the eliminator, but was hopelessly handicapped out of the final which was won by Laly on a 3-litre Aries at 68.81 m.p.h. Campbell, who finished second in a 2-litre Bugatti, was disqualified for exceeding his car's average in the eliminator by more than ten per cent and Charles Faroux, Clerk of the Course, promised that the handicap rules would be altered for the following year. The English driver George Newman was placed second in his Salmson and Brisson's Lorraine-Dietrich was third.

The sprints in 1928 consisted of the 900 metres along the front at Le Touquet, a rather unexciting 1-kilometre hill-climb at Wimille, and then a return to the traditional flying 3 kilometres on the switchbacks of the St Omer road. Fastest along the front was a Type 35C GP Bugatti (29.8 seconds) driven by 'Valcourt', a pseudonym, said *The Motor*, hiding the identity of Bielovuci, the first airman to fly across the Alps in 1910, his aircraft being a Bleriot. Unfortunately the history books generally concede this honour to belong to a Peruvian, Georges Chavez, who was killed at the end of his flight in his Bleriot in 1910. Second fastest was Mme Jennky (30.6 seconds) on a similar Bugatti to 'Valcourt's'. In the hill-climb Charlier's yellow Type 35B GP Bugatti, with its finned tail, was fastest (33.8 seconds) with 'Valcourt', now in a supercharged Type 43 four-seater Bugatti, being the fastest sports car driver (37.8 seconds).

Two tragedies marred the 3-kilometre sprint, first a woman spectator was injured and later died in hospital after the bonnet of Delzaert's Bugatti flew off and struck her, and secondly 'Valcourt' lost control of his GP Type 35C Bugatti on the switchback, went sideways across the road, cut half a dozen bicycles clean in half and mowed down two brothers, one of whom was killed, before the Bugatti overturned in the forest, momentarily catching fire. 'Valcourt' was thrown clear, but was badly cut about the face. After this the sprint was abandoned.

The Light Car and Voiturette GP was this year renamed the Trophée National and cars of up to 2 litres were eligible for the 12-lap, 279-mile race, although Gauthier's Type 35C GP Bugatti was the only 2-litre car running. From a massed start in beautiful weather, Malcolm Campbell's 1½-litre, straight-eight GP Delage kept in front of Gauthier for the whole race to win from him by 7 minutes at 72.52 m.p.h. Scaron's 1100 c.c. Amilcar Six finished third, 20 minutes behind Campbell. During his 3 hours 50 minutes drive, Campbell achieved the fastest lap ever for the Boulogne circuit of just under 78 m.p.h. in 17 minutes 51 seconds and loudspeakers replaced M. Berretrot to announce all these excitements, though the trumpet still blared from the top of Mont Lambert.

In the 12-lap Georges Boillot Cup race, Philip Taylor's Austro-Daimler was a non-starter as his elder brother Cyril, responding rather drastically to parental pressure to prevent their younger son racing, put a hammer through its radiator the night before the race. Under a new handicap system the big cars had to give away 3 seconds for every c.c. of their engine capacity over the smaller cars, with the result that Tim Birkin waited an hour and five minutes in the sunshine in his blower 4½-litre Bentley after the limit 750 c.c. d'Yrsan, driven by its constructor Raymond Siran, had set off. It was soon apparent that a likely winner would be amongst the fastest supercharged 1½-litre cars, Louis Dutilleux's 8-cylinder Type 39A GP Bugatti with road equipment, Malcolm Campbell's similarly equipped 4-cylinder Type 37A GP Bugatti or Maurice Harvey's sports 4-cylinder front-wheel-drive Alvis. This car's independent suspension paid off going through the twisty and bumpy roads in the villages, and Harvey put in a notable fastest lap of 19 minutes 17 seconds at just under 73 m.p.h. However, Dutilleux twice pulverised the Coupe Boillot lap record set up as long ago as 1922 by Bablot's big Hispano-Suiza, leaving it at 74.72 m.p.h. with a lap in 18 minutes 35 seconds. Harvey retired at half distance after being passed by both the Bugattis, which also overhauled Rousseau's 1100 c.c. Salmson. Two Amilcar Sixes driven by Miss Maconochie and Beris Wood dropped back and retired. Then, dramatically, both Bugattis retired, first Campbell on the tenth lap after leading whilst Dutilleux refuelled, and then Dutilleux himself when holding an unassailable lead on the last lap, leaving victory to Ivanowski's supercharged 1½-litre Alfa Romeo at 69.65 m.p.h., with Rousseau's Salmson second and the other team Alfa Romeos of Attilio Marinoni and Cyril Paul third and fourth. Birkin finished fifth, after putting up the record Coupe Boillot average speed of 73.16 m.p.h.

When Mrs Ruth Urquhart Dykes finished tenth and last, having suffered a blown cylinder head gasket on her 12/50 Alvis, she was not only the first woman driver ever to complete a Coupe Boillot race, but also the last driver to race on the Boulogne circuit. The interest in the Boulogne races once shown by the local people had now completely fallen off, and the fatal accidents in the speed trials, coupled with the news of the extremely serious crash at Monza the previous weekend involving the deaths of Emilio Materassi and twenty-two spectators had made motor sport decidedly unpopular, so races were never held again on the historic Boulogne circuit.

Mr Pickett's annual dramas were now played out.

Speke My Mind

L. J. K. SETRIGHT

Laurel, sienna, damson, saffron, the fifteen hundreds go out
onto the gold-grey pavé.
More capacity; you can find it in the boot
or look for it in the engine.
The more things change, the more they stay the same;
so what has become of the thirteen hundred now?
Wasn't it Car of the Year, and what did it do?
This has longer wheel travel;
shall we therefore travel longer,
Bolster and I, driving and searching
for fat Flemish fingers pointing whitely down the warm whaleback
from Knokke to Toledo?
Pooh-pooh the pavé
while the four-link axle, dead as Pindar, follows faithfully
faithfully following a tradition
the thirteen hundred was never meant to start.
The front coils seat on noise insulating washers
which must stop the noise of the engine from reaching the road—

the cobble-striped wander-ridged concrete-and-sidewinds that leads
to coffee and hooch and a smoke, and doubtless
a bushel of frites if we're careless enough to ask.
What would the thirteen hundred do out here?
What would it be doing here, indeed,
and it the bijou town carriage for gentlemen
bijou and bourgeois
driving felt-hatted and scanning the Knightsbridge kerbs
for wives who window-shop there and buy in Holborn,
smug in the polyurethane gleam off the walnut veneer and the jazz
snazz chromium bezels round dials that are there
to prove it's an engineering job. It cornered hard
and handled wickedly and withal
the harsh celery-bite ride that is good
for the upper lip and the kidneys
and is for ever England
—or Eire, seeing the back end
was independent.
But we are in Belgium and it has no terrors
and the thirteen hundred was never like this, unless you mean
stiff. But it's new,
isn't it? Fresh out of Speke via Coventry,
and fresh for that matter out of brakes
because someone has come before us like a lout
to his wedding and could not bear
to let bashing wait upon bedding.
I hear you, Leyland, this is no car
for the masher and thrasher, it's one for the road
and one for absent friends
and one for the folk who are careful and modest and canny
folk who care for luxury but do not care for it
if it troubles the conscience. It looks like a Triumph but not
like all the others and not like the thirteen hundred
which could be its big brother six after nosing a cliff.
That's how we saw ninety, nosed over a cliff.
Not really, but the high eighties are really the limit,
you know, of its aspiration; and after five twelfths of a minute
you'd be breaking our blessed political law of the land
which the car seems reluctant to do
after all its zeal to reach it. Yet we never slowed down
for cliff-precipitous potholes or gullies or cowpats
but only for cows themselves matching our own
mild full-flanked dun-coloured manner on the ruminant road
and to look for the country-wise way

round saturnine roadworks that played hell
with our route card.
                    Saturnalia would be more fun
in the Toledo which wears its favours sidesaddle, its badges asquint
on a butcher's-slab rump which shouts out Triumph
even to those who can't read and don't know
a Standard Ten axle when it jumps up in their faces.
No jumper, this, no paracyclic Autolycus
leaping at every unconsidered trifle:
four splayed links again, but a live thing driving
and holding the train that cloaks the name's nobility
in super self-effacing pug-faced normality.
Toledo and super swordsteel (forgetting the Birmingham trash
of gilded paper knives at ten quid a dozen)
are one and the same
to men who don't hail from Solingen—so
they give us polyvinyl to sit on,
pull at, wind, or take such shocks as the black plastic underriders
like rheumy Lloyds men sending their effigies to a funeral
cannot insure against. Oh God!
Oh Speke! Lord, for thy servant heareth:
Toledo is a nice name, and affords
a sop to the vanity of a pride-stripped people
more headed than any Cerberus. All right,
the Toledo is a nice car that handled far better
than ever seemed likely on four-inch whiteknuckle rims
or even seemed right for a penny-plain buzzbox.
Yes, you can hear it. Hear it spin
to that solid-bottomed falsetto that we know
the old twelve-ninety six triple-journal can sing
till the polyprop fan goes blue in the face.
A motor, this, with unburstable guts; and it seems to breathe
the muggy Belgian heat into its vitals and draw therefrom
such vigour as makes it respond to the spur
with a spurt that begins where the fifteen hundred's leaves off.
and carry on into ninetyish regions not deemed
accessible by those who should and must know better.
Was it the wind?
Or the speedo's flattering gaze
out of the matt wood gauge-plank and sporter of eyeballs?
or the decline and fall
of a road that sank imperceptibly
as are doing the Heralds?
Not gutless, anyway, this one; spineless, rather.

What has become of the chassis? Red-inked, it lies
in the profit and loss accounts, where engineers
and accountants have buried it, with all the cost
and weight and height and flexure that went with
a far-from-perfect cruciform.
If Christ faltered beneath His
can Leyland bear their cross much longer?

This unique road test report in blank verse, on the Triumph Toledo and Triumph 1500, is based on an occasion when L.J.K. Setright and John Bolster tried out these then-new cars in Belgium, shortly before they were publicly announced.—Editor.

An acquaintance of mine called his old Ford Popular The Virgin. I think it was because he never got very far with it.—Ralph Thoresby in 'Motor'

I Won't Take My Coat Off,
I'm Not Stopping

L. J. K. SETRIGHT

It was King Canute or Kanut (though he was not such a Knut as historians often suggest) who was first in our history to say 'Stop!' to something that would not. The sea, of course, just kept on keeping on, and the King had to plodge hastily back to dry land, thus inventing Knutsford.

But some people will never learn. Centuries later, it was Tennyson who kept on keeping on, crying 'Brake, brake, brake, On thy cold grey stones, O Sea!' without of course achieving the slightest effect. The bitter fact has to be faced: there are some things that you simply cannot stop, even though you threaten them with a six-letter word beginning with F.

Some cars, for instance, have this sort of interminable reputation. One such was the 30/98 Vauxhall, better remembered as the beginning of the sports car than as the end of the AGM (ante

General Motors) era. I remember a chap in the Vintage Sports Car Club with a particularly lively 30/98, handsomely and—as it transpired—conveniently built as an open four-seater. Most of them were open cars, though enthusiasts for the model insist that it was to facilitate baling out in times of flood rather than baling out in times of stress. Anyway, there it was, a lusty 90 m.p.h. 4½-litre car with splendid steering but nothing much in the way of retardation other than a surely considerable wind resistance; and there was this chap, driving furiously in pursuit of some end that now escapes me but cannot have justified the means. (*The driving is like the driving of Jehu the son of Nimshi, for he driveth furiously*, said the watchman in Second Kings; but he was obviously not to be trusted, for Jehu was the son of Jehoshaphat and therefore the grandson of Nimshi. Thus was invented the Generation Gap.) Storming through a sleepy West Country town, he found people and vehicles in the market place, so he ratcheted the hand throttle slightly open and stood up in the driving seat, waving his arms in agitated manner and crying wildly 'No Brakes!' (Jehu, of course, would have shouted 'Baal out!') Whereupon the people and the vehicles scattered before him and were divided hither and thither, so that the Vauxhall went through on clear road.

He had the right idea, that chap. If you are in a hurry, leave the brakes alone—they only make you go slower. Nuvolari used to maintain this as a principal tenet of his faith, and once demonstrated the theory during practice for a Grand Prix somewhere. Having put in some very fast laps in a Maserati, he then had half the brake linings removed and proceeded to lap even faster. It was an inevitable corollary of such a technique that he would finish a race with his brakes in near-perfect condition (you should have seen his tyres!) while his rivals would end up with their brakes almost useless.

Whatever Nuvolari might say, most drivers were prepared to concede the desirability of slowing down on occasions; but the state of the car designers' art was, until the 1950s, such that most braking systems fell far short of the ideal. Even then, there were some who took extraordinary steps to ensure that their brakes did not work too well. Daimler-Benz, for example, were so

worried about the possibilities of brake grab or fierceness in the
GP Mercedes-Benz of 1954-5 that they cautioned drivers to use
them gently to begin with, lest a sudden accumulation of heat
might crack the vast light-alloy drums or their steel liners.
Furthermore they provided in the cockpit of the Merc a set of
plungers that the driver could press to meter small doses of oil
into the brakes so that they would not work too fiercely. And
who but Daimler-Benz would even think of using brake linings
of three different brands (Energit, Ferodo and Textar), either to
frustrate the advertising department or to hedge their bets, on
the shoes of each car?

There is, as Ecclesiastes has it, no new thing under the sun.
Forty years earlier (before the W.196 Merc, I mean, not before
Eccles) an even more distinguished Vauxhall carried in its
instruction book the injunction 'If foot brake has been fierce the
previous day, put into drum a small quantity of graphite grease
or a few spots of oil, getting same as near brake surface as possible.'
And while the Mercedes-Benz drivers were doing more or less
that around the Grand Prix circuits of Europe, in England there
was a man doing very well in hill-climbs with a pre-war ERA,
preparing for each event by brushing its brake linings vigorously
with common kitchen stove blacklead!

In those days, when Fangio was oiling the Merc around the
World Championship circuits and Broad's ERA was filling the
Prescott air with wonderful noise and a smell redolent of brown
paper and boot polish, I was not a motoring writer at all. I was
a law student, journeying up to London each day in a 1926
Cloverleaf Citroën. This was a little 5CV affair that looked like
a cross between a bathtub and a perambulator, and had a performance to match. It was astonishingly manoeuvrable, however,
and at that time was just about the fastest thing on four wheels
across London—not only because it was compact and I could see
all four corners, but also for the good and simple reason that in
the absence of any effective brakes it inevitably kept moving.
The front wheels had no brakes at all; the rear wheels took scant
notice of a pair of small drums connected to the handbrake lever;
and behind the gearbox was another smallish drum worked by
the brake pedal and magnified in its effect by the gearing, the

expensively idiosyncratic herringbone gearing beloved of André Citroën, in the back axle. The net effect of all this lot being brought into earnest use was at most a vague suspicion that the car was not travelling quite so quickly (a relative term, you must understand) as before. On dry roads, the brakes were simply too weak to work; on wet roads, the wheels locked and the car went sliding merrily onward.

This made driving an absorbing exercise, and at times an entertaining one. Traffic lights were hazardous affairs calling for anticipation worthy of a stockbroker. I remember once when my anticipation was not quite up to scratch, at a deserted junction on an Easter Sunday morning. As the Cloverleaf approached, those treacherous lights flickered to amber just at the critical moment when the point of no return might or might not have been reached. 'I don't think we saw that, did we?' I said to my passengers, pressing the Citroën up to the bit and crossing the line a moment after amber had made way for red. Nor had we seen the policeman who was lurking in the doorway of a corner pub, and who then came running out with arm and forefinger peremptorily raised. Ever a well-disciplined fellow, I sat at attention, bolt upright and looking neither to right nor to left as I urged the Cloverleaf on in the general direction of Goodwood. My passengers, however, were of less stern stuff, and looked back— to see the policeman weak-kneed and glassy-eyed, his arms and legs wrapped round one of those hefty steel pillars that used to support trolleybus wires, and into which he had apparently run full-tilt.

That policeman may today be sweeping a railway station or be Commissioner of Police for the Metropolis. In either case let me say that I am very sorry, officer, but I learned my lesson. Always think twice before you drive past a pub: you never know what you might be missing.

The life of a motoring writer is just a trifle less worrying. I have been at it for some time now, and have driven hundreds of cars, but I can recall only three or four whose brakes were really quite exceptional in being beyond exception. More often than not, a car will brake well in some circumstances but prove unstable in others. There are cars that will bring you to a neck-stretching halt from 100 m.p.h. on dry roads, but will develop a front-wheel skid if you caress the brake pedal with exquisite lightness at 10 m.p.h. on wet ones. There are cars whose brakes work well when they are cold but are useless when hot. Less common are the cars whose brakes need to be warmed to their work, like one I remember: when they were hot its brakes would practically weld the car to the road; but out on a motorway after a few miles with a 130 m.p.h. wind in the willows, the brakes would be too cool and would not respond at all—at which point, in faithful compliance with Sod's Law, a humble Bumble Thousand swerved suddenly and quite needlessly into the third lane just ahead of me. One of the tricks of the trade saved me from finding myself at the wheel of a ten-cylindered articulated eight-wheeler; and thereafter I learned to tickle the brake pedal with my left toe every so often, just to stop the brakes from hibernating.

More reassuring was the cool competence of the anchorage in a Lamborghini Miura I was once driving across France. It was a brand new car, and had to be run in gently, which meant not exceeding 126 m.p.h.: and it was at precisely this speed that I came over the brow of a main-road hill to find that the rascally French had applied Sod's Law and their own remorseless national logic to a road-works diversion, placing it and the warning sign more or less together just over the crest of the hill. Braking heavily downhill on a sweeping nearside curve of wet concrete cannot always be guaranteed to succeed, but the Miura saved the day and my neck most accommodatingly.

Rather more disturbing was a double-decker omnibus I once found myself testing. A public relations man and an engineer from the factory accompanied me, and when my decelerometer showed that the maximum deceleration it could achieve was only a little better than the legal minimum, they explained with an air of injured innocence that public transport operators did not like their 'buses to be too well-braked, the accountancy departments calculating that it was cheaper to run over an old lady than to suffer a busload of plaintive passengers all with broken arms and heads. I am still not sure whether it was a demonstration of their awareness of the need for making a good impression, or a demonstration of the perversity of Sod's Law, which caused both these worthies on my next full application of the brakes to come hurtling more or less horizontal and out of control up the central gangway from the place at the rear whither I had sent them. My object, I said, was for them to make sure that there was nothing behind; and I was using my mirror to make sure they were there. . . .

As you can see, a motoring writer's armoury of technical knowledge is incomplete without a mastery of Sod's Law. It may however be that, through spending your fifth-form days too earnestly in the study of Bernoulli's Theorem or d'Alembert's Paradox, this fundamental statement of Nature's Intent has escaped you. Quite simply, Sod's Law states that a slice of buttered toast will, when dropped, fall with its buttered side to the floor. Asked to demonstrate it, my old Professor of Natural Sciences prepared a laboratory specimen slice of buttered toast, held it aloft before the incredulous eyes of his audience, and let go. It fell to the floor, buttered side uppermost. 'That, gentlemen,' sighed the Prof, 'demonstrates Sod's Law to perfection.'

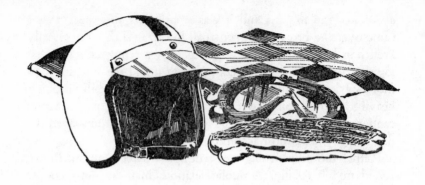

The Bull From Arrecifes

CYRIL POSTHUMUS

The greatness of Juan Manuel Fangio, five times World Champion driver, unwittingly dimmed the limelight on a compatriot and friend whose feats in motor racing deserved to be better known. The career of José Froilàn González, though shorter than that of Fangio, was almost as remarkable for its sheer press-on courage and determination as was the quintuple Champion's for sheer genius. The proud, victory-pampered houses of Mercedes-Benz and Alfa Romeo both had strong cause to rue the presence of González among the opposition, while Fangio, Ascari and Farina, Champions all, were bested by the tubby Argentinian on his great days.

Chaperoned by Fangio, he and another promising driver, Alfredo Pian, were sent under the aegis of the A.C. Argentina to Europe in 1950—two 'freshmen' to Grands Prix due to drive the Scuderia Argentina 4CLT/48 'San Remo' Maseratis. González was a short, massively-built bull of a man, with a sallow 'baby' face and short, curly hair prematurely thinning. Because of the language problem he seemed sullen to uncomprehending Europeans, but with his countrymen he was animated and cheerful, gabbling away in Spanish and working as happily on a chassis or engine as at the wheel. His girth suggested excess fat, but most of it was muscle, for he was as strong as an ox.

True, he lacked the polish of the stars, seeming visibly to force his car along, foot manifestly hard down, his great arms hauling at the wheel, the car travelling in a series of slews and slides, yet often he contrived to nurse notoriously brittle Maseratis to the finish where others broke them. Continental observers of the 'early González' mistook his do-or-die determination for 'brute force and ignorance', but he was simply practising his first law of racing—going as fast as possible. His countrymen did not call him 'the Pampas Bull' for nothing; that equally massive animal is notorious for its wild, irresistible charges, and that was how González drove in his early days.

Born in Arrecifes, some 100 miles north-west of Buenos Aires, in 1922, he caught the racing virus from his uncle Julio Perez, a prominent driver in South American long-distance road races in the '30s, but young José Froilàn preferred single-seaters which he raced on dirt tracks in his home town and elsewhere. The engines they used—U.S. Fords or Chevrolets—were rugged, cheap and easy to come by, encouraging a fierce throttle-cum-tail happiness which, coupled with a reputation for tremendous getaways, made González a spectacular attraction.

Some also called him 'Pepé', a nice friendly name, or 'El Cabezon', which literally means 'Bighead', not in the cocky sense but because of his large head and short bull neck. But nick-names signify popularity, and Froilàn González was popular as a real tiger of motor racing. In his first drives behind the fractious Trident, the Maserati broke under him, but with Fangio's advice and his own intelligence, he tempered his impulsive driving to the instruments, and early in 1950 contrived to bring an old 4CL home fifth at Palermo Park, Buenos Aires, behind four 2-litre Ferraris and ahead of newer 4CLT/48s driven by European *Maseratisti*. He also placed sixth at Mar del Plata and seventh at Rosario, feats which collectively clinched his European trip.

Painted a cheerful blue and yellow, and carried in a big blue and yellow double-decker Fiat transporter, the Argentinian 4CLT/48 Maseratis and an F.2 Ferrari certainly added colour to the European scene—and so did their drivers, the awe-inspiring Fangio and the raw but determined González and Pian, their Maseratis more often sideways than forwards as they grappled with strange new town circuits such as Pau, San Remo and Monaco. It was noticed that González cornered like Nuvolari, entering his corners very fast, braking late, and scrubbing off the speed in a long drift. His progress was often ragged and rarely consistent while his furious efforts often left him in a lather of sweat—but he was very fast.

His apprenticeship to European conditions was hectic, but 'Pepé's latent skill soon showed through, as did his tremendous courage. At Monaco 1950 he managed a remarkable fifth fastest in practice behind three of the invincible Type 158 Alfa Romeos and a works Ferrari, only to be involved in the fantastic first-lap fracas when Farina's Alfa spun at the Tabac corner and eliminated ten cars in under ten seconds. González' Maserati, knocked sideways by the Alfa, almost escaped, but its tank filler cap had sprung open, fuel slopped out, and as he braked for the Gasometer hairpin the car burst into flame. For all his bulk, González was out of the car like lightning while it was still moving, but when he saw that it was heading for a spectator enclosure he jumped back in and steered it to safety. He rolled on the ground to extinguish his burning overalls, then staggered to the pits, distractedly explaining 'El fuego! El fuego!' to all who remarked his bedraggled condition. Second degree burns put him in hospital for a fortnight.

Undaunted, 'the new boy' next placed third in that remarkable race around the ramparts at Angoulême, driving the Argentine team's F.2 Ferrari, and a week later shared a sports Simca-Gordini with Fangio in the classic Le Mans 24 Hours. They didn't finish, but it was all valuable experience. The Albi GP brought the first fruits, a Heat 2 win for González, but crafty Frenchman Louis Rosier set a higher average in Heat 1 so stuck firmly to the Maserati's tail throughout the Final to clinch victory on the added times.

El fuego dogged José Froilàn again in his next race, the Dutch GP at Zandvoort, when he stopped to refuel. The fuel was already gushing before the nozzle was in the tank, and as he cut the engine there came a 'Whoof' and the tail was ablaze. González leapt out, his trousers ablaze, while extinguishers played over the Maserati, and as the pit crew wiped the car clear of foam González donned a spare pair of trousers. Blasting back into the race, he eventually finished a heroic seventh on a very rough-looking— and sounding—car minus most of its paintwork and at least one exhaust valve.

At the end of July, 'Pepé' went back to Argentina, infinitely richer in experience if not in winnings, and established himself as *José Froilàn González & Cia; Automoviles-Camiones*, car and truck dealers, in Buenos Aires. While the new business absorbed him, destiny was busy too, preparing the next dramatic scene which was to send his name ringing round the world of motor racing. Early in 1951 two Buenos Aires GPs, one for the President Peron Cup, the other for the Señora Evita Peron Cup, were to be staged on consecutive weekends. The previous autumn, the German Mercedes-Benz concern had decided on a tentative return to racing in Free Formula events with their fabulous 1939 3-litre two-stage supercharged V.12 W163 cars. These shark-nosed silver projectiles had won all but two GPs in 1939, and rated as the acme of design perfection, more formidable even than the 158 Alfa Romeos which had reigned supreme since 1946.

Mercedes selected the Buenos Aires races for their debut—the Argentine market was an important one—entering three cars with Farina, Lang and Kling as drivers. When the news reached Italy the Ferrari team and Maserati independents decided to stay away, which left Argentinians such as Fangio, González, Galvez, Pian and Mendite guy alone to meet the German *blitzkrieg*, with their smaller, less powerful if newer Ferraris and Maseratis. With Fangio in charge, therefore, they worked out a tight, twisty course on the Costanera side of Palermo Park, in an effort to equalize their chances. Then agreement between Mercedes and Farina broke down, and ironically, the Germans hired Fangio to drive in his place!

When the ear-splitting 450-plus b.h.p. Mercedes trio made the three fastest times in practice it looked like a walkover, but to the amazement of the enormous crowd, as the race unfolded only Lang, their 1939 'tiger', managed to stave off chunky González in his chunky 2-litre Ferrari—a car known to the stable as *el corto*, the short one. Then, to the Germans' horror and the locals' joy, their 'Pepé' passed Lang on lap 23 and pulled away from the screaming Mercedes. A fuel stop let the German past again, but González re-caught him to win by 19 seconds, the Mercedes placing second, third and sixth in the order Lang, Fangio, Kling.

This was sensation enough, but in the second race, after the Germans declared they had cured the fuel troubles dogging their cars, González administered a second drubbing, winning by over 2 minutes from Kling and Lang in two surviving Mercedes! Clearly the agile little Italian V.12 was easier to handle on the twisty Costanera circuit, but González had combined fire with intelligence, and his success was enormously popular, as David over Goliath victories always are. One result was that Mercedes cancelled a projected three-car entry for Indianapolis that year; another was that Comm. Enzo Ferrari's attention focused sharply on the portly Argentinian.

González' next confrontation was with the fiery Giuseppe Farina in the Paris GP. The Italian had a well-prepared two-stage blown 1½-litre Maserati, whereas 'Pepé' had borrowed Louis Rosier's sports 2-seater 4½-litre unblown Talbot, stripped of wings and lights but a decided 'lump' on the tight little Bagatelle circuit in the Bois du Boulogne. He did his belligerent best, and with Farina's faster but thirstier Maserati making more refuel stops than the Talbot, the pair fought a ding-dong battle for the lead. Farina finally won, while 30 seconds behind after nearly three hours of heaving that heavy Talbot around came a grimed, exhausted González.

His big chance came at Reims in mid-season. The challenge to the all-conquering 1½-litre supercharged Alfa Romeos by the rival 4½-litre works Ferraris was approaching a climax by French GP time in early July. Alfas fielded four Type 159s; Ferrari fielded two twin ignition 24-plug cars and an older one with 12 plugs. Then their third man Taruffi went sick and González got the

12-plug. Playing himself in carefully, he gained a third row start, but in the race ran progressively fourth, third, then second by lap 27. Then he stopped for fuel and tyres, and Ferrari's No. 1 Alberto Ascari took the car over. That ended Froilàn's French GP, but the car stayed second to the finish and his place in the team was clinched.

So to the 1951 British GP, when González became the talk of Silverstone for an immense display of his late-braking, full-drift cornering and the first ever over-100 m.p.h. lap during practice with the 12-plug. The great Alfa-Ferrari confrontation peaked, and friend Fangio, Alfa's No. 1, became Froilàn's greatest rival. Fangio lapped at furious pace but 'Gonzo', as the British called him, gave as good as he got, slinging the big Ferrari through the turns in great beefy slides, and passed the Maestro in a wheel-to-wheel battle, while Ferrari senior drivers Ascari and Villoresi were left behind in the rubber smoke.

Thus were Alfa Romeo defeated at last, after six years of domination and 27 consecutive FI race victories, by a man new to the Ferrari team and Silverstone, winning his first Grand Prix. Europe looked at this massive *Argentino*, who could beat the masters at their own game, who had humbled, first Mercedes-Benz and now Alfa Romeo, with new respect. He followed with a model victory in the Pescara GP in Italy, Alfa Romeo being absent licking their wounds, and Fangio pit-signalling for his compatriot! Three second places and a third in the remaining 1951 races confirmed him as one of the GP élite, and as Froilàn González winged home to Argentina and his wife that October, the future looked bright indeed.

As so often happens in motor racing, things worked out differently. The change from 4½-litre Formula 1 to 2-litre Formula 2 for Grands Prix did not suit González' forceful style; he missed the power to drift, and whereas his bulk filled the big Ferrari cockpit comfortably, he positively overflowed from the F.2 Maseratis which were his 1952–3 GP mounts. He was happier wrestling with surviving F.1 cars such as Tony Vandervell's 4½-litre Ferrari Thinwall Special, or the recalcitrant but exciting 1½-litre 16-cylinder BRM. He won races at Goodwood, England, with both, took the Rio de Janeiro GP with a 2-litre Ferrari, placed second in the Italian and Modena GPs with the F.2 Maserati—and that was all for 1952.

The following season was bleak for 'Pepé' too, with but a heat win and second place overall in the Albi GP with the trouble-dogged V.16 BRM, and four third places with F.2 Maseratis to his credit. Yet 'Gonzo' tried very hard against the faster Ferraris that year; he broke, first the Spa lap record, then his accelerator pedal in the Belgian GP, while in the British GP at Silverstone Latin temperament got the better of him when, all wound up for the chase, he ignored come-in signals and had to be black-flagged with his car leaking oil. A torrent of Spanish vehemence ensued in the pits, the leak was checked, and furious Froilàn blasted back into fourth place, sharing the fastest lap with winner Ascari. Then, driving for the new Lancia sports car team, he crashed badly in practice for the Portuguese GP at Oporto when he struck an official's car full in his line at a corner. He was flung out violently, suffering spinal damage which ended his season there and then and gave him a protracted and uncomfortable sojourn in hospital.

For 1954 the 'Pampas Bull' returned to Ferrari. It proved his last full season, brought him a full share of drama, victory and disaster, and saw a new, more restrained, more consistent and very formidable González. Drama came early, in the Syracuse GP, when the dreaded *el fuego* caught up with him again. His team mate Mike Hawthorn crashed, his Ferrari hitting a wall and catching fire, whereupon González, believing Mike to be in the cockpit still, stopped and pluckily rushed to the blaze in an effort to rescue him. Fortunately Hawthorn had leapt the wall and rolled in a field to douse his blazing overalls, González spotted him, and rushed to help. Meantime his Ferrari rolled slowly forward into the blaze, and both cars were totally destroyed. Perhaps it was an ill wind. . . . González' car was the new, short-wheelbase side-tanked Type 555 Ferrari 'Squalo', which he disliked for its twitchy handling and poor steering, and he thus found himself driving the older, more wieldy Type 625 based on the 1953 F.2 car for his next few races.

Now began a winning streak. In three successive weeks, 'Pepé' won at Bordeaux, Silverstone (Heat 1 in a Squalo, the final in a 625) and Bari. He also demonstrated the 'new González' by winning the sports car race supporting the F.1 event at Silverstone, driving a big, brutish 4.9-litre V.12 Ferrari with magnificent control on a slippery wet circuit. This was a car after his own heart, recalling the 1951 GP cars, and the next feat in the astonishing 1954 González *repertoire* was to win Le Mans, the famous French 24 Hours race, with Maurice Trintignant co-driving the massive 4.9. It rained most of the time, yet the one-time Argentine leadfoot handled the car with consummate skill and delicacy, and the pair won the race by just over 2½ miles despite twenty-third hour alarums when the car lost over six minutes to the pursuing Jaguar by refusing to start.

With his back still feeling the effects of the Oporto crash, and an inability to consume a mouthful of food throughout the race because of a nervous upset affecting his stomach, this was one of González' greatest and most determined drives—and one he did not enjoy a bit. Spa, a week later, brought him more drama. His Squalo Ferrari blew up on the first lap of the Belgian GP, and he was resignedly spectating from the pits when Mike Hawthorn pulled in and collapsed over the wheel, almost asphyxiated by exhaust gases from a holed exhaust pipe. He was lifted out and given treatment, while González leapt into the car and was away, only to return a lap later, gesturing at the pipe and retching. Mechanics repaired it with sheet metal and copper wire, and he then resumed the race to finish fourth.

The French GP saw the González Ferrari again wreathed in smoke as he blew up spectacularly in the attempt to hold the sensational new GP Mercedes at Reims. The German cars finished a triumphant 1–2 to a trail of broken rivals, and when it was known they were coming to Silverstone for the British GP, such was Mercedes' reputation that the result looked a foregone conclusion. The pundits forgot that González, the 'giant killer' who beat Mercedes at Buenos Aires and Alfa Romeo at Silverstone, would be there, too, in his favourite 625 Ferrari and on his favourite circuit.

Moreover it rained on race day, and 'Gonzo' had come to like the rain. From a fantastic start he was never headed by any car. Fangio wrought wonders with the aerodynamic Mercedes, but it was a losing battle with a car unsuited to the course, and González won his second British GP, his fourth race at Silverstone, and his sixth victory in 1954. A quick journey to Lisbon ensued, for him to win a seventh, the GP at Portugal for sports cars, after a fierce duel with team mate Mike Hawthorn, both in 3-litre 750S Ferraris.

The next three Grands Prix, the European, Swiss and Italian, saw Mercedes and Fangio ascendant, with 'Pepé' taking two second places and a third, and it was after Monza that the González story struck a sudden, sombre note. His most successful season ever was drawing to a close, with but two races to go— the Tourist Trophy sports car race at Dundrod, Northern Ireland, and the Spanish GP at Barcelona. He never drove in either.

Practising for the Irish race, the notorious banks of Dundrod caught him out after only a lap and a half. Mike Hawthorn had been showing him round but González dropped back and at Tornagrough his 750S Ferrari crashed. He was cast out violently, suffering a badly wrenched shoulder and, worse, another spinal injury. 'This is the end, Mike—no more racing' he said to Hawthorn in the ambulance. During long weeks in hospital he thought hard. He had a wife and two children, and a thriving business demanding his attention, while the glamour of racing was tinged by its grimmer side—the death of his young compatriot Marimon at Nürburgring, the fiery accidents to Hawthorn and Farina, and his own. . . . Long spells in a jarring cockpit thereafter proved very painful, while to this day González' back prevents him sitting for long periods.

So this great tiger from Argentina tailed his racing off, withdrew from European racing altogether, and made only an annual International appearance in the Argentine Temporada. He made one last, abortive trip to Europe in 1956. Desperate for a top driver to meet the Ferraris and Maseratis in the British GP, Tony Vandervell persuaded González to fly to Silverstone at short notice to drive a Vanwall. Though out of training 'Pepé' managed fifth fastest practice time, and but for a last-minute change to larger diameter wheels, who knows what might have happened on his favourite circuit? As it was, the Vanwall sheared a drive shaft on the start line and Fangio, 'Gonzo's old friend, won another race.

In his last Grand Prix of all, the 1957 Argentine, poor 'Pepé' had to hand his Ferrari over to de Portago after forty-one laps, completely exhausted and in much pain. Yet the lure of racing drew him still, so he resumed racing Mecanica Nacional single-seaters over shorter distances, using a Ferrari chassis and a Chevrolet Corvette engine. This proved highly successful, but in 1960 General Motors Argentina, for whom he held the Buenos Aires agency, asked him to give up. Instead he took to sponsoring young drivers in monopostos and saloons, preferably from his native Arrecifes.

Federico Kirbus, the Buenos Aires-based journalist who kindly helped with information for this article, tells of how, one day, González was asked why he spent so much money in this way. 'Look', said 'Pepé', 'I don't like horse racing, nor do I like gambling or to spend Sunday looking at soccer. But I love the *fierros* (the 'irons' or cars), so why shouldn't I spend my money and enthusiasm helping others to race?'

Such enthusiasm and generosity comes rarely. Today there is a new generation of Argentinian racing drivers—Carlos Reutemann, Carlos Ruesch, Carlos Pairetti, Carlos Marincovich, Luis di Palma. . . . With the magnificent achievements of past masters like Fangio and Gonzalez as examples, coupled with their good-will and support today, the new men cannot fail to do well.

In a London one-way street the woman driver really got into a proper mess by trying to reverse out again—a matter of a few yards. A taxi driver yelled "Why don't you give a signal?". The reply was, very sweetly: "There is no signal for what I'm trying to do."—Rodney Walkerley

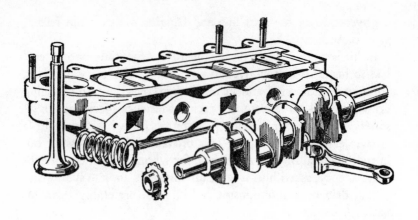

Something a Computer Can't Do

MICHAEL SEDGWICK

'*History is Bunk*'—HENRY FORD I.

Park an elderly and unusual car outside your local, and see what happens.

The fanatic will ponder over it before deciding that it won't do for Silverstone or Prescott. The pot-hunter will complain that someone has relocated the headlamps, *ergo* it'll cost a bomb to make a *concours* winner out of that heap. The investor licks his chops, and reminds you that just such a model made £3,500 at the last Sotheby sale. The family man discovers that the pedals won't fit his wife's feet. The dealer observes thankfully that he hasn't seen one of these since '38, and he'd still be lumbered with *that* if the Civil Defence hadn't requisitioned it as an ambulance. The pub bore averaged 47, old boy, with a similar machine, between Grantham and Edinburgh. But the historian will merely ask what it is *supposed* to be. Tell him, and he will inform all and sundry that it cannot be anything of the sort.

Who is this creature, and why is he suffered to exist?

He is seldom a keen motorist: grapplings with obscure and devious fact have led him to distrust every model on the market. His rarity is matched only by the tiny minority of citizens who need his services. His writings are critical studies intent on debunking the critical studies of others, be they popular novelists who credit pre-war saloons with key-starts, or fellow-historians floundering far away from their native heath. In his more snobbish moments he equates himself with the art expert or the licensed valuer, but any competent engineer can spot the work of a bodger, and does it really matter if it is period bodging or not?

In short, the motoring historian is a tiresome by-product of the Age of Specialisation and the desire to overdo knowledge. The motor car is now part of our Social Heritage, which means that people not only collect it, but pay far too much for the privilege. And for every ignorant Jonesman who contributes towards the prevailing inflation, there are at least two supercilious fanatics determined to prove their command of some aspect of the subject. These fanatics are a menace, because they are obsessional; their cars must wear correct period accessories (factory-approved, if possible), and their bookshelves are crammed with handbooks, workshop manuals and catalogues. It is bad enough to accumulate a single specimen of a chosen manufacturer's full range, but in its extreme form the mania extends to the collection of brochures in unintelligible languages. It is an established fact that a 'Silver Ghost' catalogue in French will fetch more than the same thing in Claude Johnson's English.

Cars, however, take up a lot of room, and even the hoarding of primary literature is limited by the maker's own publicity budget. Things aren't what they were. No longer do we find gems like Trojan's all-girls-together booklets, de Dion's Dicta for Doctors (you haven't really wielded a black bag if you haven't done it with the aid of one of our expanding-clutch transmissions), and Bentley's blow-by-blow accounts of victory at Le Mans. So more paperwork has to be created, and this is the historian's cue.

He is self-perpetuating. Produce a controversial article, and somebody else will be commissioned to deliver a counterblast. Back in the 1950s, we wrote about the Right Kind of Car. Then inflation struck, and a new generation of enthusiasts opted for solvency and the Wrong Kind—Clyno Nines and all that jazz. When the auction-craze arrived at the tap of a hammer, it was the historian who valued (and sometimes devalued) the fashionable Investments of the Sixties. Along with the automotive Van Meegerens, the fake Barker barrel-side tourers, and the phaetons of The School of Brewster, came the art experts, poking at wing-stays, sneaking swatches of upholstery and chips of paint, and tut-tutting over spurious door-handles. Lost Causes became an obsession: every time a badge-engineer got the sack, there ensued a Verbal Grand Prix to be first with a *marque*'s obituary. Even if some enlightened and Naderised government declares the automobile illegal, we won't be the losers. Freed of the necessity to keep *au fait* with March-Cosworths, Cortina permutations, and the Volkswagen-Renault-Fiat battle within EEC, we will subsist happily upon a diet of defunct minutiae. Consider the steam locomotive, the tram, the traction engine, and the piston-engined airliner, and you'll see what I mean.

As yet the market is limited. An art consultant can make a living out of a single painter, be it Duccio or Dali—if he is good enough. A motoring historian can't, which is why most of the true specialists make the game a hobby and not a profession. For the professional, history is being made all the time; thus he has to keep pace. Concentration on a solitary make sounds inviting, but such a safe path can embrace anything from sprags to spoilers. Maybe a great race, then? But watch it—the French Grand Prix has been with us since 1906. As if this were not sufficient deterrent, our friends on the other side of the Channel have ordained *retrospectively* that certain earlier events count towards the score, so you are stuck not only with the town-to-town stuff, but also with the 70 h.p. Panhard and even worse archaisms. In a single week you may be commissioned to write on nineteenth-century British pioneers, and on the abortive *granturismi* of the 1960s.

It is a matter of opinion which is the tougher assignment. In the first instance everyone is dead, so the winner is the man who conducts the smartest marathon tour of Britain's motoring libraries. In the second, nobody is dead: ergo, you can be landed with six unshakeable and contradictory accounts of the same circumstance—all prejudiced, and all potentially actionable. If you escape litigation, some vituperative gent will write to tell you that, thanks to your article, he has just had to pay £2,000 instead of £1,400 for such-and-such a model. (You'll get no thanks from the dealer concerned, whose views on history are probably those of Henry Ford!)

In fact, your sole reward will be a reputation for versatility, which means that you will be asked to judge a concours, or drive a microphone at one of those mammoth old-car rallies catering for Cannstatt-Daimlers and sporty Corvairs alike.

In nine cases out of ten, a judge will get the class he knows. On the tenth occasion, he'll be saddled with motorbikes, those 1930s saloons that used to be beyond the pale, or steam wagons, and once the label of Historian has been attached to him, his knowledge must extend beyond Mr Belloc's Simple Little Rules and Few. In the Lower Fourth everyone learns that if an old-school Austin Twelve has coil ignition it's a cab, that chromium plate is seldom, if ever, encountered before 1925-6, and that leather-like upholstery that doesn't breathe is plastic. At a lower ethical level, of course, holes drilled in the chassis spell Team Car, Old Boy, and plated manifolds indicate 'The Actual Earl's Court Show Model'. (Here we start sorting out the men from the boys: the former will retort that unless the car was made in 1937 or later, it can't have been at Earl's Court, wherever else it consorted with dollybirds and potted palms.) But may heaven preserve you if you try to be dogmatic about early side-valve Morris Minors or the different sub-species of Fiat Topolino.

As for Parades, these are the nearest approach I know to construing Thucydides for the Headmaster when one hasn't done one's prep. One may be a specialist in private life—but there is no time for such subtleties when one is confronted with a double row of assorted vehicles moving round an arena at 15 m.p.h., all of which have to be described. The public can't see the commentator—hence they don't realize that the racing Bugatti is concealed from him by a double-decker 'bus. The programme tells him that it is a 39A, but he musn't believe this. There aren't any left in England. In any case, someone is sure to have nicked his programme, as happened to me at the 1967 Brooklands Commem. The ensuing thirty-five minutes are best forgotten. . . .

To an oculist, as Sherlock Holmes remarked, there is no such thing as a healthy eye. To a historian, there is no such thing as a fact until it is verified. And let's dispose once and for all of the old canard that today's spate of topical works on the motor-car is going to put him out of business.

Beware of 'instant history', be this the reprint of an old buyers' guide or a glossy contemporary catalogue-book. The modern ones, in fact, are less reliable than the museum pieces, thanks to the virtual demise of the annual model outside America. There was a line of demarcation between the cars of 1930 and those of 1931: between 1970s and 1971s no such line exists, which is why the suffix letter on British number plates changes at the end of July and not at the end of December.

The clever boys will, of course, have collared a copy of one of those Trade Guides which aren't supposed to fall into the hands of the laity; but even these merely purvey the information that is meant *ultimately* to reach the public. A model is often continued to help dealers to clear their inventories: 'Owing to popular demand, our 16 h.p. sports model will be unchanged for the coming year' is no success story, but the outward and visible sign of three hundred chassis cluttering up the fields of Warwickshire. Be especially careful with super-sports cars, for homologation came cheap in the 1930s. To give a vehicle catalogue status, one spent a pound or two on a half-tone block and a few lines of type. Never mind if nobody bought the model: so much the better if they didn't try.

In the days when production statistics were veiled in secrecy, inspired guesswork was the order of the day. Industrial correspondents used to arrive at the answer by relating it to the size of a worker's Friday-night bonus, but lesser lights played the chassis-numbers game. Even then a big manufacturer can pull the wool over one's eyes with impunity. I have seen a discrepancy of thirty thousand units between two sets of 'official' figures for the same model. No, don't blame this on a computer or a scatty compositor: *both statistics are right.* It just depends on whether you include foreign licence-production or not.

Experts soon become familiar with these little dodges. Under the Third Reich the German industry published voluminous breakdown figures by make and model, but these also covered vehicles supplied to the Armed Forces, a state of affairs that could turn such Wehrmacht favourites as the vee-eight Horch into best-sellers at the stroke of a Gothic typewriter. Alfa Romeo's competition machinery, however 'stock', never counted towards their total. Above all, beware of any statistics emanating from the United States of America. Like George Washington they cannot lie, but there is a world of difference between production by calendar year, production by model year, and new home-market registrations. A factory saddled with a lemon might persevere for eight months only; this will result in a miserable model-year performance, but if the ham-fisted horror were sandwiched in between two safe, dependable family sedans, a novice might be deluded (by calendar-year figures) into thinking it hadn't been a lemon after all.

What's in a name? Very little, if you are a historian. A German who bought a Knight-engined Mathis or L.U.C. in 1914 probably imagined he was being patriotic. He wasn't: the former was about 90 per cent Minerva, and the latter at least 70 per cent Coventry-Daimler. Twenty years later the faithful Fiat Balilla called itself a Simca in France, an NSU in Germany, and a Walter in Czechoslovakia, though examples put together in Warsaw were plain Polski-Fiats. Even today, no holds are barred. Officially, no such thing as a De Soto has been made since 1960, but Dodge trucks sold in Turkey in 1972 have the name blazoned all over their grilles. Plymouth's Cricket wouldn't qualify for a Test Match: it is a Hillman Avenger. In the Antipodes all contact with reality is lost. What we used to know as a Wolseley Fifteen Hundred or a Riley One-Point-Five emerges down under as an Austin Lancer or Morris Major. I once met a Morris version of the old A105, and also recall a strange interlude with something called a Wolseley 24/80, which was a cross between the small and large Farina species from the Old Country. (The interior woodwork was splendid, and the column change diabolical, but historians aren't supposed to care about such things.)

Never claim a first for anyone, even if the maker's press department did. Their reputation does not depend on such statements. Yours does. Minerva referred to themselves as *la marque doyenne*, even when there were still two other Belgian firms in business who had been making cars long before M. de Jong had progressed beyond the bicycle stage. S. F. Edge's claims could usually be relied upon to launch an acrimonious correspondence, yet he got away with the slogan 'The First Light Six' for his 2-litre A.C. Admittedly in 1921 a 'Light Six' meant something with less than three-and-a-half litres under its bonnet, but in 1914 there had been several with 2-litre engines. Yet nobody uttered a cheep.

Moreover, history can alter. The Party Line will change overnight, just as Brighton Run cars shed a year or two when they come face to face with a competent Dating Committee. What you wrote in 1960 may no longer be true. In hack works of reference, the last two races for the Gordon Bennett Cup are still being won by *Richard*-Brasiers, whereas the 1905 cars were plain Brasier—by that time M. Richard had moved down the road to Puteaux to make Unics. (Not that this can be taken as a general guide: MM. Gobron and Brillié went their several ways in 1903, ten years before people started to call the cars 'Gobrons'.) More perilous still is the retrospective designation. 1949 pushrod Jaguars are Mk. Vs, and mark numbers were used until 1961. Nowadays 1945–48 versions are fast becoming Mk. IVs, and I have even heard allusions to 1938s as Mk. III! In the days when Britannia ruled the printing presses, foreign cars, however illustrious, bore the names inflicted upon them by their London concessionaires. Old hands are familiar with the 17–95 h.p. Alfa Romeo, the 4-litre 'Lago Special' Darracq, and the 36–220 h.p. Mercedes-Benz. To get in the Top Twenty, however, you must forget all this chauvinism, and write of the 1750GS, the 23CV *Talbot*, and something with the tongue-twisting sobriquet of 24/120/180PS. Personally I take the soft option, and call this last Modell-S—the second 'l' just to show I am with it!

Which brings us to horsepower. To any sensible person this signifies the number of horses delivered to the back axle—or at any rate to the gearbox. My own car has forty-seven of these, but under the old RAC (or American NACC) rating it boasts 10.4. By contrast, French *chevaux* are small and compact, and German PS even smaller. An 8PS sounds like an Austin Seven, but probably runs to a couple of stolid litres. Italian ones are larger than life, though not everyone played the game even by local rules. The original twin-cam touring Salmson of 1922 should have been a 7CV, but catalogues invariably called it a 10 h.p. And why did Invicta market their supercharged $1\frac{1}{2}$-litre as a '12-90'? It was taxed as a Twelve, but it certainly never had anything like ninety brake horses, and was flat out at seventy.

If you think body nomenclature is governed by rhyme or reason, try a spell as an auction cataloguer. Sunbeam's four-door sports saloons used to be 'coupés', and Rover's still are. As for that humble word 'tourer', this ought to imply a four-seater soft-top body with removable side-curtains. In British registration documents, however, it covers any type of openable style, which is why no self-respecting historian pays any heed to log-books. Nobody can object to the owner who invents an engine number because he can't find anything stamped on the unit beyond 'Drain every 300 miles', but when some County Council clerk misreads a chassis prefix and invents a new model, one gives up.

Had enough? Come with me on a voyage of discovery through the early years of a famous *marque*. Exports always bulked large, they made lorries as well as cars, had an aero-engine running in 1910, and added an aircraft department during World War I. They also raced, which means we have to keep an eye, not only on the works team, but on a whole army of obsolete behemoths ending their days in amateur and alien hands. Add the possibility of licence-production in at least four countries. And remember, *we* can't afford a computer.

We are car historians, so lorries and 'planes are a closed book to us, though we soon accustom ourselves to pastures new. But aircraft experts are obsessively meticulous, *ergo* what started as an innocent enquiry into the provenance of a 1917 fighting scout boils up into a free-for-all among the aeronautical pundits, who can't understand why an aeroplane ordered by a foreign government in 1930 wasn't officially delivered until 1938. More letters, not all of them in English, attend the exploration of some obscure army-vehicle trials in 1908 which our pet make won. By the time we discover that it was a three-tonner with shaft-drive five years before any such thing existed, we are wishing that it hadn't. Thirty letters later, our European correspondent informs us in embarrassingly copybook English that the whole affair is a mare's nest, since his country's General Staff decided that they were better off with horses after all. Never mind, the story is on file, and some day a misguided editor will ask us to do a piece on mechanisation in Ruritania. . . .

Maybe we're asking for trouble in such rarefied climes, but everyone understands racing. Not a hope. Primary sources contradict each other, nobody quotes cylinder capacities except the Americans, and when we have laboriously translated cubic inches into litres we find we've invented a few more one-offs. A subsequent search reveals that our mystery car ran in a 'stock' event, which means that theoretically it was something out of the catalogue. Maybe it was, but is it the '07 (with side valves in a T-head) or the '08 (with pushrods)? While we ponder this weighty problem, somebody else comes up with a bore and a stroke, in inches, of course. The litreage is right, but alas for our hopes, a long-dead stenographer has transformed an undersquare unit into something dramatically oversquare. As if this were not enough, the machine it ought to be was hill-climbing in Austria that June, and so can't have been racing in Massachusetts in the second week of July. Pursuit of this line of enquiry merely serves to convince us that all the people who saw the car in the United States were ufologists *manqués*. So there is only the foreign-licence game to cheer us up.

Here we start at a disadvantage. We are corresponding in four languages, and speak only two. The German-speakers come up with something that has too few PS for the period, a Hungarian tells you that five hundred chassis of unspecified type were assembled in Czarist Russia, and a letter from Spain agrees with the quantity, but asserts that the make is wrong. The Austrians say no, nothing of the sort was made in Franz Josef's domains before 1913, and then separate assembly lines existed in Vienna and Budapest. Gold at last? It seems so, especially when the

Veteran Car Club tells us that a member has just imported such a vehicle from Bosnia. The owner will let us see it, too, but it turns out to wear a dirty great plaque on the bulkhead which proves it wasn't made anywhere in the Dual Monarchy. Eight weeks later, all we have to show for our diligence is a file eight inches thick, crammed with negative information, plus a collection of muddy photographs too recondite for any editor. It may be terribly one-up to tell your public that the Type-A Mitsubishi was only a Tipo Due Fiat with a Japanese accent, and even more so to suggest (as an irreverent colleague once did) that an obvious NAG was really a Stoewer-Mathis, but neither will keep the wolf from the door.

And so it goes on. The last straight-eight Dodge was made in 1933, but there was one on show at Earl's Court in 1938. Some Abadals from Barcelona are Imperias from Liège, but none of them are Hispano-Suizas, even if the under-bonnet view isn't readily distinguishable from an 'Alfonso's'. Others were made in Liège, but not, it would seem, by Imperia. I have just discovered that about twenty years ago a certain manufacturer turned out two thousand more vehicles than the season's *national* total, and no amount of show-going will teach me just how many ways there are of personalising one's Capri. Somewhere in Fordland a computer is doubtless hard at work programming the 1975 range, but this omniscient brain is geared to Fords alone. Neither it nor its myrmidons have heard of Imperias, Abadals, or even Tipo Due Fiats. Historians have—which is why their job is something a computer can't do.

A Little Doesn't Go a Long Way

SANDY SKINNER

Anyone with half an eye can see that there has to be a market for a top-quality small car. Happily, half-eyed people tend to stick to more obvious ways of making money, like mass-producing family tin boxes or floating dodgy offshore-funds; so the gentleman's carriage on a reduced scale has stayed a specialist's playground.

The logic is obvious. Despite the determined efforts of governments all over the world to get their corporate paws on cash, a fair amount of the stuff has stuck with the people who earn or otherwise acquire it. Ferraris, Lambos, and Royces are saleable—in fact, there is probably much more of a waiting list for them than for more bourgeois transport. But while any of the £10,000 barouches are fine for a fast blast South to the sun, or even for a prestigious appearance outside the Royal Ballet, they're a bit much for less formal occasions. No matter how rich you are, filling the tank can get to be a bore, and as for trying to park twenty feet of Phantom V in Birmingham on a wet Wednesday—all right, the chauffeur copes. Think about driving a Daytona on the North Circular at half-past five, then.

So you need a small car. So go and buy one; there's plenty on the market. The trouble is that few are quite the thing in which one would wish to be seen. Engineers may have done a good job, but it's usually all too obvious that the cost accountants and value analysts followed on to do their foul work. There's the alternative of an expensively dolled-up version, black windows, coach-stripes and all, which proves the proverb about silk purses and sow's ears; or you can have a small, specialist sporting machine, ideal for anyone with well-cooled eardrums who lives close to the factory, and leaving room for a brace of dwarves travelling in pre-natal positions.

Perhaps the whole concept of a good small car is chimerical. The Vintage Sports Car Club in its corporate wisdom—and that's not something to argue with lightly—won't let anything under 2 litres into the Pomeroy Memorial Trophy event, which is designed to find the best all-round touring car. The theory is that a machine of less than $4\frac{1}{2}$ litres is a cyclecar and anything under two can hardly be dignified with the name of car at all. The fact that a D-Type Jaguar recently came within an ace of winning, and is about as suitable for touring as a rocket-propelled monocycle, must have been a slip; and anyway, they can always change the formula.

If, perish the blasphemous thought, the vscc is wrong, then it ought to be possible to sell something with the nippy handling and parkability of a small car, plus reasonable performance and the sort of finish and appointments which a gentleman would expect. It should be distinctive, and reflect its owner's taste, which is an adman's buzzphrase for shouldn't be too common, and can be fairly expensive. A decent head of steam is necessary, and a low noise level essential.

Anyone can see that this should be a commercial proposition. And any number of people have come unstuck trying.

Right back in the Veteran era, better meant bigger except to the Lanchester brothers, who had the wit to distinguish between personal transport and a scaled-down locomotive and built their

enchanting and idiosyncratic flat-twin to prove it. Over a period
the brilliant basic design was gradually shorn of its cleverest
features to produce something conventional which wouldn't
frighten the motor-buying public, and there you were—forty
horse power.

Much the same happened to Royce. A charming twin grew
into a 30-horse Six prone to crank breakage before it even got
out of the factory gates, and if the even bigger Ghost was a vast
improvement, its specific performance was sadly retrograde
compared with its little brother.

Of course, there were honourable exceptions. The most distinguished, almost inevitably, was Ettore Bugatti.

The story of how the Type 13 ran second to a monster Fiat
in the badly supported 1911 Grand Prix de France has been told
far too often, and is pretty irrelevant anyway. The rather odd
regulations made it necessary to run the Bugatti against an un-
distinguished mixed bag in the big car class, where its success
was mainly due to reliability and well-balanced design.

W. F. Bradley, doyen of correspondents, summed the car up
beautifully in *The Motor* in 1910, when he wrote 'The designer
of this little car has, indeed, made no attempt to compete with the
low-priced popular models already on the market, the price for
the Bugatti being higher than any other car of equal horse-
power offered to the public. The reason is that the new production
stands in a class by itself. Mr Bugatti . . . has sought to produce
what may be termed the motorcar pony, but a pony that is fit to
stand comparison with the most costly product of the best
factories. . . .' Apart from the curious concept of a factory-built
pony, an excellent summing-up of the first Pur-sang.

Naturally, it was very expensive. The Motor Car Index quoted
the UK price in 1909 as £350, a figure which must be treated with
considerable reserve if only because production started in 1910.
With a really civilized body, £600 was probably nearer the
mark, and various British authorities wondered publicly if it
could possibly be worth the price or if the whole affair was an
Italo/Germano/Gallic joke in rather poor taste.

In fact, the little Bug wasn't such a bad bargain. You didn't
get much metal for your money, but you got plenty of top-class

engineering. Tyre costs were a fraction of those on a monster, and the car was so well made that maintenance costs could be expected to be low. And, of course, it did forty to the gallon.

Buyers were unlikely to be worried by such considerations. Nearly 350 discriminating people bought themselves a Type 13 before the Kaiser war, and laid the foundations of the Bugatti cult. They got a startling combination of performance and refinement, the sort of delicacy of control that had never existed before, and first-class road manners. Reading the contemporary 'impressions'—which are far too vague to be called road tests— the most striking point is the way that high speed handling and stability are stressed at a time when most people were obsessed with top gear flexibility and a smooth ride. Le Patron had started something big.

After the war, Bugatti went off at a slight tangent. The Type 13 grew up into something larger and/or fiercer, and eight cylinders went into production and culminated in the monstrous—in every sense of the word—Royale. Numerically the Type 13 was reasonably successful, particularly considering the restricted market of the time, but it would be hard to say how profitable it was. Ettore's finances were always obscure; all that is known for certain is that while there was always money for wine and bloodstock at Molsheim, there were occasional problems with the electricity bill.

While Bugatti's impressive, advanced, and dubiously practical aero-engines spread his design philosophy, few people seemed keen on taking up the idea of the superlative small car. Perhaps the best-known effort was by Lionel Martin, who was so impressed that he decided to build a British equivalent; the quality was there all right, but it's a pity he went in for side-valves.

In France the honoured S. A. des Anciens Etablissements Secqueville-Hoyau, sub-contractors to the aviation industry, alleged manufacturers of Bugatti aero-engine bits, and incurable optimists, decided to have a go. They produced a particularly well-engineered 10 h.p. model with an unusual arrangement of inclined side valves, and a reasonable chassis specification. Electric starting was standard, very clever for a small car in 1919, and the radiator would have been familiar to Henry Royce.

Advertisements of the time featured an enchanting miniature coupé de ville, and *Light Car and Cyclecar*, better attuned to the barbarities of the British cyclecar, went into raptures over the quality.

With a touring body, it cost £595. You could have three Morris Cowleys for the money, or even a Frazer Nash plus a Morris for basic transport when all the chains had dropped off. At least one Secqueville-Hoyau was sold in England, since Bunty Scott-Moncrieff told me that he had driven one and thought it was a foul little car; perhaps it was a little down on steam compared with his blown Mercedes. The firm folded in 1924.

When the price war of the 'twenties was followed by a world slump, it might have been reasonable to assume that most designers would have concentrated on simplicity and cost-cutting. Most of them did, but Tim Ashcroft of Lagonda was one of those disagreeing.

Lagonda in the 'thirties probably held a record for making less money from more model types than anyone else. The Vintage 2-litre had quietly vanished, but by 1934 the 3-litre, 3½-litre, 4½-litre, and Crossley-engined 16/80 were all available. Ashcroft apparently felt this range needed extending, and produced a small car having nothing in common with any other model.

The Rapier must have been expensive on tooling. The chassis was straightforward enough, with excellent brakes and a pre-selector gearbox; but the engine was a little jewel. Instead of the slightly agricultural pushrods of the bigger Lags, it used twin overhead camshafts and a massive crank assembly. Safe revs. were 6,000, which was just as well because the car in general and engine in particular were overweight, making a low final drive ratio essential. The story goes that the motor was originally to be in light alloy, and that iron was substituted at a pre-prototype stage.

Lagonda was wedded to the original Bugatti concept of a top-quality small car as opposed to a baby racer. To make it quite clear that they were staying out of competition, the engine was built with the odd capacity of 1104 c.c., which at least eliminated the embarrassment of taking on Fred Dixon's Rileys.

The Rapier appeared at the 1933 Motor Show, and followed normal British motor industry practice by getting into production ten months later. In 1935 Lagonda suffered one of its periodic attacks of insolvency, and set an unusual record by becoming the only firm to date to have won at Le Mans while in the hands of a Receiver. New management decided to concentrate on developing the $4\frac{1}{2}$, so Ashcroft moved down the road to Hammersmith to build the Rapier. The radiator badge was changed and, significantly, the capacity was reduced to within the 1100 c.c. limit.

Commercially, neither firm did too badly. About 350 cars were built, perhaps 200 or so by Lagondas and the rest in a sporadic sort of way up to the outbreak of the war. Lord de Clifford tweaked and raced 'De Clifford Specials', and the standard cars carried a good range of pretty coachwork at not outrageous prices. It was, and is, a very pleasant car.

Somehow the Rapier was one of those models everyone praised and not enough people bought. The 1934 prices of £368 for a tourer, going up to £408 for a foursome coupé, weren't bad when a Magnette could cost close on £400, and offered nothing like the refinement; of course, you could always have a Wolseley Hornet for under £200, but no potential Rapier buyer would have looked twice at a Hornet anyway. From the competition angle, its weight was against it; commercially, the answer is probably that it's hard to sell good engineering. A tart-trap body by SS draped over sadly agricultural Standard components had more sex-appeal than all Lagonda's camshafts.

The beautiful engine only came into its own after the war. Paul Emery and Daniel Richmond both applied two-stage supercharge and extracted phenomenal outputs, the Emery car in particular being a formidable competitor in immediately post-war voiturette racing. Lightened, tuned, bored-out and generally dealt-with Rapiers are a force in Vintage racing, but they mostly cant catch the hot Rileys. Which sounds like a repeat of an old story.

Motoring history, like all history, goes round in circles. After both world wars a mechanically-minded, car-starved populace would buy anything that rolled. Certainly post-1945, quality wasn't a particularly fashionable concept; if the makers had remembered to screw on all the more vital bits, however insecurely, you didn't complain. Britain was well into the 'fifties before the scene brightened.

Two developments helped the specialist builder; welded tubular frames, which permitted enterprising chassis design, and glass-fibre coachwork, which made short production runs economic. The result was a flood of some of the nastiest devices seen since the 1919 cyclecar boom.

Most designers went on a light weight jag; since on the whole they didn't know what they were doing, the resulting confections fell to bits with great and awful regularity. Glass-fibre gives plenty of scope for the compound curve, resulting in bodies looking like the product of irregular liaison between a Mighty Wurlitzer and a barrage balloon—they tended to be painted post-operative pink, too. Several firms prospered making advanced small cars of very high performance, but they should really have included the list of names of your local friendly welders in the instruction book. And standards of trim and finish varied from dire to atrocious.

The man who stood out from the mob of exponents of bad taste and erratic manufacture was David Ogle. Like Bugatti, he applied design sense and determination to a wide range of interests; unlike Bugatti, he succeeded in building a team which survives him to carry on his work.

Ogle made his name in the 'fifties designing for the radio industry, which was leaving the bakelite coffin stage and aiming for effective form and function. David Ogle Associates carried out some impressive work from a little studio in Stevenage, but Ogle was determined to try his hand at cars. The first product from the new Letchworth base was a variation on the Riley 1.5 which wasn't anything to get excited about. It looked all right by the standards of the time, it had quite a clever rear suspension and it cost rather a lot. Four were built, but it was never developed because Ogle had had a much better idea.

The Mini-Cooper was new, and for all its mechanical virtues still looked like any other Min. Ogle was determined to use it as the basis of a baby GT car which would offer discriminating customers the sort of appointments they enjoyed in their Ferrari or Aston, but would increase their chances of finding a parking space. David Ogle Ltd. was formed, with John Ogier and Sir John Whitmore, both competition enthusiasts, on the board.

Ogle took the floor pan and scuttle of the Mini and reinforced these with a massive bulkhead assembly, deep steel sills, and a square tube rear structure to form a hefty chassis accepting Mini subframes. The body simply kept the wet out, and contributed no significant stiffness to the structure. Unfortunately, BMC was not particularly impressed. Ogles were unable to buy the bits they needed at a manufacturer's price, making it necessary to offer the car as a 'conversion' to an existing Mini. The plot was for a customer to buy a Cooper, keep it six months to avoid purchase tax problems, and then hand it over. The tin top-hamper was chopped off, and he received an Ogle in exchange.

The body was the attractive part. An extended nose killed the 'boxiness' of the original, and gave vastly improved aero-dynamics. The sleek little two-seater coupé ended in a bumble-bee tail, with a big, curved rear window. Inside, wind-up windows replaced the Longbridge horrors, and instrumentation well up to private aircraft standards lived in a binnacle ahead of the driver. Low, comfortable seats were used, and trim was of a very high standard. Leg room was adequate for six-footers, and luggage space wasn't too bad.

Ogle was determined to do the thing properly. Detail develop-ment was continuous, and improvements were fitted retro-spectively to customer's cars—a pleasant contrast to most specialist manufacturers, who tend to lose interest very sharply the moment the cheque has been cashed. He insisted on, and got, top quality workmanship. Naturally, intelligent use was made of production parts. The screen was Riley 1.5, the rear lights Rootes, and the door handles Auntie Rover. But clever design produced a unified whole.

All this cost the happy owner £550, which sounds reasonable until you add in £640 for the Cooper. You could buy a lot of car for £1,190 in 1962; the MGA coupé, with more engine but sur-prisingly similar accommodation and performance, cost £50 less and was available from stock. Worst of all, the Ogle may have been too cheap. The firm lost money on every car they sold— John Ogier used to claim that it would have been cheaper to give

£300 to every potential buyer and tell them to go away, thus neatly trebling the alleged unit loss on vintage Astons, while according to Tom Karen, now Managing Director, it was underpriced from the point of view of sales policy. 'If we'd slapped on another £500, the typical buyer would have bought it just the same, and he'd have felt he had something very special indeed.'

Part of the trouble was the problem and cost of obtaining chassis parts. This might have been easier after 100 cars had been built, but David Ogle's tragic death in a car crash intervened. Production stopped in 1964, with 66 cars complete.

Happily, the design team carried on. The Ogle-bodied Daimler SP250 was a sensation at the 1962 Motor Show, and the body design was developed for the Scimitar. Quite apart from the large amount of design and prototype work for Reliants, Ogle continued to handle car design for other organisations, the most recent product being a staggeringly handsome special body on a DBS Aston chassis for the 1971 Montreal Motor Show.

More than ten years after its birth, the little Ogle is still a superb road car. The lines have completely failed to date—the sure sign of good design. Most of the survivors have been uprated with Cooper S mechanicals, and in this form well over 100 m.p.h. is on tap, with superb handling and braking. Noise level is acceptable, and if the car shows its age in such details as the absence of really effective ventilation and demisting, these can always be modified. And there can be very few small cars of the period which are still certain crowd-pullers parked at the kerb.

So we're back on the old question; why can't you sell a top-quality small car? Cost may be against them, but if an Italian footroaster is saleable, and presumably profitable, at £10,000 plus, why not a scaled-down British equivalent at perhaps a fifth of the figure? It could be that the Company Secretary won't believe that anything that small can cost so much, or it could be the sort of snobbery which forced the best London barometer makers to sign their work with cod-Italian names. Perhaps it's pure conspicuous consumption; bigger has to be better. Anyway, it's a pity.

GREAT NOVELTY

For Sale. A valuable patent and great novelty. A comfortable small car called the Bernon-Morelle which is convertible into two motor cycles; it takes to pieces and can be stored in a cupboard. No garage required. Having two independant engines, if one breaks down you come home with the other. Full particulars, Bernon-Morelle, 58 Westbourne Grove, London, W.
Advert in trade journal, Dec. 1923

The tyre manufacturer supplies the tube and the cover. The quantity of compressed air necessary to make the tyre pneumatic is not supplied by the tyre maker. *It is the duty of the tyre user to supply and maintain the correct air pressure.*
Tyres, a book for Armstrong-Siddeley owners, 1934
This perhaps confirms what one has always thought about Armstrong-Siddeley owners. Andrew Maclagan

CLEVER

Morris Mini-Cooper . . . high ratio back axle. Cars for Sale in 'Autocar'

In Mitigation

PATRICK MACNAGHTEN

One of the many deficiencies of my education was that I was not brought up to be in awe of policemen. Respect for the Law, yes—awe of policemen, no. Not that our local policeman in the Devonshire village in which I spent my childhood was an awe-inspiring figure. A large, jovial man much given to flexing at the knees, he could often be found in our kitchen, wiping a head of beer from his moustache with the back of an appreciative hand. I regarded him as a sort of supernumerary manservant like the chauffeur and the gardener. One must be polite and friendly but nobody ever suggested that one ought to be in awe. Awe was an emotion reserved for the gardener who would brandish a hoe in a terrifying manner whenever my tricycle did a three-wheel drift round a corner of his newly-raked gravel.

In those happy far-off days one only dimly comprehended that the police were the dedicated ruthless enemies of the motorist. It was, of course, common knowledge that RAC men would not salute when there were police traps about but I was quite incapable of associating 'the police' with our own friendly constable. Indeed, I always hoped that the RAC men would fail to salute, but of course they never did. I was only driving by proxy then, so I could afford to take a detached view.

When, round about my ninth birthday, I first ventured on to the public roads, loosely in control of a car, I always first took care to ascertain the whereabouts of my friend the policeman, and to go the other way. But this evasion was delicacy on my part, not fear. I just did not want to put my friend in an embarrassing position. I also was careful to take the parson with me, to lend an air of respectability to the whole enterprise. Even at that tender age I think I must have had a flair for crime. Besides, he owned the car.

On our little jaunts we never did meet the policeman, tactful and understanding man that he was. But we took no chances. My exploits took place on a long, open stretch of road laid by the Romans and untouched since, where anything blue could have been seen for miles. Up and down I would drive, extracting the last ounce of urge from the parson's car, which was an 11.9 h.p. Citroën with an open touring body. It was elderly even then, and gifted with no great performance. A stayer, not a flyer. But it gave me more innocent (well, fairly innocent) fun than anything I have driven since. The highlight came one day when, in ideal conditions of wind and tide, the speedometer momentarily indicated eighty. I yelled with excitement and the parson yelled too—but his motivation was apprehension. It was the chauffeur who pricked that particular bubble. A stern solemn man, quite unlike the merry policeman, he took a gloomy pleasure in pointing out that the speedometer was calibrated in kilometres. It was, I suppose, the first great disillusionment of my life.

But it was disillusionment only with things mechanical. It had not then occurred to me that there could possibly be anything sinister about a body of men who included my amiable friend among their number.

Nor did my first brush with the Law do much to tarnish the image. It happened some three days after I obtained my first driving licence. I was driving my mother's Fiat Balilla and having a terrific dice with a Lancia Augusta when I was stopped by a policeman who enquired whether one so young ought to be driving at all, let alone at that outrageous speed. Proudly I flourished my brand new licence. And in those days licences were impressive documents, bound in hardback like Mr Batsford does. The policeman scrutinised it closely until my companion leaned across me and said 'Oh do hurry up. We're having a tremendous race with that Lancia.'

Innocent as I was, I knew enough to realize that that was no way to address the Law. My companion, I may say, did not end his life chained to the wall of some foetid dungeon, but in fact went on to be a most successful and famous playwright. But he never writes thrillers. He doesn't know enough about the police.

I waited apprehensively but the policeman just handed me back my licence and laughed. Image still untarnished.

During the war I became a little less naïve and I fought the Military Police with far more enthusiasm than I fought the enemy. But they, of course, were not blue policemen—really a rather pathetic imitation. The years of 'Yes, Officer, No, Officer' accompanied by the ingratiating smile were still hidden in the future.

A few blots appeared on my escutcheon from time to time, usually connected with speed limits, but the policemen concerned booked me more in sorrow than in anger. Poor fellows, they have an unpleasant job to do, was more or less my attitude. Let us not be too hard on them. I was sure that my friends who complained of being victimised by the police had only themselves to blame. 'You're too truculent,' I would say. 'No wonder these poor policemen get angry. You should be polite. Try to remember that they are the servants of the public and treat them accordingly.' I have since learned that it makes not the slightest difference. If anything, rather the reverse. The policeman who charged me with some trifling infringement of some absurd speed limit did so in spite of the fact that when asked for my address I gave it care of a judge with whom I was staying. In spite of or because of?

The scales finally fell from my eyes over that monstrous affair when a policeman on a motorcycle (they're always the worst) nipped out from behind a lorry which I had just overtaken and accused me of driving at some ridiculous speed. 'Why don't you use these?' he demanded, clouting my wing mirror. 'Oh I do, Officer, I do,' I replied soothingly.

'In that case you must have seen me behind you.'

'What, tucked in behind that great lorry?'

'Don't argue. You saw me all right. And you deliberately accelerated. Trying to take the mickey out of the Law, that's what you're up to.'

'Officer, I assure you—' I began. But it was no good. Two quid.

I was still smarting under the grave injustice of it all when I was driving with a friend through a small town. The car was a new MG and my friend was not unnaturally keen to see how it would go. 'See how fast you can take that corner,' he suggested. The corner in question was fairly tight, with the camber sloping the wrong way, but one could see round it and nothing was coming the other way. In fact the only car in sight was a grey Austin which was following us out of the town. A quick nip down to third, plenty of throttle, shave the offside apex of the corner, just a suspicion of reverse lock, and away we went, passing the derestriction sign at an accelerating eighty-five. We got behind a slow lorry after that and we were trundling along at about twenty miles an hour, unable to overtake, when the grey Austin came pounding up, lights flashing, siren wailing.

'It's a blond policeman,' said my friend. 'What?' 'A fair cop. Ha ha.'

Actually there were two of them but I was far too agitated to notice the colour of their hair. It was the colour of their car which rivetted my attention. A *grey* police car! Of all the dastardly, unsporting, mean, shabby tricks. I was so struck all of a heap that I dropped my glove from nerveless fingers. The junior inquisitor obligingly picked it up.

'Oh thank you, Officer. Most kind of you. Thank you very much indeed.'

'Licence please,' said the senior inquisitor. I fumbled in my pocket and dropped the other glove. The junior inquisitor picked it up.

'Oh thank you again, Officer. Really, you are most obliging.'

'Insurance please,' said the senior inquisitor. I dived to the pocket of the car and in doing so happened to drop a glove. But this time I put my foot on it. I really couldn't go through all that again. Unfortunately the junior inquisitor was too quick for me. I apologised, of course, and, as I pointed out at the time, a new finger nail would no doubt grow to replace the shattered one.

When the dust had settled and the senior inquisitor had uttered his awful warning I felt sufficiently restored to ask him whether he thought the local magistrate would content himself with a caution. The inquisitors exchanged smiles. At least, I think the junior inquisitor was smiling. It was difficult to tell as he had his finger in his mouth at the time.

'Hot on speeding, his worship is.'

'Well if he fines me I shall only pay on one condition.'

The policemen drew a little closer, and their demeanour stiffened. Evidently they were not used to bargaining with the criminal classes.

'I'll only pay it if you promise to use the money for painting your car black.'

I would not like to give the impression that I go in fear of the police, certainly not when they are on foot. I must admit that a shiver runs down my spine when I see a gang of them lurking in a car in a side street. They may be simply listening to pop music on the radio but to me it always seems that they are menacing and sinister, up to no good. But when I meet one in the street I can look him straight in the cold fish-like eye with any man. Not for me the nervous glance over the shoulder, the swift nipping down an alleyway when one looms up. (The verb 'loom' might have been invented specially for policemen.) In fact only the other day I felt bold enough to rebuke one. I was waiting dutifully for the lights to change at a pedestrian crossing— being uncarred at the time—when a policeman slipped through the traffic towards me. 'You are setting me a bad example,' I said sternly. 'Crossing against the lights.'

'Oh well,' he said. I went on my way rejoicing, my head held high and a spring in my step.

But I must confess that it was not ever thus. I was once driving down the Sidcup Bypass, off on a jolly jaunt to Monte Carlo when suddenly out of the darkness there boomed a resonant voice. 'That car with the rally plates. You are exceeding the speed limit, as you very well know.'

A policeman looming in the flesh is one thing. A policeman booming, disembodied, is quite another. At the terrifying sound of the Voice of Doom I experienced, after the first wild shock of panic, the deepest humiliation of a lifetime of shame. It even made me slow down.

But I must be fair. As long as they leave me alone I think the police do a fine job harrying miscreant motorists. Unfortunately they seem to lack discrimination. A woman I know told me that she had covered the length of M.1 in an incredibly—literally incredibly—short time. 'And we had a picnic on the way. There's a splendid lay-by, stretches for miles.'

Now, if I had halted for a light luncheon on the hard shoulder of a motorway I should undoubtedly have been clapped in irons. Rightly so, too. But some people are immune, like my friend who has the strange misconception that the police will never hound a professional driver. After dining out he always puts his wife in the back of the car and drives serenely home wearing a chauffeur's cap. And the ridiculous thing is that nothing has ever happened to shatter this dream world of his. If I ever dared to don a chauffeur's cap I would immediately get done for impersonation or misrepresentation or fraudulent conversion or something. No, I have to face the fact. I am singled out for persecution. Though even I have my moments. I was once struggling to park a rather decrepit and very ancient Rolls Royce when a policeman held up the traffic for me. . . .

It was to restore my self-esteem after the Sidcup Incident that I acquired this elderly Rolls Royce, a gentle docile creature with an air of faded grandeur like a retired butler gone at the knees. One day this splendid old vehicle glided to a halt (voluntary) and, putting about half a ton of mascot in my pocket, I went about my business. When I returned the car had gone. Seeing my evident distress, a sympathetic taxi driver suggested that it had been towed away by the police. 'I bet it was a good car. The copper on this beat's a communist and he only takes Rollses and Bentleys.'

His surmise proved correct, but the Rape of the Rolls had not been easily accomplished. The gallant old car had put up a courageous fight and I think they must have used a crowbar to force down the window. In doing so they had sheared the winding mechanism and I had enormous fun claiming against them. I won in the end but it was a Pyrrhic victory because by that time I had sold the car, its window shored up with a folded cigarette packet.

Shortly afterwards I was holding forth on the iniquities of the police to the proprietor of a garage situated beside a dual carriage-way on the outskirts of London. (I would like to be more specific but we criminals have to cover our tracks.)

'Of course they have a difficult job,' he said. 'For instance there's a forty limit on this stretch of road and they find it impossible to enforce. The local inspector told me they've had to give up trying.'

Three days later I drove down that road at eleven o'clock at night. It was raining hard and there was no traffic except me and one car behind me. I was travelling at a sedate sixty miles an hour when this car suddenly swung out and started flashing blue lights. I need not give the squalid details. Suffice to say that a few weeks later I received a document commanding me to send ten pounds to a nearby Court. Needless to say, this document was phrased in peremptory terms, with never a 'please' or a 'would you mind' in its whole turgid length.

I sent off my cheque by return of post and departed thankfully for the Continent, where I had a carefree holiday—or as carefree a holiday as a man can have when he has just been mulcted of ten pounds. It was not until I was returning through Swizerland that I again fell into the hands of the police, due to some trivial infringement of a speed limit. I had always previously conducted my defence in my native tongue and I saw no reason to alter the habit of a lifetime. So when the *agent* asked me if I understood French I replied firmly 'Nong'. But he was, like all policemen, a tenacious man. With great artistic skill he mimed my misdeeds. Unfortunately the makers of the car I was driving had thought-lessly marked kilometres as well as miles on the speedometer face and this made the man's task easier. When he pointed to the figures with his great spatulate thumb I realized that the game was up. Useless to go on shaking my head and spreading my hands in simulated incomprehension. As soon as he saw that I was defeated the policeman moved in for the kill. '20 francs', he wrote in his notebook and thrust it under my nose. I was agreeably surprised and paid up without further ado. He gave me a receipt and while he was writing it out I rehearsed a little speech.

'Thank you,' I said in faultless French. 'It's a lot cheaper than in England.'

Of course that man ought to have been an actor. I have never seen a face register astonishment speedily followed by indignation so unmistakably. Then he broke into a great bellow of laughter. All the same I was relieved to cross the frontier some half hour later.

I arrived home about midnight and was still asleep at eight o'clock next morning when the bell started pealing. Hastily snatching up a dressing gown I went to obey its summons. On the step was standing a large policeman, large even by police standards. I know that the first signs of old age are when you notice that they're getting very young men into the Force these days, but I think I must be gifted with eternal youth. All policemen look the same to me—stern, granite-faced and ageless. This particular specimen went through my details of identification like one intoning a liturgy. Then, 'I have a warrant for your arrest,' he added chattily.

'A warrant? For me?' I stammered.

' 'Sright. Non-payment of fine of ten pounds. You'd best come along o' me.'

The idea of being marched up the street with gyves upon my wrists, like the late Eugene Aram, did not appeal. Besides, I hadn't had breakfast.

'I shall do nothing of the sort. I paid the fine by cheque a month ago. If the magistrate has embezzled it that's none of my business.'

This spirited defence shook the policeman but he quickly rallied.

'No cheque received,' he said stubbornly. But I pressed home my advantage.

'As soon as the banks open I will telephone and find out if the cheque has been passed through my account. And if it has I shall proceed against you for wrongful arrest. Against the magistrate too, of course, but particularly against you.'

Under this onslaught he wilted visibly. But training told.

'Delaying tactics won't do you no good. Charge of obstructing the Law, I wouldn't be surprised.'

We glared at one another. Then I decided to make a concession.

'If you like I'll show you the cheque-stub,' I offered. 'I've got it handy.'

The effect was extraordinary. He didn't actually smile, granite not being constructed to facilitate smiling, but he softened perceptibly.

'So you really did send it?' he asked surprised. 'You're not just making it up?'

He winced as he received the full blast of one of my looks. All the same, he was still cautious.

'The cheque-stub isn't evidence.'

'I know that. But if the cheque's been through the bank that is.' There was still some fight left in him.

'And what if it hasn't?' he enquired. I thought for one glorious moment that he was going to add 'pray?' but he didn't.

'In that case I'll give you another one.'

'Oh you will? Well, that's all right then. Save a lot of trouble.'

'Yes.'

'Look,' he said. 'Meet me at the Police Station. Say ten o'clock.

But meet me outside. If you put your nose inside they'll lock you up. Ha ha.'

'Ha ha.'

My Bank Manager, who has a warped sense of humour, laughed heartily when I rang him up.

'No, it hasn't been presented,' he said. 'Will you take my word for it or shall I send you a statement to Wormwood Scrubs?'

With my collar turned up and my hat pulled down over my dark glasses I hovered furtively outside the Police Station. Dead on ten the policeman emerged and took my cheque. Like the Bank Manager, he seemed to find the whole thing funny.

And that—up to the time of going to Press, of course—was my last Inquisition. Oh no, there was one more. I was stopped by a motor cycle policeman the other day.

'You were doing eighty-five,' he announced.

'Oh was I? Was I really? Well, yes, actually I suppose I may have been doing a shade over seventy.'

Suddenly it struck me that there was something familiar about the man. Surely I had seen that round jolly face and that walrus moustache before? When he flexed his knees I was certain.

'You weren't by any chance the village constable in Devonshire thirty years ago were you?' I asked.

'Thirty years ago I was in my cradle in Huddersfield.'

'Then was it your father? Or your grandfather? A great-uncle perhaps?'

But he did not find the conversation gripping.

'No,' he said shortly. Then he turned aside and remounted his motor cycle. I let out a sigh of relief. But I was even more certain that he was the reincarnation of my old friend. Such tolerance is rare, and the similarity of appearance was so great as almost to rule out coincidence. I was nearly sure and when he uttered his parting words I was convinced. Across the years came the echo of that well-loved voice.

'You want to watch it, squire.'

Modern Times

Reflections on the Grand Prix scene

DAVID HODGES

It seems to be fashionable in some quarters to denigrate just about everything to do with modern Grands Prix—cars, races, drivers—with a persistent 'fings ain't what they used to be' inference. The old days were the good days is the theme, to the point that it is presented as established fact.

This attitude was perhaps understandable in the late 1950s—after all, a well-ordered and understood state of affairs was rather rudely upset by an unlikely bunch of down-to-earth practical men. Cooper and Climax, Brabham and Surbiton, was an unpalatable collection of names to observers weaned on the Greats. The Coopers did not work from high-flown principles, and nor did Jack, grafting away on the then hardly-appreciated art of tuning his car for circuits, the fire-pump background of the power unit was not aristocratic, the green and white cars did not look imposing. But the Coopers and Brabham (let's not forget Jack's part in the Cooper Grand Prix story) achieved a great deal: they completely changed the face of Grand Prix racing. And while Bugatti, Colombo, Jano, the Maserati brothers, Uhlenhaut—many illustrious men, in their varying ways—advanced the application of the motor car to racing, they did less than that.

Recognition of the Cooper achievement was grudging, and a little resentment seems to have lingered, to be echoed in querulous belittlings through to the years of the 3-litre Formula. Yet it seems quite possible that we may come to look back on the mature years of the 3-litre Formula as a golden era. True, we won't be comparing like with like any more than the nagging critics of everything modern about racing, for times change. But, happily, Grand Prix racing has broadly kept pace with the times—it has not been struggling to recover lost appeal, as have some of the tradition-bound, and declining, sports to which its critics are perhaps attuned?

This is not to deny that many past racing cars were splendid machines, or to belittle the achievements of great drivers. A great deal of course hinges on intangibles, on impressions rather than facts. But as impressions of past eras all too often seem to be represented as facts, there is some very relevant hard evidence which might be admitted to temper nostalgia?

If the editor can bear the sight of a table in a *Bedside Book*, it is a useful device for comparing the sizes of cars, and can give an idea of their potential, minimal yardsticks for relating them in perspective. The examples are representative of periods generally agreed to have been high water marks in Grand Prix history, and of recent history. They are taken from four of the six formulae preceding the 3-litre Formula (thus the 2-litre, 1953–54, and 1½-litre, 1961–65, Grands Prix are ignored; both perhaps are more memorable for drivers, especially Ascari and Clark, than for machines).

	Auto Union C-type	Mercedes-Benz W125	Mercedes-Benz W163	Alfa Romeo 159	BRM T15 (Mk II)	Mercedes-Benz W196	Maserati 250F	Lotus 49B	Ferrari 312B
Wheelbase (inches)	110	110	107	98	91	87	87	95	94
Track, front/rear (inches)	56/56	58/55	58/55	50/54	52/51	52/53	50/49	60/61	60/61
Max. power (b.h.p.)	520	645	480	425	485	290	270	420	460
Weight (pounds)	1,810	1,640	1,970	1,710	1,625	1,430	1,380	1,180	1,200

The cars have not been selected to make a case one way or another, and by common consent most are 'classics', or will one day be regarded as classics. They range from extreme examples of the muscle-bound German machines of the mid-thirties, through an example of German science at the end of that decade, and the last supercharged cars.

Comparisons are always interesting, and at face value these undermine some cherished beliefs. Have our rheumy old eyes been deceiving us? On this basic dimensional evidence we should perhaps think of the classic $2\frac{1}{2}$-litre front-engined cars as roller skates! Rough and ready power/weight ratios do not flatter them, either, and very much to the point they equate a latter-day Ferrari very closely with those awesome German cars of 1937.

Now, while that Ferrari flat-12 produced more sheer b.h.p. than any other engines on the 1970 grids, the other 12s and the V.8s were not far behind (the championship actually fell to a Cosworth V.8-engined car). The gulf between extremes on grids in the past—between Mercedes and Bugattis in the 1930s, Alfas and Gordinis in the 1950s, for example—just did not exist through the 1960s into the present decade. Well into the 1950s, remember, some constructors were producing cars with front-rank pretensions which in appearance and specification might have come fresh off the drawing boards of voiturette designers in the 1930s. Happily, in modern Grand Prix racing there is no room for the really second-rate. . . .

But, urges nostalgia, at least almost to the end of the 1950s cars were recognizably in a direct line of succession, they could be directly related to what had gone before, at least back to Dieppe in 1912; now the noble line of GP cars has been reduced to a collection of ugly projectiles, rear-engined specials thrown together by a band of mad plumbers. Well, beauty is in the eye of the beholder, and much depends on whether one is prepared to look more than skin-deep. There is surely no virtue in a car being front-engined, and inefficient? In terms of fundamental efficiency, and hence fundamental mechanical beauty, that W125 was just not in the same class as the 312B, which no more than properly reflects a gap of over thirty years (and those midterm 2½-litre cars come out pretty poorly again). It is sometimes suggested that the appearance of the current generation of formula cars would be enhanced if the wheels were enclosed; the probable result of this can be seen in action, in the present generation of sports-racing cars. Now they *do* look alike, do they not?

As for the occasional denigratory use of 'special', provided cars are special, what pray is wrong with a gridful of 'Specials'? Try a dictionary definition, rather than motor racing jargon usage, wherein 'special' seems to have a tatty backyard connotation. What have all Grand Prix Mercedes been but specials, and did not the first Vanwall proclaim that it was the Vanwall Special?

Robin Herd gave the critics a handy round of ammunition in his admittedly apt reference to the British Standard Grand Prix car, but in truth there was more variety on the 1970 grids than there was in 1956, in appearance and in mechanical make-up, despite the too-common bought-out engines and transmissions. But if Messrs Duckworth and Hewland produced equipment which did the job, was it a flaw in racing that it should have been used? Had comparable proprietory equipment been available to constructors in earlier decades, it seems unlikely that it would have been spurned!

There is indeed a ring to some of the great names of the past. One suspects that 'Ford' still sounds nasty to some people, and that they cannot bring themselves to think of Cosworth of mundane Northampton in the same way they once did of those glorified Italian speed shops which turned out exquisite pieces of machinery, apparently the end-products of native artistry. The blinkers are on again, for Ford's role has not been simply to have their name cast onto Grand Prix engines for all to see, and Cosworth engines have always been effective racing units, which is more than can be said for some past Italian engines!

With the best will in the world, we are not going to see the great and honourable names from history return to the Grands Prix, unless regulations so way out that they force constructors to build 250F replicas are introduced, or more possibly there is a move to frame regulations around production-based components. For so long as it remains a pure racing class, Grand Prix

racing is too far removed from the everyday motoring world
for it to be a forcing ground for general motoring development. In detail it can contribute to general automotive technology; more broadly, 'the racing car of today is the production
car of tomorrow' theme once dear to motoring writers is surely
dead? Competition breeding with direct application is now the
province of other sporting classes—rallying can throw up developments which will benefit the average family-box driver
within a year, whereas he might have to wait a decade for a
Grand Prix development to work through the pipeline to the
traffic jams.

For broad justification there is prestige, and plain vulgar
advertising. In image-changing terms, the Ford investment in
Grands Prix must be one of the great advertising success stories of
our time, and a similar result could hardly have been achieved
through a similar expenditure on conventional product advertising.

At an international level, in this day and age when objects can
be shot into outer space, there are better ways of demonstrating
national technological prowess than were available to Germany
in the 1930s.

Advertising, of the Italian automotive industry or cigarettes,
puts into motor racing the hard cash which is essential to its
continuation at an advanced level. So let's grin and bear cars
painted like cigarette packets (and pause to reflect that this is
better than swastikas painted on tails, or recall that had the one-
time requirement that cars be painted in the national colours of
their entrants been adhered to, there would have been an awful
monotony of green in recent years!). And let us spare only a
passing shudder at the 1972 arrival of the Grand Prix Special,
in name as in every other respect—after all the only currency
thereby debased was that of tradition, one we should be very
wary of in a sport which is supposed to be in tune with all times!

A short list of outstanding or significant cars can easily be
produced—everybody has their own ideas of those which were
outstanding in conception, performance or impression left
behind. In this it is realistic to assume that the early Monaco
Grands Prix were the first which in all respects would be recog-

nizable to a modern enthusiast with absolutely no knowledge
of racing history—a supposition which can be upheld if the 1924
Lyon race is agreed to be the last of the great Grands Prix
according to the original conception, and the intervening period
as the Grand Prix dark age.

From the 1930s one Italian and three or four German cars are
automatic selections, the Alfa Romeo Tipo B, the Mercedes W25
because it introduced a new era, the W163 and W165 which
were the technical culmination of a breed spawned to advertise
something infinitely more evil than tobacco, and an Auto
Union-C type perhaps, because it was most successful as well as
showing clearly the way ahead.

'*As the last seconds tick away all eyes are on the starter's flag.*'

From the last supercharged period, a supercharged car and an
unsupercharged car, the Alfa Romeo 158/159 and the unblown
Ferrari which eventually conquered it (in dispassionate retrospect
1951 was surely the only worthwhile year of that formula?).
No, not the BRM—too much of its reputation hangs on whimsy
about smells and sounds, and those on precious few occasions
before it became ineligible for front-line racing; perhaps the old

Mercedes équipe could have persuaded it to work, perhaps Bourne could today, but in the 1950s they couldn't, and facts are facts (the first V.12 Matra also made a lot of exhilarating noise, but nobody is going to recall it as a great car because it was noisy and didn't work very well).

Moving on, the Mercedes-Benz W196 was by any standards an outstanding car, and incidentally as surely built for advertising purposes as was, say, its 1908 Mercedes forerunner. The rather rudimentary (by direct comparison) Maserati 250F very soon surpassed the W196 in circuit performance, and has its secure place in history. And in comparing the 1954–55 and 1956–57 Mercedes and Maserati performances there is some food for thought, is there not? There was obviously development potential in the W196, and one must assume that had it been raced in 1956 and 1957 Daimler-Benz would have ensured that it was kept ahead of the opposition. And yet . . . it won races, to be sure, but in its first year usually only by the grace of Fangio's skill, and seldom by the margins which might have been expected; it was not the universally superior machine it perhaps should have been when the spare-little-expense effort it represented is borne in mind. Compared with the 1939 W165—surely the supreme Mercedes racing car?—it was too fussy and over-elaborate, one suspects out of caution almost too clever by half. Despite all the fuss over such wonders as desmodromic valve operation, for example, nobody has subsequently found a need for it on Grand Prix engines, revving at appreciably higher speeds. Possibly we should temper the reverence customary when it is described?

Then came the Coopers, and the world turned upside down—or rather front to back. What a pity Mercedes did not stay in racing, if only for the fun of seeing their reaction to Cooper impertinence!

Interesting, is it not, that only the Maseratis and the Coopers were really commercial ends in themselves, as were the Bugattis of an earlier age (although, be it noted, the record shows that they were much more successful against front-line opposition than any Bugattis ever were when pitted against teams, from Alfa Romeo and Talbot to Mercedes and Auto Union).

Already we can see that in the seventh decade of GP racing only

Lotus have built cars which have stood apart on the merit of true originality: the 25, 49 and 72. There has been virtue in others—for example, the Brabham and Tauranac creations just because they were so simple, and so successfully defied the Lotus end of the technological spectrum. In a few years we will be able to look back and assess in perspective; meanwhile let us not condemn the new breed too hastily.

Races for Grand Prix cars have become briefer and briefer, although mercifully we seem to be passing the nadir of the hour and a quarter Grand Prix. But the average modern Grand Prix probably has as much to offer as a spectacle as most in the past, encompassed in a shorter period, and this too is surely in tune with the times? However significant some races may have been in the evolution of motor racing, for the average spectator in the 'seventies most of the great contests of the past would seem monstrously boring if they could be re-enacted today. The European calendar is thick with events, and only when the Grand Prix was an Occasion was there spectacle in every Grand Prix (even though there may seldom have been two cars in sight at any one time on a stretch of circuit). Perhaps the nearest latter-day equivalents of the average Grand Prix of the 1930s have been average CanAm races, which by all accounts have been pretty dull affairs (spectacularly powerful cars, and a team which in efficiency has made the legendary pre-war Mercedes outfit look second-rate, have not made for interesting racing).

Overall standards are higher. Some facts? In 1951 more than half a minute separated the fastest and the last timed driver on the 23-car French Grand Prix grid; in 1961, 22 seconds separated pole-position man and the 26th and slowest driver; in 1971, 10 seconds covered the 23 drivers. Even more to the point, 19 seconds separated the fastest ten in 1951, three seconds the fastest ten in 1971—and this was an unusually wide gap, for on nine of the 1971 Grand Prix grids less than two seconds covered the first ten drivers. The average of the times covering the first ten on the grids for the six principal races in 1951 was 23 seconds. And at the blunt ends nowadays there is sometimes a scramble to qualify by split seconds. The whole business used to be a mite less competitive. . . .

Men are no longer men, apparently, when they cannot be seen to be wrestling with extrovertly difficult machines, teetering on the edge of disaster. Well, it would be a pretty poor reflection on designers if they did still produce machines which led to such exhibitions, for these would be totally at variance with the advancing automotive times. The edge is still there, mark you, the difference being that it is a much sharper edge than that known by the front-engined, narrow-tyred brigade. If physical effort is to be any criterion for an activity revolving around machines, well, today's professionals can put just as much physical effort into a race as their predecessors—one has only to look at drivers climbing out of cockpits after 80 laps around the Monaco houses to realize that this modern race has been just as demanding as it was 15 years earlier, over 100 laps but at an average 15 m.p.h. lower.

There can be no questioning the skill, artistry or bravery of the modern generation. Relating it seems to be the problem, since some of the visual yardsticks valid to generations of trackside observers were quite suddenly lost in the 1960s, when designers radically changed car behaviour. But the ability to hold a precise line for lap after lap is still evident, it is possible to detect effort by suspension movements more subtle than outrageous wheel-lifting, the above-average driver who has the ability to lead almost any race from the front is still with us. Too often over-looked is the fact that a high degree of skill extends further down the motor racing pyramid than once it did, that the chances of an amiable amateur picking up points in any championship with international pretensions are remote indeed (in a similar vein, although in a sense it might once have been admirable that a chap in an umpteen-year-old obsolete car should have been 'in the points', there is another side to that coin, and such an achievement was rather to the shame of contemporary racing, was it not?).

Every decade has its landmark drives, and true enough we will not see the like of past epics again. But as far as conditions will allow of comparison, modern drivers do put in drives of comparable merit. Nuvolari's 1935 German Grand Prix stands out, and so does Fangio's in the same race in 1957, and so should Stewart's in 1969—one cannot be set against another, each in its time was a triumph over different sets of exceptionally testing conditions at the Nürburgring.

If hair on the chest is a qualification for motor sporting greatness, for counterparts of an earlier racing generation one should perhaps nowadays look to the hard core of professional rally crews. Times change.

The trees of petty politics, and a mist of nostalgia for a past which in truth was only patchily splendid, can mean that sight of the wood is lost. On the whole, the Grand Prix world of the early 1970s has been vibrantly alive: the machines have greater performance potential than any in the past; races have seldom been dull 'right down the field', however they may sometimes have been dominated from start to finish at the front; while the drivers may at times have appeared a milksop generation, once a flag falls they can and have driven as hard and professionally as their predecessors. Probably few of us would be pleased to be transported back to an earlier generation of racing, once there and faced with the realities of the good old days.

Commander Pursey asked the Minister of Transport whether he was aware of the uncertainty felt by people who park boats on the highway at night; and to what extent, under his lighting regulations, such boats rank as vessels at anchor, requiring white stay and stern lights, as vessels aground or not not under command, requiring two red lights, or as wreck-marking vessels requiring three white lights.—'Highway Times'

Invest At Your Convenience

MARTYN WATKINS

Basically, one supposes, the motor car is just a convenience. (There is a fondness in some walks of life for labelling things 'His and Hers' which could, in this context and with slight modification, have unfortunate connotations, but the general idea ought to be clear.) Most people buy cars simply because it is convenient to have one's own private transport, but there are other reasons for doing so: because cars are fun, because in ever rarer cases they are beautiful, or more rarely still because they represent a sound investment. That in itself is a phrase which probably sounds like the ring of doom to that remarkable animal, the motoring enthusiast, but the simple fact remains that if cars—some cars, that is—are chosen carefully the lucky owner can find himself with an appreciating asset on his hands. He may even enjoy owning the car—an added bonus which should, in the terms of contemporary enlightened thinking, give him at least a small feeling of guilt.

What cars are going to be worth keeping, in the fond hope that one day a convenient millionaire is going to burst through the door and press huge sums of money upon its owner in exchange for an outdated, outmoded and outworn heap of ironmongery, is a subject of much obscurity. Once upon a time one could be fairly certain: classic cars of great beauty, inspired design or outstanding performance could be relied on to be sought after by the next generation, but nowadays it isn't so easy. Over the past few years some fairly odd cars, though no doubt admirable vehicles set against their purpose and their place, have appreciated in value to an astonishing degree: who would have thought that the bug-eyed Sprite, for instance, would have gone up in price over the past few years? It was certainly an endearing little car which gave a lot of people, including the writer, a lot of fun in days gone by. But an investment—well, really. . . .

Strolling round a Motor Show, trying to decide which of the anonymous assemblies of steel and chrome might be worth buying to lay down, so to speak, like wine, is an amusing, if somewhat frustrating, pastime. What exactly do you look for? Elegance of line? A potentially dangerous pitfall: judging by the numbers of people who bought one, the Chrysler New Yorker of the middle 'fifties might have been thought beautiful at the time, but would anyone do anything but shudder nowadays? What about high performance, then? Again, a transitory thing, of relevance only in contemporary context in many cases— although there are undoubtedly some cars about whose road performance is unlikely to be much exceeded at any time in the foreseeable future.

Whatever the guiding lines, there are some cars about which one gets a feeling, indefinable but apparent enough. A short list of half a score or so likely candidates comes pretty quickly to mind so far as the writer is concerned: an AC 428 because it is good-looking, fast, beautifully-made and typical of its time; a Ginetta G15 because, in a different way, it too is typical of its time and combines good looks with ingenious design and relatively good performance—it's among the best sorts of protest against the contemporary lack of distinction in small cars. Then a Jensen FF, for all the reasons that the AC provides but **for** the additional reason that it was the first road car to feature four-wheel-drive in anything like an acceptable form. All-wheel transmission isn't going to be with us in numbers for a long, long time—if ever, so the first example is a natural choice. Then the Ferrari Dino, an obvious all-time classic if ever there was one—a jewel of a car in just about every sense. And because it is still one of the only 'real' sports cars—the logical extension of thought behind a vintage Bugatti, say—one would have to have a Lotus Seven: an even better bet, from the investment standpoint, now that it has a glass-fibre body, although the earlier aluminium panels were reasonably corrosion-proof. Sheer brutality—in the best sense of the word—makes the V8-engined Morgan Plus Eight a pretty good idea, too: another real sports machine, but less agile, if faster and more powerful than the Lotus. Somehow, the Morgan is what the vintage sports car was all about. Most of the time it is pretty unlovable, with heavy steering, an unforgiving gearbox, minimal weather protection and not much room for luggage: an immensely masculine car which will always have an appeal for a particular sort of driver.

At the other end of the scale, one feels that a Monteverdi might be worth investing in—probably the 375L. The only car made in Switzerland, built by a direct descendant of the composer, big, fast, luxurious and sporting—and inevitably very rare—these points are going to keep the price of that one fairly high, for sure. And also big, luxurious and relatively fast, but about as far removed from a Monteverdi as a tin of sardines from a packing case, what about a Range Rover? Like the Land Rover, it seems to be virtually indestructible, and carries much more of an aura which suggests that the occupants are in the course of one of their frequent trips to the odd couple of thousand acres they happen to inhabit in the heart of good fox-hunting country. It's also a pretty remarkable piece of design ingenuity and just has to go down in motoring history as one of the great designs.

Another pair of cars which share the outstanding advantage, when it comes to longevity, of glass-fibre, corrosion-free bodywork and which both have qualities which might well make them of interest to a serious collector are the Reliant Scimitar GTE and the 3-litre Marcos. Both of these might well make it onto the list: both are fast, both handle very well and both share an easily-maintained, fairly lightly-stressed power unit of humble, and therefore common, origin. The Ogle-designed Scimitar of pre-GTE days has already proved its ability to keep its price high on the second-hand market, but one is less sure about the current GTE: although it has a strong following, one wonders whether its unusual (albeit trend-setting) sports-estate car coachwork, like that maybe of the Marcos in a slightly different way, won't be altogether too *outré* in ten years' time.

With or without them, there we have a handful of cars which might well form a useful 'cellar'. It would be nice to have these cars in one's own collection, just to have them there and drive them around when the mood came upon one, and to hell with the re-sale price. But one has to be practical, and since this collection, bought new this year, would set the buyer back something close to forty thousand quid—well. . . . Of course, anything that's really worth having has got to be paid for, and you don't find any Rubens in Sainsbury's: what counts in the long run, tragically, is fashion, and this tends to take precedence in the cash market over quality far too often for a purist's peace of mind.

Looking at the list again, one can't help feeling a twinge of regret that there are no competition cars featured in it. It's just a sad fact—or maybe it's progress, which can often be just as sad—that there has never been anything to replace the Aston Martin DB3S, or the 'C' and 'D'-type Jaguars of fifteen years back—superb race-winners which could still be recognised as real cars by anyone, rather than the single-purpose design freaks which are their contemporary counterparts. No-one is going to say that a Can-Am McLaren, or a Porsche 917, is anything but very close to the ultimate so far as high-speed motoring is concerned, but any of these that find their way into the collections of the middle nineteen-eighties will sadly end up as museum pieces, like the rather pathetic single-seaters which so often sit gathering dust with labels on them, peered at by uncomprehending spectators who are often incapable, poor souls, of remembering or even visualising what these savage monsters must have looked and sounded like in a grid-full of Vanwalls, Mercedes or Maseratis. No—cars that can be seriously con-

sidered for our list have to be reasonably likely of still being used
for their original useful purpose fifteen years hence—by anyone,
rather than by the handful of delightful people who still race
yesterday's Formula I machinery and the like.

'Still reasonably likely' is, unhappily, the only degree of
definition that can be employed in the light of modern legislative
thinking: none of the cars on the list are fitted with airbags
which deafen and suffocate the occupants in the event of a minor
prang, none of them are radar-controlled as to course and speed
and, although all of them can be driven by maiden aunts, the
majority are quite difficult to drive well, if full use is to be made
of their performance and road behaviour. Obviously, no great
skill is necessary to get a Range Rover from A to B, but to feel
that thrill of satisfaction that comes from getting the best, the
absolute best, out of a Ferrari Dino, a Lotus Seven or a Morgan
Plus Eight, you need to be a Driver, not merely a motorist. And
this is another underlying reason for their inclusion which hasn't
been mentioned before: they have strong characters. This may
sometimes make them wilful, even a shade unforgiving, but
no truly great car has ever suffered a fool at the wheel. In time to
come, when all cars (if cars are still allowed), have degenerated
into a uniform dullness, requiring about as much positive action
from the driver as travelling by train or hovercraft, there will
still be some who will hark back to the days when driving was
something in which to take a pride—a skill to be developed and
honed, a challenge to be met and overcome.

From a practical point of view, our list has to be pared a shade:
not too many people, one assumes, are likely to be frantically
keen on shelling out £40,000 on a random handful of motorcars,
however pretty their colours may be. What could be bought for
£10,000—still a pretty healthy sum, of course? Unfortunately,
you couldn't quite manage the Monteverdi, unless you could
claim a cash discount. A new 375L will set you back £10,500
in round figures, and they don't exactly flood the secondhand
market as yet. The A.C., the Jensen or the Ferrari, plus one or
two from the cheaper end of the list, would fit the bill—the Dino
is cheapest of the three, and one of these new, plus, say, a Morgan,
a Lotus and a Ginetta from the secondhand sales department

would probably leave you with a handful of change for buying polish and wax. If you start at the cheaper end of the list, of course, you can launch out with shiny new cars and only your own strength to resist the temptation to wear them out yourself will affect the long-term value! A Morgan Plus Eight, for instance, plus a Lotus Seven and the Ginetta—under five thousand for the lot; for the same money, near enough, how about a Reliant and a Marcos?

Of course, no-one's saying that these cars are the only ones that will appreciate in value, or be worth collecting from any other point of view. Everyone has his or her own ideas on the subject, but it seems reasonable that the same guiding principles have to apply: quality, performance, originality of design, a feeling of 'period'—and, above all, *character*. The last is probably the most difficult one to establish, and by no means every car which meets the requirements of all, or any, of the first four measures up when it comes to character. If it comes to that, one can think of a good many cars which have character in abundance but which fail as candidates for the collectors' list on some or all of the other points. For instance, the Fiat 128, or the Mini-Cooper 'S': both have more character than they need, but one would hardly expect to find them in a connoisseur's collection in fifteen or twenty years' time. But most Alfa Romeos have it, while contemporary Aston Martins, in the writer's opinion, lack it. The BMW 2002 has it, and both an Alfa and a BMW might well fit into the list for some people. The Datsun 240Z has as much of it as any car has any right to, and this would definitely be a candidate for any longer list that the writer might compile.

Somehow any list of this sort seems incomplete without a Jaguar but, despite their undoubted excellence from just about every point of view, the writer isn't going to have one on *his* list, thank you very much. The XJ6, or the V12 'E'-type, are all much, much better cars than the XK120, or the D'-type, but in spite of high scores on every other count they just don't seem, any more, to have sufficient personality—they are anonymous cars, somehow. The same goes for Mercedes—even the 280SL or the mighty 6.3-litre saloon. But if no Mercedes are to appear,

Germany might easily contribute a Porsche 911 or the remarkable NSU Ro80, the qualities of performance, excellence of design and construction and character, as well as 'period', being more than adequately represented by either of them. Would one include the Vw-Porsche? On balance, probably not—one would rather have a 'proper' Porsche, although if the 914 is made in small enough numbers it might qualify, from a purely practical point of view, on rarity grounds alone.

It is, maybe, a solemn thought that really very few makes or models crop up on a list of collectors' cars made today, and also how few names there are to choose from. A good many marques don't appear at all—no Lamborghinis, no Maseratis, no Mercedes; not a Bentley or a Rolls-Royce. On a less exalted level, no Triumphs, Rovers, Renaults—not a Simca or a Vauxhall. This, it can be assumed, is a reflection on the sorry fact that there are very few factories left who are capable of the intention, or the capability, of building great cars—cars which will have an enduring appeal and quality. Basically, as was accepted at the beginning of this essay, the motor-car must be assumed to be a convenience.

Then there was the sign on the back of the Corvette in a supporting race at Riverside that said "To pass, please blow engine".

Eoin Young in 'Autocar'

Signs up outside a garage in large, permanent flood-lit letters:
Number one: "Self service".
Number two: "Service is our business".
Can't they make up their minds?—Ralph Thorseby in 'Motor'

Air on a Shoe-String

ANTHONY BIRD

The present regulation about the permitted minimum depth of tyre tread sends the statutory titter running round the dwindling band of 'shoe-string motorists', like myself, to whom any vestige of tread pattern was once a luxury. There were those of us who worried if the canvas of their tyres was visible, but the real shoe-string motorist had no option but to press on until the wind itself was showing.

The true shoe-string motorist must be one who started car owning well before the war, when it was possible to buy a 'runner' for as little as twenty-five shillings. I know it is still possible to buy an old banger for the equivalent of a pre-war tenner, but what with the MOT test, the tin-worm and many other things it is no longer possible to run it on practically nothing a year as we used to do.

The pre-war shoe-stringer had to be able to do all his own repairs; he had to develop a nose for obscure breaker's yards where long-obsolete bits could be bought for shillings and an instinct for finding grandly-named back street 'tyre depots' which specialised in gleaming, black-leaded 're-cuts', with suspiciously spongy walls, at five shillings apiece. He also had to have a knack for finding obscure garages which stocked mysteriously dark and treacly 'commercial' oils at fourpence a pint. Beyond always buying the lowest grade of the cheapest brand, there was not much he could do about petrol prices, but with a nice old-fashioned low-compression engine it was possible to add a certain amount of (untaxed) paraffin without making the engine unstartable, or the exhaust so evil smelling as to attract the attention of some over-zealous constable.

I became a car-owner in old-banger-land in 1932 when, still ineligible for a car-driver's licence and unknown to my parents, I bought a half share in a ten-year-old Trojan, in partnership with a slightly older youth who shared with me the joys of sweeping floors and running errands at the Standard Telephones & Cables factory in Colindale. Indeed, we jointly owned three successive Trojans for these prize denizens of banger-land only sunk to our price limit of thirty shillings when their driving chains and sprockets were worn to the limits of the adjustment. It was possible to get another two or three thousand miles out of a decayed Trojan by filing the teeth of the sprockets and by heating and bending the adjusting device, but these were very temporary expedients. It was useless to hunt for chain and sprocket sets in breakers' yards as they would be equally worn, but we were able to come to an arrangement with our friendly neighbourhood car-breaker who suffered from galloping halitosis and a weakness for Trojans. When our current Trojan would scarcely climb the slightest gradient without the chain jumping, we would coax it back to him and he would allow us ten shillings against the purchase of another at thirty bob or so. On the third occasion I recall something unethical being done with number plates because of the lack of a registration book. . . .

This pre-war experience with Leslie Hounsfield's brain-child, the only car ever made with connecting rods designed to bend at every revolution of the crankshaft, stood me in good stead in 1953 when, still in need of the cheapest possible motoring,

I bought a 1928 ex-Brooke Bond tea van for use in my antique business. With this I achieved a minor triumph of shoe-string motoring by driving from Doncaster to Lydd with a broken back axle. This was quite in the spirit of Trojan's famous slogan 'Can You Afford To Walk?', made possible because the machine had a 'solid' one-piece driving shaft, with no differential gear, running inside a one-piece axle tube. The sprocket wheel for the chain drive was attached to the shaft beside the off-side wheel hub, whilst the solitary drum for the foot brake was at the other end of the shaft beside the near-side wheel. The hand brake acted on a little pulley on the reduction gear, and consequently took effect via the chain, but as it was always soaked with oil from the chain it was not much use. With the axle shaft bust roughly in the middle three things happened: the broken halves of the shaft tilted in their bearings and set up so much friction that every slight incline reduced the beast to a bottom gear crawl (the Trojan had only two speeds and low speed really was low), secondly the drive was only taken on the offside rear wheel and the footbrake only acted on the nearside wheel. Even one-wheel braking was not consistently available because on right-hand bends the near-side bit of the shaft, with the wheel and brake drum, floated out of contact with the brake shoes. It was a tedious journey but not uninteresting.

The poverty of the shoe-string motorist dictated his choice of car. It had to cost no more than ten pounds and preferably less than five. Very big old cars could then be bought, often in superb condition, for practically nothing. I wince at the memory of Kaiser Wilhelm's 1911 Labourdette-bodied, walnut-panelled 90 h.p. Renault which I could have had for £8, but how could I pay the tax on all those horses or satisfy its alleged 6 miles-a-gallon thirst? The shoe-stringer had to be content with Baby Austins, Morris Cowleys, Swifts, Cluleys and such like and, purchase price apart, preference was given to pre-1930 cars because their design and construction, generally, made them easier and cheaper to keep in order than post-vintage stuff. For example, as the first thing to give trouble in an old banger is the electrickery, and a new battery was an unattainable luxury, one tried to find a car with magneto ignition, and of sufficiently elderly design to have a decent fixed starting handle—none of the nasty new-fangled detachable things.

With his magneto and his starting handle it mattered not to the shoe-stringer that the battery never was man enough to work the self-starter, and he soon grew accustomed to strange electrical phenomena, such as dimmer controls which caused the horn to blow or horn buttons which lit up the dashboard lamp. Switches which switched on nothing but a shower of sparks and a nasty smell of burnt rubber were commonplace, and the shoe-string motorist had to find a night-time compromise between driving quickly enough to keep the dynamo charging at its full rate (of a pitiful 8 ampères) and cautiously enough to find his way by headlamps which could not look a glow-worm up the backside without blinking.

After the second world war I was fortunate enough for some years to run pre-Kaiser war cars for everyday purposes and was freed from the tyranny of decayed electrics; oil and acetylene gas lamps are much better suited to the shoe-string motorist than electricity.

Lack of money not only governed the shoe-string motorist's choice of car but also influenced the way he drove. I always drove as much as possible at the car's natural 'best speed'; this is the magic point which was more easily sensed on old cars than moderns, where inertia forces balance combustion forces and the stress on tired old bearings is at its minimum. Too-exuberant cornering or too-frequent braking had to be shunned in order to avoid unnecessary wear on tyres and brake linings. If some piece of clottishness forced one into using the brakes hard the first reaction was, 'Dammit, there's another tuppence off my linings', and I had to learn the gentle art of clutchless gear changing when I owned a 1927 Humber Nine which was in very fair condition except for a grumbling clutch withdrawal thrust bearing which was on its last legs. Using the clutch only to start the car from rest prolonged its life and avoided the need to buy a new thrust bearing, which would possibly have cost more than the thirty-five shillings I paid for the car.

Because his 're-cut' tyres, however glossily black-leaded, were only whited sepulchres the shoe-stringer became a dab hand at changing wheels and mending punctures. Although I have had only two punctures in the seven years since I bought my first (nearly) new car I still cannot get out of the habit of allowing 'ten minutes for a puncture' when planning any journey of more than about fifty miles. This, added to my natural punctuality, results in arriving madly early for appointments for which the other participants are invariably late.

Unless forced to it by some major disaster like a broken crankshaft, the shoe-string motorist simply could not afford to abandon his broken-down car by the roadside and seek professional help or go home by train. Therefore a comprehensive kit of decayed and battered old tools was essential, together with a large box of 'might-come-in-useful' oddments such as old bolts, nuts, washers, bits of metal, rubber pipe, part-worn gaskets etc. One never knew what might come in handy, and I felt very pleased when I restored life to a broken-down magneto by folding a bit of rubber from an old wiper blade into a suitable shape to wedge into the contact breaker to take over the duty of the broken spring. This got me home a matter of about thirty miles, and I still feel uneasy on the shortest journey unless I know my tool kit includes a reel of copper wire, at least one spare sparking plug as a talisman and the *vade mecum* of old-banger-land, a big roll of 'insulting tape'.

Water cooling systems were another source of anxiety in banger land, and your true shoe-stringer always plumped for a car with thermo-syphon cooling if he could. This did away with one source of inevitable trouble, the water pump, and a nice old-fashioned fixed-head engine, if it could be found, also abolished the nuisance of leaking head gaskets. One of the best inhabitants of banger land was the Jowett; it was invincibly reliable and long-lived and, because the snobbery about two-cylinder cars reached right down to the shoe-stringers, it was usually cheaper (by as much as fifteen shillings perhaps) than a comparable four-cylinder car. The only snag was that Jowetts did not have magneto ignition, but this was a small disadvantage to set beside the boon of their pump-less and fan-less thermo-syphon cooling. It is certain, incidentally that if any designer now suggested making a car with natural circulation cooling he would be carried away to the nearest bin; but fifteen million Model T Fords managed perfectly well with thermo-syphon systems, to say nothing of innumerable heavy goods vehicles and thousands of Renaults, Charrons, Morris Cowleys, Jowetts and many many more.

Most shoe-string motorists had pet receipes for dealing with slightly leaking radiators. Some favoured porridge oats, some liked corn-flour; there were those who spoke highly of Colman's mustard and others who pinned their faith, if that is the right expression, to white of egg. Those near the plutocrat end of banger-land could lash out 2/9d on a tin of somebody's patent 'Neverleak', but that represented nearly three gallons of petrol, and was not for the likes of me. I found the mustard and oatmeal treatment certainly efficacious at stopping small leaks but also apt to stop the circulation, and when I bought a 1924 Jowett for fifty shillings from the original owner in 1938 he was honest enough to confess to a leaking radiator for which, he said, I would find twopenny packets of Hudson's Soap Powder a sovereign remedy.

It was quite true, and the Hudson's Soap would 'hold' the leak for two or three months, without clogging the circulation, and would then need renewing. I once flushed, re-filled and re-Hudsoned my radiator, in preparation for a journey to Cornwall, and was guilty of *lèse-majesté* as a result. What happened was that I found myself in the front row of a line of traffic held up at the Edgware Road-Marble Arch junction. The traffic lights were switched off, several policemen in Number One uniforms controlled the traffic and the wrought iron gates in the Arch itself were open, so it was obvious that royalty was expected. We were held up for a good ten minutes and I dared not switch off my engine because, inevitably, the battery was too far gone to do more than cause the starter pinion to engage with a plaintive moan. So the water grew very near to boiling point, there being no fan, and I had unfortunately filled the radiator right up to the level of the overflow pipe. As we waited a wisp of steam blew off from the pipe and soapy water began to bubble gently from the ill-fitting mascot on the radiator cap. Then, a well-known sit-up-and-beg Daimler appeared from the Bayswater Road, with a well-known flowered toque in the back. As it swept through the Marble Arch I saw the opportunity to fulfil a life-long ambition, and whilst the policemen still had their arms raised in salute I let in the clutch and puttered in pursuit of Majesty through the Arch to a chorus of shouts and police whistles. It was a very naughty thing to do, but irresistible, and the loyal citizens in the park were treated to the sight of their favourite Royal person, followed as usual by a blue cloud of sleeve-valve Daimler exhaust smoke which was not thick enough to obscure a shabby old Jowett copiously blowing bubbles from unexpected places and smelling like an insurrection in a Chinese laundry.

The modern equivalent of the shoe-string motorist is made to feel anti-social. A recent letter to *Motor* said haughtily: '... anyone who cannot afford to run a safe car should not run one at all', and another in the same issue said: '... recent analysis showed that of 413 vehicles involved in accidents, just over half had defects which could have contributed to the crash'. 'Could' seems to be the operative word and conjecture of this sort really will not do in connection with anything put forward as a serious analysis, and the previous letter overlooks the fact that a 'safe' car is only safe in the hands of a safe driver. The statistics which purport to show that old vehicles are involved in proportionately greater numbers of accidents than newer ones, fail to take into account the ages, driving experience and other characteristics of the drivers. Nobody defends the use of patently unworthy cars or lorries, but it is too easy to look at road safety matters entirely through Nader-spectacles. The Nader-view focuses too closely upon the shape of a door latch or the thickness of the padding and too little on raising standards of human performance. A 'bad driver', one without inherent road sense who drives by rule and not by instinct, will probably have a prang sooner or later no matter how many self-inflating air-bags the over-inflated wind-bag Nader may force upon him, but a good and conscientious driver can coax an old banger through the heaviest traffic on bald tyres, with feeble brakes and soggy steering because he will make allowance for these failings and drive accordingly.

The rock-bottom shoe-string motorist just could not afford to have an accident, and the disadvantage of driving an old car with two-wheel brakes amongst all the four-wheel-braked

moderns sharpened his wits. This particular disadvantage became
more apparent after the war as traffic increased and speeds rose.
Because I had then become hooked on the vintage or veteran
type of car for its own sake, and could not afford to keep one
just for fun, I did all my everyday motoring between 1946 and
the late 'fifties mostly in such Edwardians as a 1912 Charron,
a 1910 two-cylinder Renault and 1909 four-cylinder ditto,
sandwiched between briefer spells with a 1923 Morris Cowley
and a 1924 Panhard-Levassor. Interspersed with these were spells
varying from a few days to a few weeks on other oldies including
a 1905 Adams-Hewitt, which shed a half-shaft at Tranent, its
ignition coil at Newcastle, several teeth from its final drive
sprocket in Newark and its track rod on Huntington Bridge;
a 1912 Model T Ford, which shed a hind wheel outside Ealing
Town Hall; a 1904 De Dion Bouton, which shed a universal
joint in the Fulham Road and a 1911 racing Delage which shed
sweetness and light wherever it went. Only once on these, and
never on my pre-war bangers, did I fail to reach my destination,
even though it was literally 'under my own steam' when a fan
blade went through the radiator of the Ford and all the chewing
gum in Rottingdean would not seal the leak.

All these cars but the Panhard-Levassor had two-wheel brakes
and all had narrow section high-pressure beaded edge tyres. In
wet weather there is no better combination than narrow high-
pressure tyres and back-brakes-only for teaching one to use the
brakes sparingly, and to bear in mind Dr Lanchester's dictum,
in his 1902 *Driver's Manual*: 'But remember, whatever the
state of the road it is *bad driving* to navigate sideways'. The down
grade from Hyde Park Corner to the gates at the top of Consti-
tution Hill presented a particularly nasty combination of gradient,
camber, curvature and highly-polished wood-block paving and I
used to plan my route carefully on wet mornings in order to get
round into the road to Belgrave Square without having to use
the brakes. I did come unstuck one morning, and had to do a little
sideways navigating when I found the gap between two buses
which I planned to use was blocked by one of those little canvas
houses workmen put up in busy streets so that they may drink
their tea in comfort. Fortunately it was unoccupied.

One of the ills which did not afflict pre-war cars, whether they were mere bangers or prized vintage, Edwardian or Veteran specimens, was the tin-worm or rust. There might be superficial corrosion of mudguards, valances and so on, but rust-weakened structural members were unknown and most of the ten, twenty, fifty-or-more year old cars I have owned still had their original exhaust pipes and silencers intact. If any motor industry tycoon wishes to produce a motor car which will not begin to disintegrate from corrosion after a couple of years, I will gladly tell him how it may be done on payment of a million pounds.

There were times when unexpected gremlins almost defeated my ambition never to have to abandon a car by the roadside. One of these gremlins attacked on Christmas Eve 1946, when I was using the 1923 Morris Cowley. Although it had done well over 100,000 miles this excellent motor car gave me no trouble in another 35,000 beyond occasionally getting its carburettor choked with muck from its dirty petrol tank. Until Christmas Eve, that is, when I stepped into the car just before midnight to set off from Pimlico to my flat in Ealing. I pressed the starter button (yes, I even had a decent battery on that car), the silent dynamotor did its stuff and the engine started whereupon I pushed the clutch pedal down against the usual amount of spring pressure and found that I could not engage any gear. Although the clutch pedal action *felt* normal, I discovered later that the pressure plate was firmly locked to the clutch shaft because, by a fluke, it had jammed on worn splines when I switched off the engine on arriving at my office that morning.

So there I was cotched, with the last 'bus gone and a good car with a smoothly running engine but, in effect, no clutch. Taking advantage of a slight down gradient I managed to push the car from the offside and clamber aboard whilst it was still moving at a walking pace; this was just enough to enable the gear lever to be snicked into the first speed position with the engine running but without the cog wheels fighting. The rest was easy, provided I did not have to stop again, because 'clutchless' gear-changes, up or down, were very easy on old-fashioned 'crash' gearboxes in the pre-synchromesh days.

I took every back double I could think of to avoid T-junctions, right turns and traffic lights and all went well until I had to cross Kensington Road near Olympia. As I approached from the Cromwell Road the wretched lights turned to red when I was about 150 yards from them. I changed down to second, then bottom and let the car creep along at tickover speed but the light was still red when I reached the junction—and it is a slight up-grade there so there was little hope of being able to push myself off again. There was no traffic about, except a taxi waiting for the lights on the opposite side of Kensington Road, but I was deter-mined not to chance 'going over the red'; however, the road is nice and wide there and old Cowleys have a good lock, so I solemnly made three slow circles in the width of the street whilst the taxi-driver civilly removed his cap.

The lights then changed and the next hurdle was Shepherd's Bush Green. I took one back double which enabled me to dodge the first set of lights; the second set were at green and stayed green and the third set obligingly changed to green when I was about fifty yards away. Given a bit of luck I knew the rest of the journey would be easy, but as I accelerated a little to make sure I could pass the lights before they changed again a gentleman swayed from the kerb and fell flat on his face in front of my car. There was nothing for it but to slap the gear lever into neutral and clap the brakes on. For a moment I was afraid I had hit the man, and jumped out to see if he was hurt. He was not, for-tunately, and I had not hit him. He was middling drunk but lucid enough, as I helped him to his feet, to assure me that it was all his fault. He was, indeed, in affable mood, as was the inevitable policeman who materialized out of nowhere. After hearing what had happened the copper cheerfully joined forces with the drunk and pushed the car at a nice brisk walking pace so that I could again slip into gear and resume my clutchless journey. There was no malice in bangerland on that Christmas morning.

Motoring in the 21st Century

HENRY N. MANNEY

When you consider the strides made in motoring development during the last seventy years, it boggles the mind to contemplate what is yet to come. There are those individuals who point to the prevalence of four wheels, fossil-fuel engines, and mass-produced tin boxes as evidence of Curly's song 'She's gone about as fur as she can go' but then similar prognostications have been made about technical developments from the bow and arrow down. In his day the celebrated J. S. Bach was supposed to have demonstrated just about every possible variation on the theme but the no less celebrated W. A. Mozart demonstrated that there was quite a bit left to say. In our own era musical comedies and pop tunes mined so diligently on the moon-spoon-june motif that the vein should have been long since exhausted but today's musicians, certainly not any more talented, continue to dig away aided intermittently by side issues like air pollution, maryjane, hair, and Vietnam. Clearly the human race, once it has got hold of a pleasurable idea, will continue to worry away at it even if the results cannot always be regarded as progress. This last conclusion will be fought to the bitter end, of course, by advertising agencies whose financial well-being depends on change for change's sake.

Casting a jaundiced eye into the motoring future shows that one of two things will happen; either we will have a vast pullulating undisciplined mess (with a primrose Austin Seven at the head of the queue) or a Buck Rogersian scene with rocket cars, private helicopters, flight belts, roller-coaster tracks for 'cars', and pretty girls in short skirts with odd goggles and flowing sleeves (those we have already—Ed.). At any rate private motoring isn't going to be much fun, aside from looking at the girls. Science fiction these days has a nasty habit of turning into reality within a dozen years or so and already plans are in the works for magnetic bands in the motorways to keep the vehicles in a given lane, automatic distance control, automatic speed control, automatic feeds on the input ramps, and coming soon an equally automatic device that will refuse entry to a main road unless the car is fully roadworthy (via sensors in critical places) and furthermore, fully loaded with 'essential' passengers. As any fool can plainly see, megalopoli cannot operate without tight control, and tight control demands an ever increasing bureaucracy. Government bureaux have always been nobly ready to step into the breach, assume extra controlling work, and incidentally increase their numbers thereby. You may be sure, therefore, that while the private motorist is battling the web of regulation, slightly different, slightly better vehicles bearing only one or two fat-cats will be seen swishing silently to their destinations. The hoi polloi will go by clean, comfortable, cheap, and well-organized public transport. After all, it is for the good of the country.

The sheer numbers of people and the spread-out nature of megalopoli will necessitate some kind of regulation of private drivers, largely because most of the great cities of the Western world have suffered the same disease of decentralisation. Advances of modern medical science means that many babies live who would formerly have died in childhood; these naturally grow up into adulthood and even more naturally demand a place to live. The land pirates are only too happy to buy up farmland (since the farm boys have generally gone to the cities and their parents have been taxed out of existence) on which to put rows of tickytacky houses, conveniently close to the cities and yet appealing to residual race-memories by leaving a few trees scattered about. All of this window-dressing is very carefully researched down to the last square inch of grass and the last centimeter of mass-produced mullioned window. Kickback-hungry politicians are equally happy to bend the rules a little bit having to do with minimum distance between houses. And so all the shacks are sold to families who, naturally, finding themselves many miles from any shops but the Company Store, buy yet another car to get about. Seeing all this money floating around loose, the big downtown emporiums put up shopping centers and then, finding a former country road clogged daily, the highway improvement and motorway people get into the act. As satellites get further and further out, more and more people buy cars, and as sure as eggs are eggs one fine day they all get on the road together.

Every reader, I fancy, has been out for a drive and found the highway littered with too many people. Some of those, it is easily apparent, are unfit to drive for one reason or another depending on the judgment of the saint driving the car *we* are in. Clearly the old fogies, those possessed of marginal intelligence (such as supporters of another football team), the drunks, the young, the pushy drivers, the snails, and types smoking large cigars and wearing fancy shirts should obviously be relegated to buses. One may also include those who apparently have lost grip on their reason but since most of us have fallen temporarily into that category from time to time, the line has to be drawn some-where. Ideally, the roads could well do without the demonstrably accident-prone, those ladies of post-menstrual vintage who take twenty-three goes to win a licence, habitual drunken drivers, and that sort of anti-social chap who is always motoring through red lights. It is easy to say that the old folks should go too but all of us know old folks who not only get along very smartly but manage to keep the wings unbent. The powers-that-be of the 21st century may well decide to do away with all marginal drivers like these, even as our insurance companies would like to, in order to keep the road free for Efficient Workers of Producing Age and to cut out unprofitable paperwork. Powers-that-Be tend to get the bit in their collective teeth and so, in addition, you can expect to see permits doled out on the premise of occupation, geographical location, social attitude, and whether the applicants have ever visited Disneyland or not. This last qualification played an important part recently in the filling of an important government post in Washington. You may well larf. They feel that visiting Disneyland has an important bearing on group conformity. And thank *you*, George Orwell.

In certain parts of the world where too many drivers exist already, some of these restrictive practices have already been tried under the sacred heading of Safety. Many of us would be walking if a wise head had not whispered in the Governor/President/Premier's ear that something like 95 per cent of drivers are also voters. Taking a man's licence away for no really good reason is liable, in these days of wavemaking and general dissatisfaction with our rulers, to set up ripples unheard of a few years ago. Therefore it is no great surprise to find that machinery is already in operation to do away with essentially private motoring via psychologically subtil and many-pronged attacks, based on the automobile itself. You may well have heard of Nader, right? And safety cars, right? And smog gear, right? Aha. Any engineer will tell you that the steadily increasing safety requirements will shortly make it impossible to build an automobile that is not only within a competitive price range but is practical and safe. For example I recently tried a pair of 'safety cars' built to the orders of the Government which were not only set up like a NASCAR stocker as far as suspension and tyres were concerned but weighed something over 2,000 lb above normal. Granted a good deal of refinement but the machine is still impractical, not only for public taste but for public use for anyone else but A. J. Foyt. And we won't go into airbags which allegedly go off like a magnetic mine, not only blowing all the glass out of the car but in one case, I understand, decapitating the dummy. Likewise the smog gear requirements are becoming tighter and tighter to the point of being ridiculous.

For example the Mercedes folk, who certainly build sanitary machinery, are forced to put a whacking great V.8 in their nice saloon as the lovely 3.5 six won't pull the skin off a rice pudding with smog gear installed. Therefore Mercs put in the V.8 which, with smog gear installed, doesn't go as well as the nice 3.5 six. The pattern is quite clear, Watson; as the smog requirements become tighter (even if you live in the middle of airy Snetterton) pretty soon engines won't produce enough power to haul the excess weight and rolling resistance required by the Safety people. Just like driving a Flying Standard 8 again and who wants to go back to that?

Another facet of this attack by the bowlerhat army is that of traffic control. Now everyone sees the need for a certain amount of traffic control via stoplights, stopsigns, and so forth otherwise getting centrepunched at your favourite main road intersection would be so commonplace as not to be mentioned. Imagine, if you will, downtown any city with no traffic lights at all. Just like Italy and no right-thinking Anglo Saxon will hold still for that. Nevertheless the authorities have been staging a great number of computer runouts on traffic patterns already in Southern California, for example, and the results are very interesting as straws in in the wind. Take, if you will, traffic lights as a dadgummed nuisance to anyone trying to get from A to B in a decent time but a necessary evil nonetheless. In California, as elsewhere, they are used in a punitive manner to hold traffic down to crawling pace on shop-lined roads by making the one ahead of you turn red when the one you have just left is green. This can have many underlying reasons, ranging from the local merchants' wish that you gaze idly at the displays while sitting immobile, or else to enforce a lower speed limit than the speed limit signs actually say. Then there is the entrapment gambit; on several stretches of highway near here it is absolutely impossible to make two lights in a row without exceeding the legal speed limit. All the local motorists know this and so do the local rozzers, who lurk about in great numbers. Since it is obviously impossible to make the lights travelling at a legal speed, if you make two lights you are breaking the law, right? Motorists are also channelled onto the crowded main road in another ploy which ensures that side

roads and back doubles are so festooned with stop signs and
lights slamming red in the motorist's face that he loses too much
time going around. Therefore the reagans in their rolling popcorn
machines are waiting for him. But surely the Highway Patrol
is there to catch dangerous wrongdoers and make the world safe
for us all? Perhaps. The traffic cops had themselves a strike in
San Diego, California, last year which produced a high thin
scream from the county government that it was losing some
$7,000 a week in revenue from traffic fines. *Revenue.* Think
about that. In actual fact the money garnered from traffic fines,
ranging anywhere up from $20 a whack, is already budgeted for
and spent in running the county and State governments. And
already some bureaucrat has been heard mumbling about
'harvesting' the traffic flow to increase the 'revenue base'. And
don't think that it only happens here in America.

In the official mind, controlling traffic is either ensuring that
it is stopped dead, moving at 15 m.p.h., or comfortably channelled
onto motorways (both urban and intercity) where it can be easily
supervised by whirlypigs. The private motorist is a nuisance in
that he sometimes prefers to motor through towns on normal
roads and dislikes said towns being split, despoiled and otherwise
buggered about for motorway construction. Not too long ago
a certain town put up a fight against the motorway menace for
the above reasons, thinking rightly that there were quite enough
motorways already. There was a lot of legal scrapping and
eventually, in a referendum, the motorway project (a State one)
through that town was voted down by a large margin. I will not
go into all the diabolical manoeuvres but note it be said that a bit
before the referendum came due, little men with clipboards were
at all the major intersections along the motorway route and
shortly afterwards the most colossal traffic jams ensued. Why?
The periods of the lights had been changed so that what smooth
traffic flow existed had been loused up. Why? So that the un-
thinking voter would conclude that there really was a need for a
motorway to avoid total paralysation. Nevertheless, no serious
person around that town doubts that the Official Mind will
finally get its way and the town will be spoiled, simply because
the Official Mind, looking forward to the 21st Century, wants

to keep everything tidy, pigeon-holed, organized, and contrary to the wishes of as many private motorists as possible. The purpose, therefore, of increasing regimentation as implemented by increasing stoplights (ignoring the lucrative kickback angle) is to make the individual stop and stop and stop again, reminding him that he must be a good boy and do as he is told, otherwise by the threats of fines, rising insurance premiums, and loss of licence, he is going to catch it. Thus conditioned, the motorist, most independent of the voters because of his mobility, will tend to accept What Is Good For Him. This docility is not so much based on force, as guerilla bands all over the world have shown that force often doesn't do the job, but on a planned campaign to make everyday living awkward and above all to take the enjoyment out of motoring via dull cars and channelisation. Most of us drive because we enjoy it, as it certainly is easier and cheaper to take the Tube. Are you listening, George?

Motor racing in the 21st Century is already casting its shadow long before thanks to the Grand Prix Drivers Association. Ignoring the fact that the first duty of a constructor is to make the racing car hold the road and the first duty of the conductor is to keep it there, miles of expensive Armco have sprouted around the most beautiful courses in Europe. A lot of arm waving goes on about dangerous locales like Spa and Monte Carlo but ignoring the fact that Spa and Monte Carlo are the Big League and meant to be the maximum test of skill, nobody or nothing (except the drives of ego and greed) forces the driver into the car or to go too quickly at some particular place. A modicum of common sense simply must be applied. If such-and-such a car is dangerous in the wet because its oversize tyres aquaplane or because it isn't set up properly, then it should be a matter for the organisers and/or the GPDA to safeguard the lives of both drivers and spectators by making appropriate changes. The only objection comes, as usual, from those whose pocketbooks will be hurting.

Sooner or later the Officials will decide whether motor racing is valuable from a panem and circenses viewpoint or whether it is dangerous in the sense that it gives ordinary motorists a touch of the old pizazz. If kept on, it will undoubtedly continue in the manner now in vogue with drivers buried well in the bodywork,

meaningless advertising slogans instead of marques, and a development completely away from anything closer to normal use than
a moonship. There will be, in addition, smaller engines in a mild
state of tune, full silencing equipment, and a regulation (vide
USAC) that any car losing vital fluids shall withdraw forthwith.
Long races at slow speed with no refuelling or pit stops are ever
so much duller than the usual sort. Excitement makes the natives
restless, especially if they can't see much from behind the barriers
and across an acre of plowed field. The whole point will be that
racing will really not be very interesting but just barely better
than no racing at all. Reformers, as you have probably noticed,
hate to have anyone actually enjoy himself.

Fortunately the human animal is quite resilient. Already certain
individuals who are tired of plastic knobs, fake padding and seat
belts like *la toile d'araignée* have turned to the cars of yesteryear.
Not only the choice goodies paraded by Clutton and friends but
Model A Fords, Terraplanes, La Salles and even Packard Clippers
God save the mark. It is difficult to see how these gentle road-
going coelacanths will fit into the Better and Organised Society
as their leisurely mode of progress, although perfectly adequate
in wads of traffic, will surely draw the wrong sort of attention by
being different. They are meant for deserted country roads but as
progress overtakes us, deserted country roads will undoubtedly
be phased out as wasteful to the national economy. An indication
of the future lies in the large and jolly fraternity of off-road
motorcyclists in California; before most of the middle west
moved out, these happy souls would sally forth into suitably
vacant deserted ground and have at it. Due to the spread of
suburbia, their sheer numbers, some unfortunate flicks, and a
propensity for removing silencers, the cycle hounds are now
finding themselves chased out of even remote patches of wild
desert. As a result, large cycle parks have sprung up where the
lads may do wheelies and endoes to the heart's content, un-
pursued by grim gentlemen eager to bust them. Sort of a game
preserve for motorcyclists, as it were. It is likely that the purely
private motorist, sick and tired of clogged expressways, will pay
his fee and return to automobile parks sited at convenient intervals. There will have to be different sections, of course, for

those who want to have a little race, those who like the dune buggy thing, those who like to do a little pub crawling, those who like to drive through folklorique towns, or simply those who like to picnic on a grassy hillside underneath the trees, suitably accompanied by pretty girls in long dresses and Dolly Vardens. But it will be expensive.

The only hope, really, lies in the Officials' realization that they cannot afford to run a government without the vast sums paid in by the uncomplaining milch cow of a motorist. Without him there will be no road tax, government insurance premiums, licence fees, automobile inspection fees, and last but not least the enormous wad of taxes brought in by the purchase of tyres, batteries, radios, and other accessories, not forgetting petrol, oil, and the vehicle itself. And what will all the police do? They will have to catch burglars instead of sitting comfortably by their radar sets smoking tax-free cigarettes. The most powerful lobbies against municipal public transport, an inevitable corollary of heavy motoring restrictions in the Official State, have been the oil companies and the automobile clubs, both organizations swinging a considerable amount of clout. Those organizations will not be slow to point out the great loss of steady revenue concomitant with barring all but Privileged (and levy-free) vehicles from the roads. Rather like throwing the baby out with the bathwater, eh?

Wouldn't it be amusing if the motorist's comparative freedom continued into the 21st Century simply because of old-fashioned money? Won't the planners be livid? We can hang about in the Shades and laugh.

TYRE DESCRIPTIONS ACT

"This bus going to City Centre?"
"No, man."
"But it says 'City Centre' on the front."
"Man, it says 'India' on the tyres, but we're not going there."

'Autocar'

RADICAL BUT A BIT LATE

There is no future for the motor car and the quicker the motor manufacturers, the motoring organisations and the public at large realise this, the better it will be for all concerned.—Letter in local paper, November 1965

SURPRISE

Ettore Bugatti was an Italian who made cars in Molsheim, Alaska.

American periodical

A special type of madness is required to see the virtues in ancient vehicles as outweighing their manifold disadvantages. And to endeavour to restore a mouldering pile of corruption to its original beauty (mainly in the eye of the beholder anyway) requires a fixity of purpose of monumental fatuity.
C. H. de Whalley, 'New Scientist', 66/4/65)

Having rammed a Lambda
It would have pleased Vincenzo
To know I got bent so. . . .
Porsche Post and Lancia Journal